Languages of the Mind

Languages of the Mind

Essays on Mental Representation

Ray Jackendoff

A Bradford Book
The MIT Press
Cambridge, Massachusetts
London, England

Second printing, 1993

© 1992 Massachusetts Institute of Technology

This book was set in Palatino by Asco Trade Typesetting Ltd., Hong Kong and was printed and bound in the United States of America.

Library of Congress Cataloging-in-Publication Data

Jackendoff, Ray S.
    Languages of the mind: essays on mental representation / Ray Jackendoff.
        p.   cm.
    "A Bradford Book."
    Includes bibliographical references and index.
    ISBN 0-262-10047-9
    1. Human information processing. 2. Mental representations. 3. Psycholinguistics.
4. Cognitive science. I. Title.
BF444.J333   1992
153.2—dc20
                                                                          91-45159
                                                                              CIP

Contents

Introduction

Over the past several years I have had occasion to write papers and give talks on a considerable variety of topics growing out of the overall position worked out earlier in my *Consciousness and the Computational Mind* (*CCM*). Some of them have addressed particular issues set by a conference, others have dealt in more detail with questions treated only tangentially in *CCM*, and still others have extended the approach to new domains. It seemed appropriate to bring a few of them together into this volume, where they cumulatively form a broader picture of how that position can be elaborated.

As I thought about what might make the collection cohere, a number of themes emerged. The first is a reaffirmation of the value of studying the mind in terms of formal symbolic descriptions of information structures. For linguists this should be no surprise, as linguistics has always dealt in these terms, calling the enterprise the description of "linguistic structure" or "linguistic competence." However, it seems to me that there has always been suspicion of this enterprise in other branches of cognitive science, most recently in the claims of the connectionist school that symbolic theories misrepresent the fundamental character of the mind. Chapter 1 in particular discusses the relation I see between connectionist theories and formal symbolic theories, and the reasons why I do not find them mutually exclusive approaches.

One of the most important issues in the study of the formal symbolic description of mental structure is the expressive power of the formalism. Formal descriptions permit one to see whether what one claims for a mental capacity can actually be accomplished, and whether the resources of a mental capacity can be appropriately constrained. This theme plays a role in practically all the chapters in various ways.

At the same time, I part company with much of the philosophical tradition on symbolic theories of mind, in that I see them purely as theories of combinatorial structures in the brain, lacking intentionality of the kind stressed by such philosophers as Jerry Fodor and John Searle. This theme arises in chapters 1 and 2, and I return to a more concentrated comparison of these contrasting views in chapter 8.

The second theme of the book is the modularity of mind and how it can be further articulated. *CCM* proposed a view of modularity roughly along the lines popularized by Jerry Fodor, but differing from Fodor's view in several respects: (1) The domain specificity of modules is a consequence of the formal representations they operate on. Thus modularity of processing is determined precisely by the forms of mental representation being processed. (2) Central representations as well as input-output representations are modular. (3) In addition to specifying the modules themselves, a theory of mind must also specify the routes of communication among modules in terms of "correspondence rules." (4) One can investigate structural parallelisms between different modules as a way of gaining insight into the possible evolution of the mind. The upshot is that one can begin to articulate a kind of "mental anatomy," in which the different kinds of information structures and their relations can be sketched in some detail. Chapter 1 lays out this theme of the book, and chapters 4, 6, and 7 elaborate further aspects of it.

A third theme of the book is that it is indeed possible to articulate a theory of the central levels of representation in the mind, in particular the level of conceptual structure. This level has been a preoccupation of mine for most of my career, and much of the broadening of my work into other domains has been in the service of putting the theory of conceptual structure on firm philosophical and psychological foundations. Chapter 2 summarizes the basic organization of conceptual structure as I understand it; a great deal more detail appears in my book *Semantic Structures*. Chapters 3, 4, and 5 provide some further angles on conceptual structure. However, what I believe to be the most substantive advance appears in chapter 6, written in collaboration with Barbara Landau. Here we develop some important details of the way in which conceptual structure communicates with another of the central levels of the mind, spatial representation. This builds on the preliminary suggestions about such a connection made in *CCM*; it leads toward a clearer understanding of how it is possible for us to talk about what we see, and furthermore why we talk about what we see in the way we do.

Most work in cognitive science has concerned the linguistic and visual faculties. Three chapters of the book concern application of this overall approach to domains of human experience not within the traditional purview. Chapter 7 is an extension of my work with Fred Lerdahl on musical cognition, examining how musical grammar bears on the problem of music parsing. Under the assumption that musical and linguistic parsers should follow roughly similar principles of organization, this argument is germane to choice among linguistic parsers as well. Chapter 5 is a bit of speculation on how the theory of mental representation could be applied to issues in psychodynamics (the contemporary form of Freudian personality theory). Chapter 4 concerns an issue I have secretly ruminated about for many years and on which I have finally had the courage to come out of the closet: the possibility that the modules of mind include a faculty specifically devoted to social cognition, and that such a faculty can be studied along lines quite parallel to those for the study of the language faculty.

Finally, there comes the necessity to reflect on what it all means—on the consequences of this approach for our overall view of the mind and of human experience. Chapter 8 develops this theme, making use of many points brought out in the previous chapters.

As these papers were originally written to stand alone, there is a certain amount of duplication in their expositions. I have let it stand, in order to allow the reader to browse among them at will. For those chapters that were published previously, I have for the most part made only minor alterations to suit the present setting, in particular providing cross-references among chapters.

Each chapter carries with it appropriate acknowledgments and attributions. However, a few more general acknowledgments are in order. First, I must express my deep appreciation to the Max-Planck Institut für Psycholinguistik and the University of Nijmegen for honoring me with an invitation to deliver the Nijmegen Lectures in December 1989. The friendly reception accorded the lectures, which included chapters 1 and 8 and parts of chapter 4, led to the initial impulse to assemble the present volume. Of all the wonderful people in Nijmegen, I must especially thank Pim Levelt, Melissa Bowerman, and Janet Randall for being terrific hosts and terrific colleagues.

Over the past few years, I have had the privilege to participate in an informal discussion group with Dan Dennett, Marcel Kinsbourne, and Nick Humphrey. These free-wheeling discussions have ranged through consciousness, perception, brain damage, artificial intelligence, linguistics, piano playing, and more, often all within a single hour—quite a stretch. The experience, besides being tremendous fun, has strengthened my conviction that each of the constituent disciplines of the cognitive sciences needs the others in order to tackle the Big Problems—and that it is possible, with practice and good will, to talk productively across disciplinary boundaries. I think Dan, Marcel, and Nick feel the same way. Their influence is clearly present in the spirit of this volume. Perhaps most importantly, their example has given me courage to discuss in print many of the topics in this volume that are off the beaten track. I hope they don't regret it.

Last and most, I thank my family. The period during which I was preparing this book was personally very difficult for a variety of reasons. Elise, Amy, and Beth made it all worth it.

Languages of the Mind

Chapter 1
Languages of the Mind

1.1 Forms of Mental Information

One of the most gripping issues posed by a materialist psychology—a psychology grounded in physical explanation—is the fundamental question of how it is that we are intelligent. In the last forty years, models of intelligence based on the notion of the brain as an information-processing device, a sort of biological computer, have been particularly influential and productive.

In light of this emphasis, a crucial subquestion emerges: *Over precisely what kinds of information are computations in the brain carried out?* That is, what categories, distinctions, and relations must be encoded in mental information structures in order to account for behavior, experience, and intelligence?

There seem to be large subcultures of the cognitive psychology and artificial intelligence communities where this question is not considered a central concern. Rather, there has been a strong tendency in the lore to say, "We're obviously more intelligent than animals because we have big brains, so brain size must determine intelligence. Hence, if we can build the computational capacity of the human brain into a computer, the computer will be as intelligent as we are. (And if we put in more, the computer will be smarter!)" Although estimating the raw bit capacity of the brain is an interesting exercise in establishing overall boundary conditions, it does not really get us any closer to discovering what the brain actually computes.

An earlier version of this chapter was given at the Symposium on the Computer and the Brain, held at Arizona State University in April 1987 in commemoration of John Von Neumann's 1957 monograph *The Computer and the Brain*. It was published as "Languages of the Computational Mind," in J. R. Brink and C. R. Haden, eds., *The Computer and the Brain: Perspectives on Human and Artificial Intelligence*, pp. 171–190, Elsevier, 1989, and is republished here in its present form by permission.

The present version was prepared as the first of my Nijmegen Lectures in December 1989 at the University of Nijmegen and the Max-Planck Institut für Psycholinguistik. Much of the paper is a précis of positions discussed at greater length in Jackendoff 1987a.

This research was supported in part by NSF Grants IST 84-20073 and IRI 88-08286 to Brandeis University.

Sheer size is not enough; as is well known, a big computer is only as useful as its programs.

Such a quantitative approach to the brain is characteristic of the information-theoretic perspective in which early cognitive science developed. The origins of this perspective are seen clearly in Norbert Wiener's (1954) *The Human Use of Human Beings: Cybernetics and Society*, where he discusses the way the mathematics of information theory grew out of thermodynamics. For Wiener, information is equated with lack of uncertainty, hence with deviation from randomness. In his essentially statistical conception of information, it is the amount, not the character, of information that is of interest.

Unfortunately, this tendency continues today. The information in the brain often seems to be regarded as somewhat like a liquid that is poured from one container (say short-term memory) to another (say long-term memory), perhaps being filtered on the way or being combined with other liquids. Certain containers are of limited size (for example, following Miller (1956), short-term memory is often said to hold 7 plus or minus 2 units of information, whatever that is), and any excess liquid poured into that container spills off into forgetfulness. Often the major question with respect to the form of mental information is taken to be how knowledge can best be encoded in order to facilitate its storage and retrieval in real time, that is, what constraints are placed on information by processing. This way of approaching the issue subordinates the study of form to the study of processing.

However, such an approach is inherently insufficient. To understand the workings of the mind, we must study not just the *quantity* of information in the brain but also, very specifically, the *forms* of the information the brain processes, stores, and retrieves.

Let me try to clarify what I mean by the form of information. Basically, the notion of information is significant only against the background of a space of possibilities or states available to the device receiving the information. This space will have an inherent organization—different independent degrees of freedom, each with an inherent range of possibilities, either discrete (binary or n-ary) or continuous (analogue). In essence, this space can be thought of as the device's space of hypotheses about how many different ways the world can be. An input received by the device may enable it or cause it to choose a location or region in this space of possible states. Thus a stimulus serves as information for the device just insofar as it drives the device into a particular state. This state, regarded against the background of the organization of the total space of states, constitutes the device's *representation* of the stimulus: for the device, this state encodes how the world *is* in the context of all the ways it might possibly be.

By a *form of mental information*, then, I mean an organized combinatorial space of distinctions available to the brain. When we as theorists use symbols to state a theory of mental representations, it is not the symbols themselves that are significant, but rather the distinctions possible in the system of symbols we use: these are claimed to be homologous to the organization of the relevant subsystems of brain states.

I believe that this is about the *only* sense we can make of "information" in a materialist psychology. In particular, we cannot begin building a theory from the notion that mental representations are connected to the world by a supervening relation of "intentionality" that transcends physical mechanism, a notion advocated by philosophers of mind otherwise as disparate as Jerry Fodor (1987) and John Searle (1983). I will come back to this issue in chapters 2 and 8.

The overall description of the forms of mental information is constrained by some fairly obvious boundary conditions:

First, information *entering* the mind comes in many different forms, for example spatial arrays of light intensity provided by retinal receptors, temporal patterns of sound frequencies provided by the ears, spatially arrayed patterns of pressure detected by the skin, and so forth.

Second, information *leaving* the mind is primarily in the form of patterns of stimulation to muscles, since it is through movement (including the movement of the vocal tract in the case of language) that we act on the world. The brain's stimulation of glands probably may also be regarded as a sort of information leaving the mind.

Third, none of these forms of input and output information suffices to explain the way we understand the world in terms of objects, their motions, our actions on them, and so forth. Rather, such aspects of our understanding must be encoded in an integrated modality-independent form that I will call a *central format*. (There may be more than one central format, as we will see later on; but there must be at least one.)

Fourth, since these different forms of information interact, the mind must have means for translating or transforming information from the input forms into the central format, so that we can perceive and understand the world in modality-independent fashion. It must also have means for translating from the central format into output forms, so that we can use our understanding of the world as a basis for acting.

These basic boundary conditions motivate various questions about the overall organization of the information in the mind, for example: How many different forms of information are there altogether? How do we differentiate them? What are their distinctive characteristics? What is each one used for? What formal relations permit information to be translated from one form to another? How are these translations accomplished in real time? In the course of trying to answer such questions, we are rapidly led to an overall view of intelligence that goes beyond simple brain size. Rather, it emerges that the power of the brain is in part a result of having many different specialized forms of information—many different "languages of the mind," each with its own repertoire of primitive distinctions and its own principles of combination, and each with its own contribution to the richness of our understanding of the world.

1.2   A Survey of Known Languages of the Mind

I would like to engage in a brief guided tour of the forms of mental information about which something is known, drawn from the faculties of language, vision, and music. I will use the term *level of representation* as a more technical term for a distinct form or "language" of information structure. (Other terms in the literature with approximately the same intent are Kosslyn's (1980) "format" and Marr's (1982) "stage of representation.") I will speak of forms of information that are relatively closely related to sensory input or motor output as *lower* or *more peripheral* levels of representation, contrasting them with *higher* or *more central* levels, which have relatively greater degrees of abstraction, integration, and cross-modal character. Given the picture painted so far, we would like to be able to say that thought, as we intuitively understand the term, consists of computations over a fairly central level of representation.

1.2.1   Language

Let me start with the language faculty, where intuitions about forms of information are most robust, and where there has been the longest tradition of studying the faculty in these terms. It is generally agreed that three distinct forms of information are invoked by the language faculty: *phonology*, or sound structure, *syntax*, or phrase structure, and *conceptual structure*, or meaning. Their relationships are indicated in figure 1.1. (To forestall misunderstanding, I should say at the outset that the arrows in this and subsequent figures indicate formal relationships or mutual constraints that obtain between levels of representation, not temporal order of processing.)

Consider first phonology. It is well known that the sound structure of language is not a simple analysis of the acoustic signal or a list of motor commands to the vocal tract. We experience the sound structure of language as a linear sequence of discrete words; in turn, the words can be divided into a sequence of discrete syllables, and the syllables into a sequence of discrete speech sounds. By contrast, the acoustic speech signal (or auditory input) and the motor activity involved in producing speech display no such discrete segmentation. For example, the word *attack* and the word sequence *a tack* are acoustically and motorically identical in ordinary speech. In the sentence *Bill sat on a tack*, there is no space between

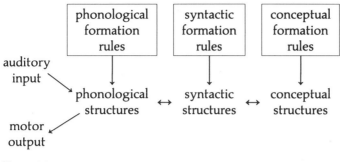

Figure 1.1
Forms of linguistic information

the words *a* and *tack* either in the acoustics or in the motions of the vocal tract, even though we "hear" (more properly, *understand*) a word boundary there. It turns out, in fact, that the relation between the acoustic signal and the "heard" speech sounds is extremely complex, even after one has compensated for speaker-to-speaker differences in the character of the voice, differences in rate of speech, and so forth. (This complexity is one of the reasons that it has been so difficult to devise a reliable automated speech decoder, one of the leading goals of artificial intelligence since the late 1940s.)

One fundamental tenet of the computational theory of mind is that *whenever a psychological constancy exists, there must be a mental representation that encodes that constancy.* Let me call this methodological assumption the *Tenet of Constancy.* If one does not accept this assumption, one is in effect regarding the psychological constancy as an unprincipled accident. In the present case, the form in which speech is perceived, regardless of the vagaries of the incoming acoustic signal, constitutes a set of constancies of the classical type, analogous to size, shape, and color constancies in visual perception. The sound *p*, for instance, is perceived as a *p* no matter in what position it occurs in the word, no matter in what position it occurs in the sentence, no matter who is speaking, no matter at what distance the sound is spoken. Thus the Tenet of Constancy leads to the conclusion that there is in the mind a level of representation—a form of mental information—that explicitly encodes the segmentation and discrimination of speech sounds. This level is what is traditionally called *segmental phonology*: a linear sequence of discrete speech sounds, concatenated into syllables, the syllables in turn concatenated into words.

Recent connectionist theory (e.g. Rumelhart and McClelland 1986) often claims not to need a theory of mental representation in this sense. However, I believe that the Tenet of Constancy still applies to connectionist theories of mental processing. In particular, even if information is distributed throughout a neural network as a set of connection weights, it is necessary for apparent psychological constancies such as speech sounds to be instantiated as constancies of particular connection weights somewhere in the network. Otherwise the theory implicitly claims that the regularity and constancy of speech sounds from one occurrence to the next is more or less an accident.

According to contemporary phonological theory, the speech sounds of segmental phonology are not themselves primitive. Rather, they are decomposed into *phonological distinctive features*. These features encode the dimensions of variation among speech sounds, such as consonant versus vowel; voiced versus unvoiced (*b, d, g, z* are voiced, *p, t, k, s* unvoiced); nasal (*m, n*) versus nonnasal (*b, k, s*); constricted lips (*oo, w, p, m*) versus unconstricted lips (*i, e, k, n*); and so forth. It was pointed out by Roman Jakobson and his associates (Trubetzkoy 1939; Jakobson 1941; Jakobson, Fant, and Halle 1952) that phonological distinctive features play a crucial role in determining the patterns of sounds found across languages of the world, in determining patterns of historical change in languages, and in determining patterns of acquisition of sound systems by children. It has been pointed out more recently (e.g. Fromkin 1971; Garrett 1975) that they also play a role in determining patterns of speech errors. This variety of functions shows that the encoding of segmental phonology in terms of distinctive features is not just an artificial notation that happens to be convenient for describing language. Rather, by assuming that the distinctive feature system is the informational framework in terms of which speech sounds are mentally encoded—the space of possibilities among which speech sounds can differ from one another—we can explain the patterns in many different facets of linguistic behavior.

On the other hand, an encoding of segmental phonology is not sufficient to explain the sound pattern of language. There must also be a way to translate phonological form into motor output, so that language can be spoken, and a way to translate auditory input into phonological form, so that heard language can be understood. (The acoustic-to-phonetic translation is the domain of acoustic phonetics; the phonetic-to-acoustic translation is the domain of articulatory phonetics.) These principles of translation, or *correspondence rules*, are indicated in figure 1.1 by arrows between the relevant forms of information. Notice that phonological structure serves both in speech perception and in speech production. Thus it is cross-modal—a multipurpose representation, more central than the auditory input and motor output.

There are a number of other components to the sound structure of language—components often ignored by nonlinguists. One is *intonation*, the "melody" to which a sentence is spoken. In English, intonation is normally used to highlight or focus various aspects of the sentence and to signal differences such as that between declaratives and yes-no questions. On the other hand, in so-called tone languages (such as Chinese and many West African languages), intonation is part of the intrinsic pronunciation of each word, along with the sequence of consonants and vowels. Another aspect of phonological structure is the *stress contour* of words and sentences, for instance the difference between the verb *perMIT* and the noun *PERmit*. This is now thought to be represented by a hierarchical organization called a *prosodic structure* (Liberman and Prince 1977; Halle and Vergnaud 1987). In addition, phonological structure must specify the *rhythm* in which the language is spoken, and this is now thought to be encoded in a *metrical grid* (Liberman and Prince 1977; Selkirk 1984; Prince 1983). Thus phonological structure must be elaborated into four independent and interrelated parts, each with its own characteristics, and each placed in correspondence with the others and with acoustic and motor information.

A second major component of the language faculty, *syntactic structure*, is built on entirely different fundamental notions. Instead of categories such as word, syllable, and voicing, syntax has *lexical* categories such as noun, verb, adjective, preposition, and adverb, and *phrasal* categories such as noun phrase, verb phrase, prepositional phrase, and sentence. Syntactic structures are traditionally notated in terms of the familiar tree structures and/or labeled bracketings of generative grammar. The primitives of syntactic structure, then, are the syntactic categories and the means of building these categories into hierarchical structures. There is much dispute in the literature on the fine details of this organization, as might be expected in a well-articulated theory; but the overall outlines of syntactic structure, and its distinctness from both phonology and meaning, are absolutely clear.

Again, the existence of a new level of representation means that there must be principles of correspondence by which this level makes informational contact with the rest of the mind. In particular, syntactic structure must be related to phonological structure. Part of this function is served by the lexicon (the list of words in the language): it specifies that a particular sequence of phonological segments, say *dog*, is a noun in syntactic structure. But there must also be larger-scale principles of correspondence that establish, for example, how the intonational phrasing of a sentence corresponds to its syntactic phrasing (Selkirk 1984; Gee and Grosjean 1983; Jackendoff 1987a, section 5.7 and appendix A). Because this set of principles of correspondence is used both in perceiving and in speaking language, it is notated in figure 1.1 as a double-headed arrow.

The third component of the language faculty is meaning. Meaning, of course, is presumably the reason for there being such a thing as language at all, since the language faculty is at bottom a device for externalizing and communicating meaning. I will use the term *conceptual structure* for the level of representation that encodes meaning. At the very least, this form of information must permit us to encode all the kinds of things we think there are, such as one's list of known individuals (real and imaginary), one's repertoire of categories into which individuals can be placed, and the tokens and types of events and situations in which individuals are understood to be taking part. These various entities collectively make up one's stock of *concepts*. They must be encoded in a form such that they can be manipulated by purely formal means: there is no further recourse to a "deeper" level of understanding. (This requirement distinguishes the present approach from truth-conditional semantics, but is altogether congenial with artificial intelligence approaches to meaning. See chapter 2 for discussion.)

In order to count as an encoding of meaning, conceptual structures must make it possible to formally define the functions that we associate with "understanding sentences"—just as phonological structures make it possible to formally define the functions that we associate with sound structure. These functions include at least the following:

1. It must be possible to determine whether a newly identified individual is or is not an instance of a known category. For example, one must be able to determine that Rover, an individual newly identified, is a dog and not a bookcase. As it happens, for most categories there are individuals for which one is not sure whether they belong to the category or not. The principles of conceptual structure must account for such phenomena of indeterminacy or "fuzziness" as well (see chapter 2).

2. It must be possible to determine the relation between any two arbitrary categories, including newly constructed categories. For example, it should be determinable that chairs are a kind of furniture and a kind of thing you can break but are not a kind of typewriter or a kind of thing you can disperse. Again, fuzziness inevitably appears, and must be an intrinsic part of the formal theory. Fuzziness of categorization may be somewhat strange in a strictly digital conception of mental computation, but it is less strange in a system that contains the possibility of continuously graded strengths of criterion application (see again chapter 2).

3. There must be a formal procedure for creating new categories on the basis of presented instances; that is, there must be a way to learn a new category concept without being explicitly taught the principles on which the category is based.

These tasks and others are involved in speaking of language understanding as a computational system. It is still highly controversial whether these tasks can indeed be encoded formally. On one hand, Jerry Fodor argues in *The Language of Thought* (1975) that ultimately the only way we have of dealing with intelligence is by treating it as a formal system; yet in *The Modularity of Mind* (1983) he seems to claim that understanding can't be studied. So there is at once hope and gloom on this issue. But to the extent that the level of conceptual structure can be systematically fleshed out (see chapter 2, as well as Miller and Johnson-Laird 1976, Jackendoff 1983, 1990, and many references therein), it seems that it must include conceptual primitives such as Object, Event, Place, Action, Property, and Amount, and principles of combination such as predication and quantification. On this view, then, thinking consists in large part of computations carried out over conceptual structures. That is, there are computations that can be formally investigated which create new conceptual structures—new ideas—on the basis of old ones.

I should perhaps repeat that work within the connectionist framework often claims to do away with the need for such a formal system. However, even if the knowledge notated formally as conceptual structure is not instantiated in a neural network in an iconic or localistic fashion, the constancies and relations built into the notation must somehow be reflected by constancies and relations (however distibuted) in the network.

On this view, then, in order to understand a spoken sentence, the brain must translate information from the form in which it is detected—auditory input—through phonological form and syntactic form to conceptual structure. In *speaking* a sentence, the brain must translate the initial thought, in the form of a conceptual structure, through the intermediate levels of syntactic and phonological structure into information in the form of motor instructions to the vocal tract. This does not mean that these translations must be accomplished in a strictly serial fashion (for a detailed reply to this common objection, see Jackendoff 1987a, chapter 6; see also Levelt 1989). Rather, it means that the translation between sound and meaning must conform to the principles of correspondence between levels in order to get from one level to the next.

1.2.2   Vision

Understanding language, of course, is not all there is to understanding the world. Another important input is the visual system. The literature has frequently adverted to the possibility of multiple levels of representation in visual processing, but to my mind the issue has been faced most directly in the work of David Marr, especially in his posthumous book *Vision* (1982). Marr claims that there is not a direct grand mapping from the retinal array to the understanding of space. Rather, as shown in figure 1.2, there are three distinct levels of representation on the way from the retinal array to the form of information that encodes spatial understanding.

The most peripheral of Marr's proposed levels is the *primal sketch*. This level encodes preliminary information about detectable local boundary elements and textures in the visual field, about groupings of various local elements in the visual field into somewhat larger units, and about movement of these elements across the visual field. Crucially, there is no notion

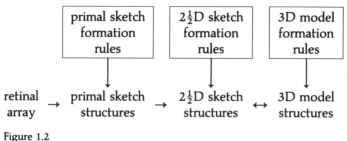

Figure 1.2
Forms of visual information (after Marr 1982)

of "object in space" in this level of representation—only the bits and pieces out of which perceived objects can be constructed farther along the line. The early part of Marr's book is concerned with working out the principles by which the primal sketch can be derived from (i.e. placed in correspondence with) the retinal array in a fashion that explains a wide range of perceptual phenomena. The exact mechanisms for this correspondence are still under dispute, but the general outline is rather clear.

Marr's next level is the *$2\frac{1}{2}$D sketch*. This specifies the shapes, distances, and orientations of surfaces visible to the viewer. Again, there is still no full-fledged notion of "object"; however, recovering the surfaces visible to the viewer and placing them in space is an important step on the way to identifying the objects being viewed. Perhaps the largest part of Marr's book is devoted to arguments for the psychological reality of the $2\frac{1}{2}$D sketch and to the principles by which it is derived from lower-level information such as parallax, binocular disparity, texture cues, and motion cues. (Again, the functions and even the existence of the $2\frac{1}{2}$D sketch are open to dispute in the literature, but something like it seems necessary.)

It is only when visual encoding reaches the level of the *3D model* that we achieve the traditional notion of "object constancy"—the fact that an object is formally represented in the same way no matter what angle and distance it is viewed from, no matter under what lighting conditions, and no matter whether it is partially obscured by other objects. It is this "object-constant" or "object-centered" encoding that permits different views of the object to be integrated and stored in memory, so that the object can be reidentified in further novel circumstances.

An important aspect of Marr's conception of the 3D model representation of an object is that it is not just a "statue in the head," but rather specifies the configuration of the object's parts relative to each other. So, for example, in Marr's analysis of the 3D model representation of a human figure, the arm is encoded as a separate part of the body, which is in turn elaborated into upper and lower arm; the lower arm is elaborated into arm part plus hand part; the hand is elaborated into palm plus fingers; and the fingers are elaborated into their joints. Thus the 3D model encodes our understanding not just of the shapes of objects but of how objects can be regarded as assemblages of parts. (A more elaborate version of Marr's decomposition appears in work of the last few years by Biederman (1987); see also chapter 6.)

Marr's levels of visual representation help make sense of much recent work on visual imagery (e.g. Shepard and Cooper 1982; Kosslyn 1980, 1987). Consider the experience of "mentally rotating" an imagined object around a vertical axis. As the rotation proceeds, new portions of the imagined object's surface come into view, while other portions disappear. This suggests that the mental image we experience has the characteristics of a $2\frac{1}{2}$D sketch: it incorporates the "visible surfaces" of the imagined object. However, in order to create a "rotating" image with these properties, one must also have a constant, viewpoint-independent encoding of the imagined object that incorporates all its parts, so that they are available to be "put into" the image as mental rotation brings them "into view." In turn, this requires principles of translation to produce the image from the viewpoint-independent representation. (These are what Kosslyn (1980) calls the "inverse mapping function.") It can be seen that the viewer-independent encoding must have properties much like (if not identical to) the 3D model representation used for visual perception.

It emerges from Marr's theory of levels, then, that producing visual images is more or less analogous to speech production—with the exception that "visual production" gets arrested at the $2\frac{1}{2}$D level, for lack of a lower-level output format. If, say, we had little television screens on our foreheads onto which we could project our visual imagery, the parallel to language would be complete. Because the mapping between the $2\frac{1}{2}$D sketch and the 3D model is used both in perception and in "production," I have notated their correspondence with a double-headed arrow in figure 1.2.

To push the parallel a bit further, notice that we frequently experience "linguistic imagery": hearing sentences in our heads. In fact, our thoughts most often come to us in the guise of linguistic imagery. It is a curious but undeniable fact that linguistic images have not only meaning but also syntactic and phonological structure, down to stress, rhythm, and possibly even intonation. In the present approach, linguistic imagery is a precise parallel to visual imagery: linguistic representations are built up from an intended meaning, but the final translation into output format is lacking. We formulate the sentence but do not actually pronounce it.

1.2.3 Music

A third faculty of mind, not generally considered in the same league as the linguistic and visual faculties, is the faculty for music. Since 1974 I have

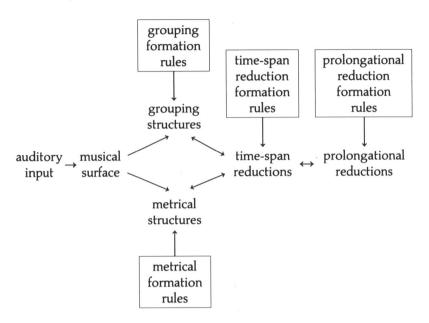

Figure 1.3
Forms of musical information (after Lerdahl and Jackendoff 1983a)

collaborated with the composer Fred Lerdahl on a theory of this faculty; our research is reported in detail in our *Generative Theory of Tonal Music* (*GTTM*). The basic question Lerdahl and I address in our work is, If a listener is familiar with a particular musical idiom (or style), what is it that enables him or her to hear a piece of music in that idiom as more than just a sequence of notes? That is, how does the listener put the notes together into a coherent organization that can conceivably be responsible for the musical affect (or emotional response)? We take this problem to be altogether parallel to the problems of linguistic and visual understanding.

As it has developed, it is necessary again to adopt an approach that makes use of discrete levels of mental representation linked by principles of correspondence (see figure 1.3). This time the levels in part encode aspects of general-purpose auditory cognition (aspects discussed in detail in Bregman 1990); but, significantly, they also encode aspects of cognition that are highly specific to the organization of music.

First of all, the auditory signal must be processed into a *musical surface*—the sequence of tones with their pitches, durations, amplitudes, and timbres. This is easy to take for granted, but it is in fact a formidable task. Just how formidable it is can be suggested by the experience of hearing a recording played backward. Our auditory system, adapted to the temporal asymmetries between the onset and the release of tones and to the asymmetries contributed by reverberation, is not equipped to compensate in the same way when these asymmetries are reversed. The result is that a backward recording is frequently incomprehensible—one finds it difficult even to distinguish separate tones. Thus considerable processing must evidently take place just in order to encode the mere sequence of tones heard in a piece of music.

But hearing the sequence of tones is not sufficient to explain how the sequence is experienced as *music*. The musical surface only provides the basis from which musical cognition can take place. Musical cognition proper involves four levels of representation. The first, *grouping structure*, encodes a hierarchical segmentation of the musical surface into motives, phrases, and sections. (This structure is in large part a product of general Gestalt principles of auditory perception; the musical case has been investigated experimentally by Deliege (1987).) The second, *metrical structure*, marks off the musical surface with a hierarchical arrangement of points in time or "beats"; very roughly, the metrical structure encodes where it is appropriate to tap one's foot or clap one's hands in time with the music. These two levels together constitute, roughly speaking, the rhythmic organization of the music.

In order to probe further into musical understanding, Lerdahl and I found it necessary to posit two additional levels of musical representation called *time-span reduction* and *prolongational reduction*. The insight behind these comes from the work of the early twentieth-century music theorist Heinrich Schenker (1935). Schenker proposed that music is organized in terms of the hierarchical elaboration of a "structural skeleton." In order to understand a piece of music, Schenker claimed, one must determine which events in the piece—which of the notes and chords—are structural anchors on which patterns of elaboration and ornamentation are hung. In the *GTTM* theory, the time-span reduction encodes such patterns in terms of the rhythmic framework established by grouping and meter; the prolongational reduction encodes such patterns in terms of hierarchically arranged waves of tension and relaxation in the music. Each reduction is a specialized form of tree structure. The two operate in counterpoint: the time-span reduction tends to reflect symmetries of phrasing in the music, whereas prolongational reduction (in Western music at least) tends to be asymmetrical, with long periods of increasing tension followed by relatively rapid relaxation. (Oura (1991) presents experimental evidence for the role of time-span reduction in remembering melodies.)

It follows from the *GTTM* theory of musical cognition that understanding a piece of music involves, at the very least, constructing all these musical structures in one's mind (unconsciously of course), just as one constructs phonological, syntactic, and conceptual structures in the course of under-

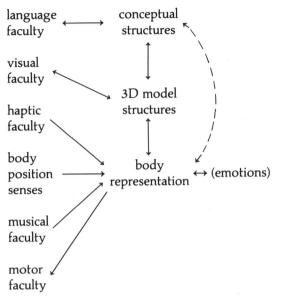

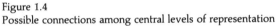

Figure 1.4
Possible connections among central levels of representation

standing a sentence. In order for this to be possible, the listener must make use of the principles that determine the translation of auditory input into the representation necessary for musical cognition. The arrows in figure 1.3 show the major routes over which this translation is accomplished. *GTTM* works out a grammar for the four musical levels and for the correspondences between them and the musical surface. This grammar, like grammars of natural languages, can be sorted out into idiom-specific aspects and musically universal aspects; chapter 7 discusses some issues of using this grammar to process a musical signal in real time. In short, the cognition of music appears to be a faculty of mind with its own characteristic properties, standing alongside language, vision, motor control, and so forth.

1.3   Interaction of Faculties

Next let us consider how the various faculties link up to form a unified understanding of the world. Figure 1.4 presents a somewhat speculative summary of the links.

A first important boundary condition on linking the faculties is that we can talk about what we see. This suggests that there must be a linkage—a set of principles of correspondence—between the visual system and the language faculty, so that visually encoded information can be translated into a form suitable for linguistic expression. The logical place to look for this link is between the most central representations of the two faculties, that is, between the 3D model and conceptual structure. I have argued (Jackendoff 1987a, chapter 10; Jackendoff 1987b; see also chapter 6) that there is an empirically interesting translation between my treatment of the conceptual structure of spatial expressions in language (Jackendoff 1983) and Marr's treatment of the 3D model; this correspondence helps solve a number of important problems for both language understanding and visual understanding. According to this picture, "abstract" thought is concentrated in conceptual structure representations and "spatial" thought in 3D model representation, with considerable interplay between the two in many fundamental cognitive tasks, not the least of which is talking about what we see.

What about other faculties? Without any firm theory in place, it seems reasonable to speculate that, alongside conceptual structure and the 3D model, there is a third central format (or perhaps a family of formats): a level of *body representation* that encodes internal states of muscles and joints, as well as the locus and character of body sensations such as pain, tension, heat, and so forth. This representation would serve, for one thing, as a way station between the intention to act, which is formulated in conceptual structure, and the form of motor commands. For instance, consider the act of carrying out an order. The order, received as a spoken utterance, must be translated into a conceptual structure by the language faculty. This conceptual structure—one's understanding of the order—would be used to determine an intended action in compliance with the order, in the form of another conceptual structure. The abstract intended action would then be translated into a 3D model representation of the spatial configuration and motion involved in the intended action. In turn, this could be used to determine what the muscles should do in order to carry the action out, a function of the body representation.

Another possible function of body representation is as a way station in *haptic perception*, the perception of shape by touch. If you pick up an object in your hands, you can tell what shape it is, just as you can by looking at it. Thus haptic perception derives shape information (i.e. information at the 3D model level) from inputs such as touch and pressure sensors in the skin rather than retinal arrays. A body representation that included information derived from skin sensors (by some as yet unknown translation) might well be a step in this process. In addition, the body representation is deeply involved in the *body position sense*, which, following the research of James Lackner and his associates (Lackner 1985, 1988; Lackner and Graybiel 1983; Lackner and DiZio 1984, 1988), is fed by such diverse sources as the visual system, the system of auditory localization, the vestibular and otolithic organs in the ears, the touch and pressure sensors in the skin, and muscle spindle receptors.

An interesting thing about all of these "bodily" senses is that we can't talk about them with much precision, even if our body awareness may be very highly developed (for instance in performing gymnastics or playing the violin). This suggests that the linkages between body representation and conceptual structure—the central format that most directly serves the language faculty—are not very highly developed, by contrast with the extremely rich 3D model—to—conceptual structure link. That is, our relatively great ability to talk about what we perceive out in space compared to our relatively poor ability to talk about the state of our bodies is a function of the ways in which the central representations are able to communicate with one another. (Hence the dashed rather than solid arrow linking conceptual structure with body representation in figure 1.4.)

So far nothing has been said about how the musical faculty links up with anything else. My suspicion is that music is linked in some way with the body representation. If there is any other cognitive activity that music is closely correlated with, it is dance, whose principal concern is dynamic states of the body. This suggests that musical affect—the emotional response to music—arises through the music's entraining body representations, whether or not one actually dances to the music—that is, whether or not the body representations are actually translated into motor patterns. In turn, this hypothesis would incorporate in a natural way the fact that tension and relaxation—fundamentally body states—are also an important component of musical cognition.

This hypothesis would also help explain the fact that musical understanding is not very verbalizable: as just noted, this seems to be a characteristic of the senses most directly linked with body representation. We tend to call musical understanding "mysterious" or "intuitive" or "irrational." These terms, however, only reflect a cultural bias against nonlinguistic thought. Musical understanding is as computationally characterizable, and as complex, as linguistic understanding. It is very much a psychological process on a par with language use, and phenomenologically just as real.

This overview of the languages of the computational mind has of course been extremely schematic. For each of the forms of information I have mentioned, there are major empirical questions yet to be answered about the tasks that the representation subserves, its formal properties, the mappings between it and other levels of representation, its development in real time in the course of perception, reasoning, and action, and its acquisition.

Some of the forms of information that I have treated here in terms of a single level may well be decomposable into even more specialized "languages." Likewise, some of the correspondences that have been notated here as single arrows between levels most likely decompose into a number of more specialized autonomous systems. Marr's decomposition of the mapping from primal sketch to $2\frac{1}{2}$D sketch is a notable example, in which there are separate mechanisms for stereopsis, structure through motion, detection of surface patterns, and so forth. Each of these uses primal sketch information to derive partial $2\frac{1}{2}$D sketch information, all of which must then be integrated into a unified perception.

1.4   Modularity and Connectionism

Whatever refinements accrue through further research, though, this general view of the mind seems altogether robust. The various specialized computational capacities of the mind are carried out, not by a single type of general-purpose device, but by a variety of computational devices, each specialized to deal with a particular form of information or to translate information from one particular form to another. This specialization is what Jerry Fodor (1983) has called the "modularity" of the mind and what Noam Chomsky (1975) has called the division of the mind into "mental organs." It seems reasonable to speculate that the many specializations found in the neural architecture of the brain constitute "hardware" adaptations to particular levels of representations and/or correspondences among levels.

The present view of the mind need not be antithetical to the connectionist approach to mental computation. Connectionist theory presents a "style" of computation and knowledge representation, but within rather broad limits it is more or less neutral about the formal organization of information being computed and stored. I suspect that the differences among forms of mental information will eventually be seen reflected in differences of architecture among neural networks, either in the brain or in a machine.

To clarify this point a little further, let me return to the "mental organ" metaphor. The fact that the organs of the body are highly differentiated into heart, liver, blood, bones, immune system, and so forth, does not deny that there are general principles underlying them all, for instance the principles of cell biology. Similarly, the fact that the computational devices in the mind are differentiated into segmental phonology, conceptual structure, primal sketch, prolongational reduction, and so forth, does not deny that there are general principles of computation from which these specialized devices are built. These general principles might well be those currently being explored with great vigor in connectionist research.

Pushing the analogy, it is important to observe that the study of cell biology does not undermine the enterprises of anatomy and physiology— rather, it supports them. By the same token (to my thinking at least), connectionist theory should not be taken to undermine the enterprise of "mental anatomy" that I have been describing here. Rather, the two disciplines are concerned with the mind at different scales of description. What would unite them would be an approach which asked how to construct different connectionist architectures that would intrinsically instantiate the organizations of information in the various mental organs. Though I think such an approach would be immensely fruitful, perhaps its time has not quite yet come. In particular, it seems to me that there are unfortunate sociological problems in cognitive science (Kuhnian paradigm clashes, if you like) that must be overcome before the empirical problems can be properly addressed.

1.5   Localization of Intelligence

So far I have said nothing about an important question often raised in discussions of the computational mind: the status of mathematical knowledge. Interestingly, John Von Neumann (1958) considered this question and concluded, somewhat chagrined, that the language of the brain is not the language of mathematics—that mathematics is "a *secondary* language, built on the *primary* language truly used by the central nervous system" (p. 82). We have now found that there are many languages used by the central nervous system. Each of them can be regarded as formal or computational, but none of them is mathematical per se. In fact, they all seem highly eccentric from the point of view of standard mathematics. This raises the interesting question of where mathematics fits in—on which "primary language" mathematics is built.

I will hazard a speculation that the intuitions out of which different branches of mathematics have developed come from different aspects of the mind. For example, arithmetic comes out of, or is an idealization of, the logic of amounts and individuation, where these are particular primitive elements in conceptual structure (Jackendoff 1983, chapter 3; Jackendoff 1991). Geometry comes out of or is an idealization of aspects of the logic of the 3D model representation, which encodes our understanding of space. Logic itself comes out of intuitions concerning the principles of inference—the computational principles that enable us to create new conceptual structures from old ones (Macnamara 1986 elaborates this point in considerable detail). Thus mathematics, which we Western academics tend to consider the quintessence of rational thought, comes out on this view as emerging from various subparts of the specialized languages of the mind, not as the foundation for all of them.

Suppose we ask, then, where our intelligence comes from—what might be its evolutionary antecedents. There is no reason at all to believe that anything like mathematical reasoning exists in other animals. So mathematics is hardly a likely candidate as the foundation of intelligence. Rather, as Harry Jerison (1973) has argued, the increase of intelligence in mammals, especially primates, seems to have to do with a better capacity for spatial cognition and action, a better ability to get around in a perceptually complex world. If you're a predator, such ability makes you better at detecting and catching prey; if you're a prey, it makes you better at detecting and evading predators. These kinds of intelligence basically involve the spatial (3D) and body representations. In fact, research by (among many others) Jeffrey Gruber (1965/1976), Ronald Langacker (1986), George Lakoff (1987), and myself (Jackendoff 1976, 1983) has suggested that the linguistic conceptualization of space underlies much of our thought. More particularly, it has been suggested by Jean Piaget (1970) and Leonard Talmy (1985) that the notion of logical entailment is essentially an abstraction of the conceptualization of the force-dynamics of objects pushing one another around in space. (See chapter 3 for some further discussion of the status of Piagetian theory with respect to these points.)

Another major factor in intelligence, one almost entirely neglected by cognitive science, is the area of social cognition. It is a commonplace that many animals have elaborate social organization. What is not often pointed out, though, is that such organization requires complex and specialized capacities for processing certain kinds of information. Dorothy Cheney and Robert Seyfarth (1985, 1990) have shown, for example, that vervet monkeys are much better at solving three-term transitivity problems when they involve social dominance hierarchies than when they involve, say, the size of blocks in a laboratory experiment. Cheney and Seyfarth conclude from this that vervet monkeys are in a sense "more intelligent" at social cognition than at what we might call "physical" cognition, and they speculate that social cognition may be a major evolutionary antecedent of our generalized intelligence. (See also Tooby and Cosmides 1989 and chapter 4.)

Yet another kind of intelligence might be called "motor intelligence." If you dispassionately observe your own hands carrying out a task as mundane as washing dishes, it is not hard to realize that a tremendous amount of computation must be involved in producing such creative dexterity. Like linguistic, spatial, and social cognition, we take this kind of intelligence entirely for granted—except when it performs an incorrect inference, and we drop a dish on the floor.

More generally, as Stephen Jay Gould has pointed out (1980, esp. 19–44; 1983, esp. 189–198), evolution does its work mostly by differentiating and specializing existing mechanisms to new purposes, "familiar bits of anatomy remodeled for a new function" (Gould 1980, 22). It seems to me that the evolution of the brain—hence the evolution of the mind—is no exception. The message of the approach advocated here is that our intelligence arises not just from our brain size, but rather from the presence in the brain of various specialized mental organs, each of which has its own particular language. (This view might be seen as a formal working out of the theory of "multiple intelligences" of Gardner 1983.)

Following this line of reasoning, the emergence of rational thought in humans in the course of evolution is therefore not merely a function of the brain growing larger, but rather a function of its growing larger in the service of abstracting and idealizing the more mundane faculties that we take for granted, such as getting around in the physical world and getting along with our fellow human beings. To understand our intelligence, or to make a computer intelligent in the way we are, we can't just skim off the cream—the part of the mind that we call "rational thought": we must attempt to understand more thoroughly the elaborate evolutionary foundations on which rationality is built.

Chapter 2

What Is a Concept, That a Person May Grasp It?

2.1 Prologue

Asking a psychologist, a philosopher, or a linguist what a concept is is much like asking a physicist what mass is. An answer cannot be given in isolation. Rather, the term plays a certain role in a larger world view that includes the nature of language, of meaning, and of mind. Hence the notion of a concept cannot be explicated without at the same time sketching the background against which it is set; and the "correctness" of a particular notion of concept cannot be evaluated without at the same time evaluating the world view in which it plays a role.

In turn, the evaluation of a world view is at least in part dependent on one's purposes. A world view incorporating a geocentric universe evidently was well suited for the purposes of the Church of the sixteenth century; a world view incorporating the Newtonian notions of mass and energy is perfectly adequate for building bridges. On the other hand, a world view incorporating a heliocentric planetary system is more suitable for the purpose of unifying the theories of terrestrial and celestial motion; a world view incorporating relativistic notions of mass and energy is more suitable if our purpose is building nuclear weapons.

My purpose is to better understand human nature. My method is to attempt to characterize the mental resources that make possible the articulation of humans' knowledge and experience of the world.

This chapter was originally prepared as the keynote lecture for the April 1989 meeting of Generative Linguists of the Old World, in Utrecht. It was first published in *Mind and Language* 4.1/2 (1989), as part of a special issue devoted to the topic "What Is a Concept?" It is reprinted here by permission. Much of it appears also in chapter 1 of Jackendoff 1990. The title owes apologies to Warren McCulloch. I am grateful to Noam Chomsky, John Macnamara, and Jerry Fodor for comments on an earlier version. I do not, however, intend to imply by this that they endorse my approach; in particular, Fodor doesn't believe a word of it.

This research was supported in part by NSF Grant IST 84-20073 to Brandeis University.

2.2   E-Concepts and I-Concepts

There is a fundamental tension in the ordinary language term *concept*. On one hand, it is something out there in the world: "the Newtonian concept of mass" is something that is spoken of as though it exists independently of who actually knows or grasps it. Likewise, "grasping a concept" evokes comparison to grasping a physical object, except that one somehow does it with one's mind instead of one's hand. On the other hand, a concept is spoken of as an entity within one's head, a private entity, a product of the imagination that can be conveyed to others only by means of language, gesture, drawing, or some other imperfect means of communication.

Precisely the same tension has been discussed by Chomsky (1986) with respect to the term *language*. He differentiates the two poles as "E-language" (externalized language, the language seen as external artifact) versus "I-language" (internalized language, the language as a body of internally encoded information). I will adopt Chomsky's terminology and speak of "E-concepts" versus "I-concepts."

For Chomsky's purpose—the characterization of the mental resources that make possible human knowledge of language—the notion of I-language rather than E-language is the appropriate focus of inquiry. Chomsky argues this point at length in Chomsky 1986, and he has in fact been quite explicit on this point at least since Chomsky 1965. The new terminology only helps make clearer an old and forceful position.

However, the choice of I-language as the focus of Chomsky's linguistic theory does not rest on a priori argumentation alone. It rests primarily on the suitability of this notion to support scientific investigation into the issues that flow from the overarching goals of the inquiry. To the extent that generative linguistics has indeed been successful in increasing our understanding of the human language capacity, the choice of I-language as the object of inquiry has been vindicated. (And notice that disagreement—even violent disagreement—among its practitioners does not diminish the fact that progress has been made. It stands to reason that, at any particular moment, the most time and energy is being spent at the frontiers of understanding, not in the areas that have been settled. Any linguist will acknowledge that the frontiers have expanded considerably over the past three decades.)

My purposes—the characterization of the mental resources that make possible human knowledge and experience of the world—is conceived as an extension of Chomsky's goals. Accordingly, an important boundary condition on my enterprise is that it be compatible with the world view of generative linguistics.

In particular, if we think very roughly of language as a vehicle for expressing concepts, an integrated theory of language and the mind must include a way for linguistic expressions to be related to concepts. If, for my purposes and Chomsky's, the notion of I-language rather than E-language is the suitable focus of inquiry, then on the face of it one should also choose I-concepts rather than E-concepts as the focus for a compatible theory of knowledge.

In this chapter I hope to accomplish two things. First, I will ground a theory of I-concepts called Conceptual Semantics in first principles parallel to those of generative syntax and phonology, and show how other approaches are incompatible with this outlook. Second, since I have stressed that a world view is evaluated by how well it suits one's purposes, I will demonstrate some actual empirical results that flow from adopting my approach. (Most of the arguments are elaborated in greater detail in Jackendoff 1983, 1987a, 1990.)

2.3   First Principles of I-Conceptual Knowledge

The fundamental motivation behind generative syntax is of course the creativity of language—the fact that speakers of a language can understand and create an indefinitely large number of sentences that they have never heard before. It follows from this observation that a speaker's repertoire of syntactic structures cannot be characterized just as a finite list of sentences. Nor, of course, can it be characterized as an infinite set of possible sentences of the language, because it must be instantiated in a finite (albeit large) brain. Rather, one's potential repertoire of syntactic structures must be mentally encoded in terms of a finite set of primitives and a finite set of principles of combination that collectively describe (or generate) the class of possible sentences. In speaking or understanding a sentence, then, a language user is taken to be creating or invoking a mental information structure, the syntactic structure of the sentence, which is organized in conformance with the principles of syntactic structure.

Parallel arguments obtain for conceptual knowledge, in two different ways. First, a language user presumably is not gratuitously producing and parsing syntactic structures for their own sake: a syntactic structure expresses an I-concept (or a "thought"). On the basis of this concept, the language user can perform any number of tasks, for instance checking the sentence's consistency with other linguistic or extralinguistic knowledge, carrying out inferences, formulating a response, or translating the sentence into another language. Corresponding to the indefinitely large variety of syntactic structures, then, there must be an indefinitely large variety of concepts that can be invoked in the production and comprehension of sentences. It follows that the repertoire of concepts expressed by sentences cannot be mentally encoded as a list, but must be characterized in terms of a finite set of mental primitives and a finite set of principles of mental combination that collectively describe the set of possible concepts expressed by sentences. For convenience, I will refer to these two sets together as the *grammar of sentential concepts*.

It is widely assumed, and I will take for granted, that the basic units out of which a sentential concept is constructed are the concepts expressed by the words in the sentence, that is, *lexical* concepts. It is easy to see that lexical concepts too are subject to the argument from creativity. For instance, consider the concept expressed by the word *dog*. Someone who knows this concept, upon encountering an indefinitely large variety of objects, will be able to judge whether they are dogs or not. Thus the concept cannot be encoded as a list of the dogs one has previously encountered; nor, because the brain is finite, can it be a list of all dogs there ever have been and will be, or of all possible dogs. Rather, it must be some sort of finite schema that can be compared with the mental representations of arbitrary new objects to produce a judgment of conformance or nonconformance.

Two immediate qualifications. First, there may well be objects for which people's judgments disagree. This does not entail that there is no concept *dog* or that people do not know the meaning of the word. Rather, since our concern is with people's internalized schemas, we simply conclude that people may have schemas for *dog* that differ in various details and that these differences too may bear examination.

Second, there may be novel objects such that one cannot judge clearly whether they are dogs or not. ("It's sort of a dog and sort of a wolf.") Again, this does not necessarily challenge the idea that one has an internalized schema. Rather, from such examples we may conclude that there is a potential degree of indeterminacy either in the lexical concept itself, or in the procedure for comparing it with mental representations of novel objects, or in both. Such indeterminacies are in fact rampant in lexical concepts; section 2.7 will discuss the characteristics of conceptual knowledge that give rise to them.

To sum up so far: Paralleling the argument from creativity to the necessity for principles or rules in syntactic knowledge, we have argued (1) that sentential concepts cannot be listed, but must be mentally generated on the basis of a finite set of primitives and principles of combination; (2) that lexical concepts cannot consist of a list of instances, but must consist of finite schemas that can be creatively compared (i.e. in rule-governed fashion) to novel inputs.

The second major issue in the foundation of syntactic theory flows from the problem of acquisition: How can a child acquire the rules of syntax on the basis of the fragmentary evidence available? In particular, how does the child induce *rules* from *instances* of well-formed sentences? This question is rendered especially pointed by the fact that the community of generative linguists (and cognitive psychologists and computational linguists and logicians), with all their collective intelligence, have not been able to fully determine the syntactic rules or English in over thirty years of research, supported by many centuries of traditional grammatical description—yet of course every normal child exposed to English masters the grammar by the age of ten or so. This apparent paradox of language acquisition motivates the central hypothesis of generative linguistics: that children come to the task of language learning equipped with an innate Universal Grammar that narrowly restricts the options available for the grammar they are trying to acquire. The driving issue in generative linguistics, then, is to determine the form of Universal Grammar, consonant both with the variety of human languages and also with their learnability.

The parallel argument can be made for the logical problem of concept acquisition, in both the sentential and lexical domains. For the sentential case, consider that the language learner must acquire not only the principles for constructing syntactically well formed sentences, but also the principles for constructing the corresponding sentential concepts. Like the rules of syntax, these principles must be acquired on the basis of some combination of linguistic experience, nonlinguistic experience, and innate constraints on possible principles. As in syntax, then, an important part of our task is to determine what aspects of the grammar of sentential concepts are learned and what aspects are innate; the innate parts must be sufficiently rich to make it possible to acquire the rest. (See chapter 3 for some further discussion of innateness.)

Turning to lexical concepts, consider that one is capable of acquiring during one's life an indefinitely large number of concepts, each of them on the basis of rather fragmentary evidence. (What evidence might be involved in learning the concepts expressed by such words as *bevel, prosaic, phonology, justice,* or *belief*?) Again, since lexical concepts must be encoded as unconscious schemas rather than lists of instances—in the case of the words above it is not even clear what *could* be presented as instances—lexical concept acquisition too presents a problem parallel to the acquisition of syntax. As in syntax, we adopt the hypothesis that lexical concepts are constructed from an innate basis of possible concepts, modulated by the contribution of linguistic and nonlinguistic experience.

But now the argument from creativity applies in a new way. If there is an indefinitely large stock of possible lexical concepts, and the innate basis for acquiring them must be encoded in a finite brain, we are forced to conclude that the innate basis must consist of a set of generative principles—a group of primitives and principles of combination that collectively determine the set of lexical concepts. This implies in turn that most if not all lexical concepts are composite, that is, that they can be decomposed in terms of the primitives and principles of combination of this innate *grammar of lexical concepts.* Learning a lexical concept, then, is to be thought of as constructing a composite expression within the grammar of lexical concepts, associating it with phonological and syntactic structures, and storing them together in long-term memory as a usable unit. (This contrasts sharply with Jerry Fodor's view that lexical concepts are cognitively primitive monads linked with each other by meaning postulates. Section 2.8 compares the two positions.)

Given the parallelism in first principles, I therefore believe that the central issue of the theory of conceptual knowledge ought to parallel that of the theory of syntax: What are the innate units and principles of organization that make human lexical and sentential concepts both possible in all their variety and also learnable on the basis of some realistic combination of linguistic and nonlinguistic experience?

2.4   Three Models for the Description of Meaning

The preceding section used the expression *concept* operationally to mean essentially 'a mental representation that can serve as the meaning of a linguistic expression'. In the present framework, then, the act of understanding a sentence S—recovering its meaning—is to be regarded as placing S in correspondence with a concept C, which has internal structure derivable from the syntactic structure and lexical items of S. On the basis of C, one can draw inferences, that is, construct further concepts that are logical entailments of C. One can also compare C with other concepts retrieved from memory ("Do I know this already?"; "Is this consistent with what I believe?") and with conceptual structures derived from sensory modalities ("Is this what's going on?"; "Is that what I should be looking for?"). That is, the meaning of the sentence can be evaluated with respect to what one believes and perceives.

The idea that a meaning is a sort of mental representation is, of course, not universally accepted. Perhaps the most prestigious tradition in the study of meaning grows out of Frege's "Sense and Reference" (1892), where he very carefully disassociates the "sense" of an expression—what he takes to be an objective, publicly available entity—from the "ideas" that users of the expression carry in their heads, which are subjective and variable. Frege's notion of "sense" underpins the approach to meaning in truth-conditional semantics (including model-theoretic semantics and Situation Semantics as subcases). This is seen clearly, for instance, in the following quotation from David Lewis's foundational paper "General Semantics":

> I distinguish two topics: first, the description of possible languages or grammars as abstract semantic systems whereby symbols are associated with aspects of the world; and second, the description of the

psychological and sociological facts whereby a particular one of these abstract semantic systems is the one used by a person or population. Only confusion comes of mixing these two topics. This paper deals almost entirely with the first. (Lewis 1972, 170)

It is hard to find a clearer statement that the purposes of truth-conditional semantics are different from those of generative linguistics, and that their world views are incompatible. To be sure, both generative grammar and truth-conditional semantics treat language as a formal system. But they differ radically in the goals they wish to accomplish through such treatment. The avowed purpose of truth-conditional semantics is to explicate Truth, a relation between language and "the world," independent of language users. In turn, the truth-conditions of sentences can be treated as speaker-independent only if both "the world" *and* the language that describes it are speaker-independent as well. Hence a truth-conditional semantics in the Tarskian or Davidsonian sense requires a theory of E-language, of language as an abstract artifact extrinsic to speakers.

As stressed in section 2.2, the purpose of generative grammar has always been to explicate I-language, the principles internalized by speakers that constitute knowledge of a language. A typical statement of generative linguistic theory, say "Sentence S is grammatical in Language L because of Principle P," is taken to be shorthand for a psychological claim, roughly "Speakers of Language L treat Sentence S as grammatical because their knowledge of Language L includes Principle P," subject to the usual caveats about attentional and processing limitations. A compatible theory of meaning must therefore concern the principles internalized in speakers that permit them to understand sentences, draw inferences from them, and judge their truth: it must be a theory of I-semantics, not E-semantics. Within a theory of I-semantics, a statement in the Tarskian vein like "Sentence S in Language L is true if and only if Condition C is met" is taken as shorthand for something like "Speakers of Language L treat Sentence S as true if and only if their construal (or mental representation) of the world meets Condition C," and it is subject to similar caveats about attentional and processing limitations. This is the basis of the approach of Conceptual Semantics, in which a level of mental representation called *conceptual structure* is seen as the form in which speakers encode their construal of the world.

It is sometimes proposed that there is no inherent conflict between the two approaches. One is about the way the world *is*, and the other is about the way we *grasp* the world. They might lead to altogether different, though hopefully complementary, insights. I see nothing wrong with this conclusion in principle: you go your way, I'll go mine. The difficulty is one of terminological imperialism, as exemplified by Lewis's (1972) widely quoted slogan to the effect that the study of "Mentalese"—in effect I-semantics—isn't *really* semantics. Along with this goes the implication that what the I-semanticist and the psychologist are doing isn't really anything worth doing. As stressed in section 2.1, whether it's worth doing cannot be determined until the results are in; as promised, I will present some. I don't care what the enterprise is called; but notice that relativistic physics *is* a way of doing physics, not some curious nonenterprise, and it did make use of most of the basic terminology of Newtonian physics despite a radical conceptual restructuring. Such, I suggest, is the case in the contrast of E-semantics and I-semantics.

It is also sometimes suggested that my characterization of model-theoretic semantics is unfair. In principle, model-theoretic semantics is neutral between E-semantics and I-semantics; even if Davidson and Lewis designed the theory with E-semantics in mind, nothing stops us from choosing a model that conforms to psychological constraints and thereby producing a model-theoretic I-semantics. Again I agree—in principle. But to my knowledge, all model-theoretic semantics, other than a few exceptions such as the work of Bach (1986a) and Verkuyl (1989), has in practice been E-semantics. And of course, the project of determining a psychologically defensible model theory is pretty much equivalent to the enterprise of Conceptual Semantics, that is, finding out how human beings actually encode their construal of the world. Again, I don't want to make heavy weather of the terminology. If some readers are more comfortable thinking of Conceptual Semantics as a very particular and eccentric brand of model-theoretic semantics, I have no objection. It is the *psychological* claim, not the name of the theory, that is crucial. (See Jackendoff 1983, chapters 2, 3, 5, and Jackendoff 1987a, chapter 7, for amplification of these points. Verkuyl and Zwarts 1990 recasts some of the leading formal innovations of Conceptual Semantics in model-theoretic terms, stressing the potential compatibility of the approaches.)

It is next necessary to differentiate Conceptual Semantics from Fodor's (1975) "Language of Thought" Hypothesis. On the face of it Fodor's position seems closer to mine: his purpose is to understand the character of mind. Unlike the model theorists, he is committed to a combinatorial mental representation in terms of which language users make inferences and formulate responses. Moreover, Fodor stresses that the performance of these tasks must be explained purely by virtue of the form of the representations. There can be no appeal to what the representations "mean." His argument is that the buck has to stop somewhere: if one is to characterize the brain as a computational device, driven by the syntax of internal representations, an appeal to meaning in the outside world amounts to an invocation of magic.

So far Fodor's story is altogether compatible with Conceptual Semantics. But now it splits in two directions. On one hand, Fodor argues (1980a) for "methodological solipsism"—the idea that the only causal determinants of behavior (including inference) are the formal properties of internal representations. This is again consistent with Conceptual Semantics, in which rules of inference do not reach out from conceptual structures to "the world" but are rather confined to examining conceptual structures themselves.

However, another thread in Fodor's work (seen especially in Fodor 1987) is his insistence on "Intentional Realism," the idea that the mental representations over which these computations take place still *do* nonetheless have further semantic content—that they are representations of propositions with real-world reference and truth-value. This view allegedly makes contact with Chomsky's notion of Universal Grammar in the following way:

> It is, however, important to the Neocartesian [i.e. Chomskian] story that what is innately represented should constitute a bona fide object of propositional attitudes.... Now, the notion of computation is intrinsically connected to such semantical concepts as implication, confirmation, and logical consequence. Specifically, a computation is a transformation of representations which respects these sorts of semantic relations.... So, Chomsky's account of language learning is the story of how innate endowment and perceptual experience interact *in virtue of their respective contents* [Fodor's italics]. (Fodor 1983, 4–5)

I find this a serious misconstrual of generative grammar. Look at the representations of, say, generative phonology. It makes little sense to think of the rules of phonology as propositional; for instance, it is strange to say that English speakers know the proposition, *true in the world independent of speakers of English*, that syllable-initial voiceless consonants aspirate before stress. This amounts to an appeal to the properties of E-language. In generative phonology as it is conducted by its practitioners, this rule of aspiration is regarded as a principle of internal computation, not a fact about the world. "Such semantical concepts as implication, confirmation, and logical consequence" seem curiously irrelevant. In short, the notion of computation need not have anything to do with "respecting semantic relations," at least in the domains of phonology and syntax.

If you have hesitations about this argument with respect to phonology, consider a slightly more exotic cognitive domain, the understanding of music. As shown in Lerdahl and Jackendoff 1983a, the factors that make a piece of music cohere for a listener into something beyond a mere sequence of notes involve complex internal computations over abstract mental representations of the piece. Fodor's insistence on respecting semantic relations seems totally out of place here: these abstract structures are part of mental life, but one would hardly want to make a metaphysical claim about there being something "real" in the world, propositional or otherwise, that they are representations *of*.

The question at issue, then, is whether conceptual structure is somehow different from phonology, syntax, and music—whether, when we enter the domain of meaning, the rules of the game should be changed, so that propositional content rather than computational form ought to be the focus of inquiry. Fodor's position, as I understand it, is that the generalizations (or laws) of psychology are intentional (that is, concern the propositional content of representations, outside the head), but that the mental mechanisms that instantiate these generalizations are merely formal computations that have no access to propositional content. For Fodor, the fact that these mental computations preserve semantic properties comes from the fact that the formal structures mimic the structure of the (nonmental) content in considerable detail. In fact, Fodor argues for the combinatorial character of mental representations precisely on the grounds that they must mimic what he takes to be the undeniable combinatoriality of propositional content. Put in present terms, his position is that we *grasp* the world the way we do precisely because that is the way the world *is*. (This argument is perhaps clearest in the Appendix to Fodor 1987.) What Fodor appears to require, then, is a marriage between the Realism of truth-conditional semantics and the mentalism of generative grammar—that is, a unified theory of E-semantics and I-semantics, mediated by the relation of intentionality, which even to Fodor is mysterious.[1]

Conceptual Semantics, on the other hand, is concerned most directly with the form of the internal mental representations that constitute conceptual structure and with the formal relations between this level and other levels of representation. The theory of conceptual structure is thus taken to be entirely parallel to the theory of syntactic or phonological structure. The computation of inference, like for instance the computation of rhyme in phonology, is a matter internal to the organism.

For Fodor, as for the model theorists, such an inquiry does not count as semantics: a theory of semantics must include a Realist account of truth-conditions and inference. Once again, I don't care too much about terminology. I would prefer that the enterprise be judged on its merits rather than being summarily dismissed because it doesn't address issues that someone calls the True Issues of Semantics. If you would rather call the enterprise logical or conceptual syntax, or the "Syntax of Thought" Hypothesis, that's fine with me. We should be clear, though, that it is as different from "straight" syntax (the grammar of NPs, VPs, etc.) as straight syntax is from phonology.

Given the meager positive empirical results of Fodor's approach, I submit that the merits of the Language of Thought Hypothesis over the Syntax of Thought Hypothesis have yet to be demonstrated.

How do the two approaches differ empirically? The difference is that Fodor insists that all combinatorial properties of concepts must be mirrored in Reality, whereas a theory of pure I-semantics is not necessarily subject to that constraint. As will be shown below, there are many structural properties of Conceptual Semantics that make little sense as properties of Reality, but a great deal of sense as properties of mind. I will therefore conclude that Fodor's insistence on Intentional Realism is misguided for the purpose of doing scientific psychology. (Chapter 8 returns to this theme.)

(Note that this conclusion is not inconsistent with Fodor's observation, seconded by Dennett (1987), that Intentional Realism is an extremely useful stance for dealing with people in ordinary life. But "folk physics" is a good stance for ordinary life, too. That does not make it a productive constraint for doing scientific physics. So why get mired in "folk psychology" when studying the mind?)

To conclude this section, I should mention the relation of Conceptual Semantics to a program of research called *Cognitive Grammar* or *Cognitive Semantics* (e.g. Fauconnier 1985; Langacker 1986; Herskovits 1986; Lakoff 1987). This work, like Conceptual Semantics, is concerned with the mental representation of the world and its relation to language. It shares with Conceptual Semantics a concern with the encoding of spatial concepts and their extension to other conceptual fields (see section 2.6). Some work in this tradition, especially that of Talmy (1980, 1983, 1985), has provided important insights and analyses to the present framework. Conceptual Semantics differs from Cognitive Grammar, however, in that (1) it is committed to an autonomous level of syntactic representation rather than its abandonment; (2) it is committed to rigorous formalism, insofar as possible, on the grounds that formal treatment is the best way of rendering a theory testable; (3) it makes contact with relevant results in perceptual psychology rather than leaving such relationships tacit; (4) it is committed to exploring issues of learnability and hence to the possibility of a strong innate formal basis for concept acquisition (see chapter 3).

2.5 Organization of Language

Next I must spend a little time sketching the relation of the putative level of conceptual structure to language. For concreteness, I will assume an overall organization of the information structure involved in language as diagrammed in figure 2.1. This organization includes three autonomous levels of structure: phonological, syntactic, and conceptual. Each of these has its own characteristic primitives and principles of combination and its own organization into subcomponents, such as segmental phonology, intonation contour, and metrical grid in phonology, and D-Structure, S-Structure, Phonetic Form (PF), and Logical Form (LF) (or counterparts

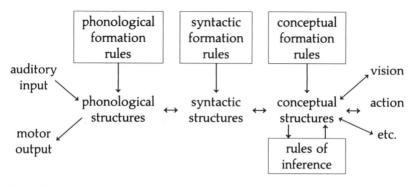

Figure 2.1

in other theories) in syntax. Each of the levels is described by a set of *formation rules* that generates the well-formed structures of the level.

The grammar also contains sets of *correspondence rules* that link the levels. The correspondence of phonological structure to syntactic structure is specified by one such set. This is, for instance, the locus of "readjustment rules" such as cliticization. The correspondence of syntactic and conceptual structures is specified by what used to be called "projection rules" (Katz and Fodor 1963), which determine the relation of syntactic structure to meaning.

Figure 2.1 also includes correspondence rules between the linguistic levels and nonlinguistic domains. On one end, there must be a mapping from the acoustic analysis provided by the auditory system into phonological structure; this mapping is the subject matter of acoustic phonetics. There must also be a mapping from phonological structure into motor commands to the vocal tract, the domain of articulatory phonetics. On the other end, there must be mappings between conceptual structure and other forms of mental representation that encode, for instance, the output of the visual faculty and the input to the formulation of action. One such representation will be discussed briefly in section 2.7 and more extensively in chapter 6.

Since conceptual structure is the domain of mental representation over which inference can be defined, figure 2.1 also includes a component called *rules of inference*, which maps conceptual structures into conceptual structures. As argued in Jackendoff 1983, chapters 5 and 6, I include in this component not only rules of logical inference but also rules of invited inference, pragmatics, and heuristics: whatever differences there may be among these categories of principles, they are all defined over the same level of mental representation. That is, there is no proprietary level of "semantic representation" at which only logical properties of sentences are encoded, with other "pragmatic" properties reserved for a different level. (This is an important point of commonality between Conceptual Semantics and Cognitive Grammar.)

It should be pointed out that, under the view being laid out here, the level of conceptual structure is not language-dependent, since it serves as an interface between linguistic information and information germane to other capacities such as vision and action. I assume, on grounds of evolutionary conservatism, that nonlinguistic organisms—both higher animals and babies—also possess a level of conceptual structure in their mental repertoire, perhaps not as rich as ours, but formally similar in many respects. The difference between us and the beasts is that we have evolved a capacity to process syntactic and phonological structures, as well as the mappings from them to conceptual structure and to the auditory and motor peripheries. These mappings are what permit us a relatively overt realization of conceptual structure—language—that is unavailable to other organisms.

Figure 2.1 as it stands contains no explicit lexical component. Where is the lexicon in this picture? Under the standard view of the lexicon, a lexical item establishes a correspondence between well-formed fragments of phonological, syntactic, and conceptual structure; that is, the lexicon is a part of the correspondence rule component. Thus we can regard each component in figure 2.1 as divided into lexical principles (those that apply within words) and extralexical principles (those that apply to domains larger than the word level). However, the basic alphabet of primitives and principles of combination is shared by the two subcomponents. For instance, Selkirk (1982) has argued that the syntactic part of morphology (word formation) consists essentially of an extension of the principles of syntax down below the word level. Similarly, in phonology, the lexical and extralexical principles of stress assignment, though different in details, deal in exactly the same kinds of formal entities.

In parallel fashion, we can ask about the relation between the grammar of sentential concepts and the grammar of lexical concepts, both of which are subsumed under the rubric "conceptual formation rules" in figure 2.1. Gruber (1965/1976) Jackendoff (1983), and indeed the generative semanticists (McCawley 1968; Postal 1970; Lakoff 1971) argue that the semantic combinations that can be expressed through syntactic phrases can in many cases also be incorporated into lexical conceptual structures. For instance, to the extent that *two times* paraphrases *twice*, or *cause to die* paraphrases *kill*, or *break violently* paraphrases *smash*, or *give away in exchange for money* paraphrases *sell*, the extralexical conceptual structures expressed by the paraphrases must be reproduced internal to unitary lexical items.[2] That is, the grammars of sentential concepts and of lexical concepts interpenetrate in much the same way as do the grammars of, say, sentential and lexical stress: they share many of the same primitives and principles of combination, even if they differ in details. In short, the division of the overall grammar into three independent levels linked by correspondence rules is crosscut by a subsidiary division in each component into lexical versus extralexical principles.

2.6   Feature-Based Aspects of Conceptual Structure

Section 2.3 argued that the central issue for a theory of I-conceptual knowledge ought to be the innate units and principles of organization that underlie human lexical and sentential concepts. I have now presented enough background to be able to sketch out three major subsystems within conceptual structure. The first involves the major category system and argument structure; the second involves the organization of semantic fields; the third involves the conceptualization of boundedness and aggregation.

2.6.1   Ontological Categories and Argument Structure

Jackendoff 1983, chapters 3 and 4, proposes a basic organization of major conceptual categories. Instead of a division of formal entities into such familiar logical types as constants, variables, predicates, and quantifiers, each of which has nothing in common with the others, it is argued that the major units of conceptual structure are *conceptual constituents*, each of which belongs to one of a small set of major ontological categories (or conceptual "parts of speech") such as Thing, Event, State, Place, Path, Property, and Amount. These are obviously all quite different in the kind of reference they pick out, but formally (algebraically) they have a great deal in common. Here are six points of similarity.

1. Each major syntactic constituent of a sentence (excluding contentless constituents such as epenthetic *it* and *there*) corresponds to a conceptual constituent in the meaning of the sentence. For example, in *John ran toward the house*, *John* and *the house* correspond to Thing-constituents, the PP *toward the house* corresponds to a Path-constituent, and the entire sentence corresponds to an Event-constituent.

Note that this correspondence is stated very carefully. As will be seen presently, the converse of this correlation does not hold. That is, not every conceptual constituent in the meaning of a sentence corresponds to a syntactic constituent, because (for one thing) many conceptual constituents of a sentence's meaning are completely contained within lexical items. In addition, note that the matching is by *constituents*, not by *categories*, because the mapping between conceptual and syntactic categories is many-to-many. For instance, an NP can express a Thing (e.g. *the dog*), an Event (*the war*), or a Property (*redness*); a PP can express a Place (*in the house*), a Path (*to the kitchen*), or a Property (*in luck*); and an S can express a State (*Bill is here*) or an Event (*Bill ran away*).

2. Each conceptual category supports the encoding of units not only on the basis of linguistic input, but also on the basis of the visual (or other sensory) environment. For example, (1a) points out a Thing in the environment; (1b) points out a Place; (1c) accompanies the demonstration of an Action; (1d) accompanies the demonstration of a Distance, independent of the object whose length it is.

(1)   a.   *That* is a robin.
      b.   *There* is your hat.
      c.   Can you do *this*?
      d.   The fish was *this* long.

3. Many of the categories support a type-token distinction. For example, just as there are many individual tokens of the Thing-type expressed by *a hat*, there may be many tokens of the Event-type expressed by *John ate his hat*, and there may be many different individual Places of the Place-type expressed by *over your head*. (Properties and Amounts, however, do not appear to differentiate tokens and types.)

4. Many of the categories support quantification.

(2)   a.   Every dinosaur had a brain.   (Things)
      b.   Everything you can do, I can do better.   (Actions)
      c.   Anyplace you can go, I can go too.   (Places)

5. Each conceptual category has some realizations in which it is decomposed into a function-argument structure; each argument is in turn a conceptual constituent of some major category. The standard notion of "predicate" is a special case of this, where the superordinate category is a State or Event. For instance, in (3a), which expresses a State, the arguments are *John* (Thing) and *tall* (Property); in (3b), also a State, both arguments are Things; and in (3c), an Event, the arguments are *John* (Thing) and ⟨PRO⟩ *to leave* (Event or Action).[3]

(3)   a.   John is tall.
      b.   John loves Mary.
      c.   John tried to leave.

But in addition a Thing may have a Thing as argument, as in (4a) or (4b); a Path may have as argument a Thing, as in (5a), or a Place, as in (5b); a Property may have as argument a Thing (6a) or an Event/Action (6b).

(4)   a.   father of the bride
      b.   president of the republic

(5)   a.   to the house
      b.   from under the table

(6) a.   afraid of Harry
     b.   ready to leave

6. The conceptual structure of a lexical item is an entity with zero or more open argument places; empirically, the maximum number of argument places seems to be three. The meanings of the syntactic complements of the lexical item fill in the values of the item's argument places in the meaning of the sentence. For instance, the verb *be* in (3a) expresses a function whose arguments are found in the subject and predicate adjective positions; *love* in (3b) expresses a function whose arguments are found in subject and object positions; *try* in (3c) expresses a function whose arguments are the subject and the complement clause; *father* and *president* in (4) express functions whose arguments are in the NP complement; *from* in (5b) expresses a function whose argument is a complement PP; *afraid* in (6a) expresses a function whose argument is the complement NP.

These observations should convey the general picture: though none of the major conceptual categories can be insightfully reduced to the others, they share important formal properties. Thus a basic formation rule for conceptual categories can be stated along the lines in (7).

$$(7)\quad \text{Entity} \rightarrow \begin{bmatrix} \text{Event/Thing/Place/}\ldots \\ \text{Token/Type} \\ \text{F}(\langle \text{Entity}_1, \langle \text{Entity}_2, \langle \text{Entity}_3 \rangle \rangle \rangle) \end{bmatrix}$$

(7) decomposes each conceptual constituent into three basic feature complexes, the third of which, the argument structure feature, allows for recursion of conceptual structure and hence an infinite class of possible concepts.

In addition, observation 1 above—the fact that major syntactic phrases correspond to major conceptual constituents—can be formalized as a general correspondence rule of the form (8); and observation 6—the basic correspondence of syntactic and conceptual argument structure—can be formalized as a general correspondence rule of the form (9). (XP stands for any major syntactic constituent; X^0 stands for any lexical item whose complements are (optionally) YP and ZP.)

(8) XP corresponds to Entity.

$$(9)\quad \begin{bmatrix} X^0 \\ \underline{\hspace{1cm}} \langle \text{YP} \langle \text{ZP} \rangle \rangle \end{bmatrix} \text{ corresponds to } \begin{bmatrix} \text{Entity} \\ \text{F}(\langle E_1 \rangle, \langle E_2, \langle E_3 \rangle \rangle) \end{bmatrix}$$

where YP corresponds to E_2, ZP corresponds to E_3, and the subject (if there is one) corresponds to E_1.

The examples given for observations 1–6 show that the syntactic category and the value of the conceptual n-ary feature Thing/Event/Place...are irrelevant to the general form of these rules. The algebra of conceptual structure and its relation to syntax is best stated cross-categorially.

2.6.2   Organization of Semantic Fields

A second cross-categorial property of conceptual structure forms a central concern of the "localistic" theory of Gruber (1965/1976) and others. The basic insight of this theory is that the formalism for encoding concepts of spatial location and motion, suitably abstracted, can be generalized to many other semantic fields. The standard evidence for this claim is the fact that many verbs and prepositions appear in two or more semantic fields, forming intuitively related paradigms. (10) illustrates some basic cases.

(10)   a.   *Spatial location and motion*
         i.   The bird went from the ground to the tree.
         ii. The bird is in the tree.
         iii. Harry kept the bird in the cage.
       b.   *Possession*
         i.   The inheritance went to Philip.
         ii. The money is Philip's.
         iii. Susan kept the money.
       c.   *Ascription of properties*
         i.   The light went/changed from green to red.
              Harry went from elated to depressed.
         ii. The light is red.
              Harry is depressed.
         iii. Sam kept the crowd happy.
       d.   *Scheduling of activities*
         i.   The meeting was changed from Tuesday to Monday.
         ii. The meeting is on Monday.
         iii. Let's keep the trip on Saturday.

Each of these sets contains a verb *go* or *change* (connected with the prepositions *from* and/or *to*), the verb *be*, and the verb *keep*. The *go* sentences each express a change of some sort, and their respective terminal states are described by the corresponding *be* sentences. The *keep* sentences all denote the causation of a state that endures over a period of time. One has the sense, then, that this variety of uses is not accidental.

On the other hand, the generalization of lexical items across semantic fields is by no means totally free. Each word is quite particular about what fields it appears in. For instance, *go* cannot be substituted for *change* in (10d), and *change* cannot be substituted for *go* in (10a). *Travel* occurs as a verb of change only in the spatial field; *donate* only in possessional; *become* only in ascriptional; and *schedule* only in scheduling.

Gruber's *Thematic Relations Hypothesis*, as adapted in Jackendoff 1972, 1976, and 1983, chapter 10, accounts for the paradigms in (10) by claiming that they are each realizations of the basic conceptual functions given in (11). (The ontological category feature is notated as a subscript on the brackets; nothing except convenience hangs on this notational choice as opposed to that in (7).)

(11) a. $[_{Event}$ GO ([   ], $\begin{bmatrix} \text{FROM ([   ])} \\ _{Path} \text{TO ([   ])} \end{bmatrix}$)]

   b. $[_{State}$ BE ([   ]), $[_{Place}$])]
   c. $[_{Event}$ STAY ([   ], $[_{Place}$])]

The paradigms are distinguished from one another by a *semantic field feature* that designates the field in which the Event or State is defined. In the cited works, the field feature is notated as a subscript on the function: $GO_{Spatial}$ (or, more often, plain GO) versus GO_{Poss} versus GO_{Ident} (using Gruber's term *Identificational*) versus GO_{Temp}. Again, not much hangs on this particular notation. The point is that at this grain of analysis the four semantic fields have parallel conceptual structure. They differ only in what counts as an entity being in a Place. In the spatial field, a Thing is located spatially; in possessional, a Thing belongs to someone; in ascriptional, a Thing has a property; in scheduling, an Event is located in a time period.

   This notation captures the lexical parallelisms in (10) neatly. The different uses of the words *go, change, be, keep, from,* and *to* in (10) are distinguished only by the semantic field feature, despite the radically different sorts of real-world events and states they pick out. However, the precise values of the field feature that a particular verb or preposition may carry is a lexical fact that must be learned. Thus *be* and *keep* are unrestricted; *go* is marked for spatial, possessional, or ascriptional; and *change* is marked for ascriptional or scheduling. On the other hand, *travel, donate, become,* and *schedule* are listed with only a single value of the field feature. Similarly, *from* and *to* are unrestricted, but *across* is only spatial and *during* is only temporal.

   Recall that in each paradigm in (10), the *be* sentence expresses the end state of the *go* sentence. This can be captured in the informally stated inference rule (12), which is independent of semantic field.

(12) At the termination of $[_{Event}$ GO ([X], $[_{Path}$ TO ([Y])])],
   it is the case that $[_{State}$ BE ([X], $[_{Place}$ AT ([Y])])].

A variety of such inference rules appear, in slightly different formalism, in Jackendoff 1976. In particular, it is shown that many so-called implicative properties of verbs follow from generalized forms of inference rules developed to account for verbs of spatial motion and location. Thus inferential properties such as "factive," "implicative," and "semifactive" need not be stated as arbitrary meaning postulates. This is exactly the sort of explanatory power one wants from a theory of lexical decomposition into conceptual features.

Each semantic field has its own particular inference patterns as well. For instance, in the spatial field, one fundamental principle stipulates that an object cannot be in two disjoint places at once. From this principle plus rule (12), it follows that an object that travels from one place to another is not still in its original position. But in the field of information transfer, this inference does not hold. If Bill transfers information to Harry, by (12) we can infer that Harry ends up having the information. But since information can be in more than one place at a time, Bill still may have the information too. Hence rule (12) generalizes from the spatial field to information transfer, but the principle of exclusive location does not. Thus inference rules as well as lexical entries benefit from a featural decomposition of concepts: the Thematic Relations Hypothesis and the use of the semantic field feature permit us to generalize just those aspects that are general, while retaining necessary distinctions.[4]

Notice how this treatment of the paradigms in (10) addresses the issues of learnability discussed in section 2.3. The claim is that the different concepts expressed by *keep*, for example, are not unrelated: they share the same functional structure and differ only in the semantic field feature. This being the case, it is easier for a child learning English to extend *keep* to a new field than to learn an entirely new word. In addition, the words that cross fields can serve as scaffolding upon which a child can organize new semantic fields of abstract character (for instance scheduling), in turn providing a framework for learning the words in that field that are peculiar to it. Thus the Thematic Relations Hypothesis, motivated by numerous paradigms like (10) in English and many other languages, forms an important component of a mentalistic theory of concepts and how humans can grasp them. (See chapter 3 for further discussion of learnability.)

2.6.3   Aggregation and Boundedness

The phenomena discussed so far in this section involve areas where the syntactic category system and the conceptual category system match up fairly well. In a way, the relation between the two systems serves as a partial explication of the categorial and functional properties of syntax: syntax presumably evolved as a means to express conceptual structure, so it is natural to expect that some of the structural properties of concepts would be mirrored in the organization of syntax.

On the other hand, there are other aspects of conceptual structure that display a strong featural character but are not expressed in so regular a fashion in syntax (at least in English). One such aspect (discussed in Vendler 1957; Verkuyl 1972, 1989; Talmy 1978; Declerck 1979; Dowty 1979; Platzack 1979; Mourelatos 1981; Link 1983; Hinrichs 1985; and Bach 1986b, among many others) can be illustrated by the examples in (13).

(13) $\begin{cases} \text{For hours,} \\ \text{Until noon,} \end{cases}$

    a.   Bill slept.

    b.   the light flashed.   *(repetition only)*

    c.   lights flashed.

    d.   *Bill ate the hot dog.

    e.   Bill ate hot dogs.

    f.   *Bill ate some hot dogs.

    g.   Bill was eating the hot dog.

    h.   ?Bill ran into the house.   *(repetition only)*

    i.   people ran into the house.

    j.   ?some people ran into the house.   *(repetition only)*

    k.   Bill ran toward the house.

    l.   Bill ran into houses.

    m.   Bill ran into some houses.   *(repetition only)*

    n.   Bill ran down the road.

    o.   *Bill ran 5 miles down the road.   (OK only on reading where 5 miles down the road is where Bill was, not where 5 miles down the road is how far he got.)

The question raised by these examples is why prefixing *for hours* or *until noon* should have such effects: sometimes it leaves a sentence acceptable, sometimes it renders it ungrammatical, and sometimes it adds a sense of repetition. The essential insight is that *for hours* places a measure on an otherwise temporally unbounded process, and that *until noon* places a temporal boundary on an otherwise temporally unbounded process. *Bill slept*, for instance, inherently expresses an unbounded process, so it can be felicitously prefixed with these expressions. On the other hand, *Bill ate the hot dog* expresses a temporally bounded event, so it cannot be further measured or bounded.

In turn, there are two ways in which a sentence can be interpreted as a temporally unbounded process. One is for the sentence to inherently express a temporally unbounded process, as is the case in (13a,c,e,g,i,k,l,n). We will return to these cases shortly. The other is for the sentence to be interpreted as an indefinite repetition of an inherently bounded process, as in (13b,h,j,m). (*Bill ate the hot dog*, like *Bill died*, is bounded but unrepeatable, so it cannot be interpreted in this fashion.) This sense of repetition has no syntactic reflex in English, though some languages such as Hungarian and Finnish have an iterative aspect that does express it.

How should this sense of iteration be encoded in conceptual structure? It would appear most natural to conceive of it as an operator that maps a single Event into a repeated sequence of individual Events of the same type. Brief consideration suggests that in fact this operator has exactly the same semantic value as the plural marker, which maps individual Things into collections of Things of the same type. That is, this operator is not formulated specifically in terms of Events, but rather should be applicable in cross-categorial fashion to any conceptual entity that admits of individuation. The fact that this operator does not receive consistent expression across syntactic categories should not obscure the essential semantic generalization.

Returning to the inherently unbounded cases, it has often been observed that the bounded/unbounded (event/process, telic/atelic) distinction is strongly parallel to the count/mass distinction in NPs. An important criterion for the count/mass distinction has to do with the description of parts of an entity. For instance, a part of *an apple* (count) cannot itself be described as *an apple*; but any part of a body of *water* (mass) can itself be described as *water* (unless the part gets too small with respect to its molecular structure). The same criterion applies to the event/process distinction: a part of *John ate the sandwich* (event) cannot itself be described as *John ate the sandwich*. By contrast, any part of *John ran toward the house* (process) can itself be described as *John ran toward the house* (unless the part gets smaller than a single stride). These similarities suggest that conceptual structure should encode this distinction cross-categorially too, so that the relevant inference rules do not care whether they are dealing with Things vs. Substances or Events vs. Processes.

It has also often been observed that plurals behave in many respects like mass nouns and that repeated events behave like processes. (Talmy (1978) suggests the term *medium* to encompass them both.) The difference is only that plural nouns and repeated events fix the "grain size" in terms of the singular individuals making up the unbounded medium, so that decomposition of the medium into parts is not as arbitrary as it is with substances and processes. Thus the structure of the desired feature system is organized as in figure 2.2. That is, the features that distinguish Things from Events are orthogonal to the features that distinguish individuals from media, and within media, homogeneous media from aggregates of individuals.

The examples in (13) provide evidence that Paths also participate in the system shown in figure 2.2. For instance, *to the house* is a bounded Path; no

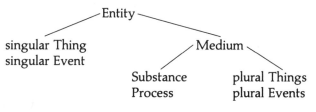

Figure 2.2

subparts of it except those including the terminus can be described as *to the house*. By contrast, *toward the house* and *down the road* are unbounded Paths, any part of which can also be described as *toward the house* or *down the road*. *Into houses* describes multiple bounded Paths, one per house. Thus the cross-categorial feature system in figure 2.2 extends to yet another major ontological category.

Here is an example that illustrates some of the explanatory power achieved through the system of features in figure 2.2: the meaning of the word *end*. For a first approximation, an *end* is a 0-dimensional boundary of an entity conceived of as 1-dimensional. So, for the simplest case, the end of a line is a point. A beam is conceived of (as in Marr 1982) as a long axis elaborated by a cross section. The end of a beam is a point bounding the long axis, elaborated by the same cross section; this makes it 2-dimensional. A table can be said to have an end just in case it can be seen as having a long axis (e.g. it is rectangular or oval but not square or circular); the end is then just the boundary of the long axis elaborated by the short axis. In the expected cross-categorial fashion, we can also speak of the end of a week (a point bounding a 1-dimensional period of time) and the end of a talk (a 0-dimensional State bounding an Event that extends over time).

However, there is an apparent difficulty in this account of *end*. If the end of a talk is a point in time, how can one felicitously say "I am now giving the end of my talk" or "I am now finishing my talk"? The progressive aspect in these sentences implies the existence of a process taking place over time and therefore seems to attribute a temporal extent to the end.

An answer is provided by looking at the treatment of the boundaries of Things. Consider what is meant by *Bill cut off the end of the ribbon*. Bill cannot have cut off the geometrical boundary of the ribbon. Rather, the sense of this sentence shows that the notion of end permits an optional elaboration: the end may consist of a part of the object it bounds, extending from the actual boundary into the object some small distance ϵ.

There are other boundary words that *obligatorily* include this sort of elaboration. For instance, a *crust* is a 2-dimensional boundary of a 3-dimensional volume, elaborated by extending it some distance ϵ into the volume. *Border* carries a stronger implication of such elaboration than does *edge*: consider that the *border of the rug* is likely to include a pattern in the body of the rug, whereas the *edge of the rug* is more likely to include only the binding.

The claim, then, is that *end* includes such an elaboration as an optional part of its meaning. Going back to the case of Events, I can therefore felicitously say "I am giving the end of my talk" or "I am finishing my talk" if I am within the region of time that extends backward the permissible distance ϵ from the actual cessation of speech. In other words, the featural machinery of dimensionality and boundaries, with which we characterize

Things and the regions of space they occupy, extends to Events as well. That's why the word *end* is so natural in either context. The main difference in the systems is that Things have a maximum dimensionality of 3, whereas Events have a maximum dimensionality of only 1, so that certain distinctions in the Thing system are leveled out or unavailable in the Event system. Only in a theory of conceptual structure that permits this sort of cross-categorial generalization can even the existence of a word like *end* be explained, much less the peculiarities of its use in so many different contexts—and the fact that these peculiarities are evidently learnable. (This subsystem of conceptual structure is treated in more detail in Jackendoff 1991.)

A general conclusion emerges from these three brief case studies. Beneath the surface complexity of natural language concepts lies a highly abstract formal algebraic system that lays out the major parameters of thought. The distinctions in this system are quite sharp and do not appear to be based on experience. Rather, I would claim, they are the machinery available to the human mind to channel the ways in which all experience can be mentally encoded—elements of the Universal Grammar for conceptual structure.

Significantly, the primitives of this system cannot appear in isolation. Rather, they are like phonological features or the quarks of particle physics: they can only be observed in combination, built up into conceptual constituents, and their existence must be inferred from their effects on language and cognition as a whole. This result militates against Fodor's Intentional Realism, in that one should not expect constant counterparts in reality for every aspect of the conceptual system. Roughly speaking, concepthood is a property of conceptual *constituents*, not conceptual *features*. (See Verkuyl and Zwarts 1990 for a formal treatment of this distinction.)

2.7   Where Traditional Features Fail

One of the abiding reasons for skepticism about feature-based semantics, even among those who believe in semantic decomposition, is that binary or n-ary features are clearly inadequate to the full task of conceptual description. These suspicions have been voiced since the earliest days of semantics in generative grammar (Bolinger 1965; Weinreich 1966) and continue to the present day (e.g. Lakoff 1987). This section will briefly mention some of the problems and the forms of enrichment proposed within Conceptual Semantics to deal with them.

2.7.1   Spatial Structure of Objects and Actions
The first problem has to do with specifying the shapes of objects. For instance, consider the lexical entries for *duck* and *goose*. Both of these

presumably carry features to the effect that they are animate, nonhuman categories of Things, that they are types of birds, perhaps types of water-fowl. But what comes next? How are they distinguished from one another? One possible factor, which clearly enters into learning the words in the first place, is how ducks and geese *look*, and how they differ in appearance. But to encode this difference in binary features, say [±long neck], is patently ridiculous. Similarly, how is a *chair* to be distinguished from a *stool*? Do they differ in a feature [±has-a-back]? What sort of feature is this? It is surely not a primitive. But, if composite, how far down does one have to go to reach primitives—if one can at all? To put a ± sign and a pair of brackets around any old expression simply doesn't make it into a legitimate conceptual feature.

This problem is addressed in Jackendoff 1987a, chapter 10, in the context of the connection between the linguistic and visual faculties. In order for an organism to accomplish visual identification and categorization, independent of language, there must be a form of visual representation that encodes geometric and topological properties of physical objects. The most plausible proposal I have encountered for such a representation is the *3D model structure* of Marr 1982. In turn, this structure can be interfaced with conceptual structure via a set of correspondence rules, as suggested in figure 2.1. This correspondence effects a translation of visual information into linguistic format, enabling us to talk about what we see.

Marr's approach is interesting because of the way it goes beyond a simple template theory of visual recognition. The 3D model is much more than a "statue in the head." It is an articulated structure that encodes the decomposition of objects into parts, the geometric systems of spatial axes around which objects are organized, and the relations among the parts. Within this framework, it is possible to represent not just single objects in single positions, but ranges of sizes, ranges of angles of attachment of parts, and ranges of detail from coarse- to fine-grained. Thus it is admirably suited to encoding just those geometric aspects of an object's appearance that are an embarrassment to any reasonable feature system.

Jackendoff 1987a suggests, therefore, that the lexical entry for a physical object word includes a 3D model representation in addition to its phonological, syntactic, and conceptual structures. The 3D model in fact plays the role sometimes assigned to an "image of a stereotypical instance," except that it is much more highly structured, along the lines suggested by Marr, and it can include parameters of variation among instances. The distinctions between *duck* and *goose* and between *chair* and *stool*, then, can appear in the 3D model instead of conceptual structure. We thereby eliminate the need for a plethora of objectionable conceptual features in favor of a geometric representation with entirely different primitives and principles of combination. It is shown that this natural division of labor is of benefit not only to the theory of the lexicon but also to the theory of visual categorization; I will not repeat the arguments here.

I should however add that the use of the 3D model need not pertain just to objects and the nouns that denote them. Marr and Vaina (1982) propose a natural extension of the 3D model to encode action patterns such as throwing and saluting. This can be used to address a parallel problem in the verbal system: how is one to distinguish, say, *running* from *jogging* from *loping*, or *throwing* from *tossing* from *lobbing*? If the lexical entries for these verbs contain a 3D model representation of the action in question, no distinction at all need be made in conceptual structure. The first set of verbs will all simply be treated in conceptual structure as verbs of locomotion, the second set as verbs of propulsion. Thus again we are relieved of the need for otiose feature analyses of such fine-scale distinctions. (Chapter 6 elaborates on the relation between conceptual structure and spatial cognition, especially in the domain of spatial relations among objects.)

2.7.2 Focal Values in a Continuous Domain

A second area in which a simple feature analysis fails concerns domains with a continuous rather than a discrete range of values. Consider the domain expressed by temperature words (*hot, warm, tepid, cool, cold*, etc.) or the domain of color words. One cannot decompose *hot* and *red* exhaustively into discrete features that distinguish them from *cold* and *yellow* respectively. The proper analysis seems to be that these words have a semantic field feature (Temperature or Color) that picks out a "cognitive space" consisting of a continuous range of values. In the case of Temperature, the space is essentially linear; in the case of Color, it is the familiar 3-dimensional color solid (Miller and Johnson-Laird 1976). For a first approximation, each temperature or color word picks out a point in its space, which serves as a focal value for the word.

According to this analysis, a percept is categorized in terms of its relative distance from available focal values. So, for example, a percept whose value in color space is close to focal red is easily categorized as red; a percept whose value lies midway between focal red and focal orange is categorized with less certainty and with more contextual dependence. Thus color categorization is a result of the interaction between the intrinsic structure of the color space—including physiologically determined salient values—and the number and position of color values for which the language has words (Berlin and Kay 1969).

Refinements can be imagined in the structure of such spaces. For example, the field of temperature has both positive and negative directions, so one can ask either *How hot?* or *How cold?* By contrast, the field of size words has only a positive direction from the zero point, so that *How big?* asks a neutral question about size but *How small?* is intended in relation to some contextually understood small standard. I will not pursue such refinements here. The point is that the introduction of continuous "cognitive spaces" in which words pick out focal values is an important enrichment of the expressive power of conceptual structure beyond simple binary or n-ary feature systems.

2.7.3   Preference Rule Systems

A different challenge to feature systems arises in the treatment of so-called cluster concepts. Consider the following examples:

(14)   a.   Bill climbed (up) the mountain.
        b.   Bill climbed down the mountain.
        c.   The snake climbed (up) the tree.
        d.   ?*The snake climbed down the tree.

Climbing appears to involve two independent conceptual conditions: (1) an individual is traveling upward; and (2) the individual is moving with characteristic effortful grasping motions, for which a convenient term is *clambering*. On the most likely interpretation of (14a), both these conditions are met. However, (14b) violates the first condition, and, since snakes can't clamber, (14c) violates the second. If *both* conditions are violated, as in (14d), the action cannot at all be characterized as climbing. Thus neither of the two conditions is necessary, but either is sufficient.

We do not want to say that the meaning of *climb* is just the disjunction of these two conditions. That would in effect claim that there are two unrelated senses of the word. If this were so, we would have the intuition that (14a) is as ambiguous as *Bill went down to the bank*, which may refer equally to a riverbank or a savings bank. But in fact we do not. Rather, (14a), which satisfies both conditions at once, is judged more "stereotypical" climbing. Actions that satisfy only one of the conditions, such as (14b,c), are somewhat more marginal but still perfectly legitimate instances of climbing. In other words, the two conditions combine in the meaning of a single lexical item *climb*, but not according to a standard Boolean conjunction or disjunction. Jackendoff 1983, chapter 8, calls a set of conditions combined in this way a *preference rule system*, and the conditions in the set *preference rules* or *preference conditions*.[5]

A similar paradigm can be displayed for the verb *see*:

(15)   a.   Bill saw Harry.
        b.   Bill saw a vision of dancing devils.
        c.   Bill saw the tree, but he didn't notice it at the time.
        d.   *Bill saw a vision of dancing devils, but he didn't notice it at the time.

The two preference conditions for *x sees y* are roughly that (1) x's gaze makes contact with y, and (2) x has a visual experience of y. Stereotypical seeing (i.e. veridical seeing) satisfies both these conditions: x makes visual contact with some object and thereby has a visual experience of it. (15b) violates condition (1) and (15c) violates condition (2), yet both felicitously use the word *see*. But if both are violated at once, as in (15d), the sentence is extremely odd. Again, we don't want to say that there are two homonymous verbs *see* and hence that (15a) is ambiguous. The solution is to claim that these two conditions form a preference rule system, in which stereotypical seeing satisfies both conditions and less central cases satisfy only one—but either one.[6]

Similar phenomena arise in the lexical entries for nouns that denote functional categories: form and function often are combined in a preference rule system. For instance, a stereotypical *chair* has a stereotypical form (specified by a 3D model) and a standard function (roughly "portable thing for one person to sit on"). Objects that have the proper function but the wrong form—say beanbag chairs—are more marginal instances of the category; and so are objects that have the right form but cannot fulfill the function—say chairs made of newspaper or giant chairs. An object that violates both conditions—say a pile of crumpled newspaper—is by no stretch of the imagination a chair. This is precisely the behavior we saw in *climb* and *see*.

A further aspect of preference rule systems is that when one lacks information about the satisfaction of the conditions, they are invariably assumed to be satisfied as *default values*. Thus the reason (14a) and (15a) are interpreted as stereotypical climbing and seeing is that the sentences give no information to the contrary. It is only in the (b) and (c) sentences, which *do* give information to the contrary, that a condition is relinquished.

The examples of preference rule systems given here have all involved only a pair of conditions. Systems with a larger number of conditions are likely to exist, but are harder to ferret out and articulate without detailed analysis. A preference rule system with only one condition degenerates to a standard default value. More generally, preference rule systems are capable of accounting for "family resemblance" categories such as Wittgenstein's (1953) well-known example *game*, for Rosch's (1978) "prototypes," and for other cases in which systems of necessary and sufficient conditions have failed because all putative conditions have counterexamples, but not all at once.

Still more broadly, Jackendoff 1983 shows that preference rule systems are an appropriate formalism for a vast range of psychological phenomena, from low-level visual and phonetic perception to high-level operations such as conscious decision-making. The formalism was in fact developed originally to deal with phenomena of musical cognition (Lerdahl and Jackendoff

1983a) and was anticipated by the Gestalt psychologists in their study of visual perception (Wertheimer 1923). There seems every reason, then, to believe that preference rule systems are a pervasive element of mental computation; we should therefore have no hesitation in adopting them as a legitimate element of conceptual structure. (See Jackendoff 1983, chapters 7 and 8, for extended discussion of preference rule systems, including comparison with systems of necessary and sufficient conditions, prototype theory, and fuzzy set theory, and for a rejoinder to Armstrong, Gleitman, and Gleitman's (1983) criticisms of cluster concepts.)

To sum up, this section has suggested three ways in which the decomposition of lexical concepts goes beyond simple binary or n-ary feature oppositions. These mechanisms conspire to make word meanings far richer than classical categories. Each of them creates a continuum between stereotypical and marginal instances, and each can create fuzziness or vagueness at category boundaries. Moreover, each of them can be motivated on more general cognitive grounds, so we are not multiplying artifices just to save the theory of lexical decomposition. And indeed, they appear collectively to go a long way toward making a suitably expressive theory of word meaning attainable.

2.8   Lexical Composition versus Meaning Postulates

Section 2.3 used the creativity of lexical concept formation to argue that lexical conceptual structures must be compositional and that one must have an innate "Universal Grammar of concepts" that enables one to construct new lexical concepts as needed. An important aspect of Fodor's work on the Language of Thought Hypothesis has been to deny lexical compositionality. Not that Fodor has offered any alternative analysis of lexical concepts that deals with any of the problems discussed in the last two sections; indeed his arguments are almost exclusively negative. Nevertheless, for completeness I had better address his concerns.

Fodor's first set of arguments (Fodor 1970; Fodor et al. 1980) builds on the virtual impossibility of giving precise definitions for most words. If definitions are impossible, Fodor argues, there is no reason to believe that words have internal structure. But in fact, this observation shows only that if there are principles of lexical conceptual composition, they are not entirely identical with the principles of phrasal conceptual composition. If the principles are not identical, it will often be impossible to build up an expression of conceptual structure phrasally that completely duplicates a lexical concept. As it happens, it appears that the nondiscrete elements of concepts discussed in section 2.7 play a role only in lexical semantics and never appear as a result of phrasal combination. Hence phrasal expansions of these aspects of lexical meaning cannot be constructed. Yet they are indubitably compositional. So this argument of Fodor's does not go through; it is founded on the false assumption that lexical and phrasal principles of composition are homogeneous.

The second set of arguments concerns processing. Fodor's supposition is that if lexical concepts are composite, a more complex word ought to induce a greater processing load and/or take more time to access or process than a less complex word. Finding no experimental evidence for such effects (Fodor, Fodor, and Garrett 1975), Fodor concludes again that lexical items cannot have compositional structure.[7] I see no reason to accept the premise of this argument. As is well known, the acquisition of complex motor concepts (such as playing a scale on the piano) *speeds up* performance over sequential performance of the constituent parts. Nevertheless, such motor concepts must still be compositional, since in the end the same complex motor pattern must be invoked. It stands to reason, then, that acquisition of a lexical concept might also speed up processing over a syntactically complex paraphrase, without in any way reducing conceptual complexity: a lexical item is "chunked," whereas a phrasal equivalent is not.

Because Fodor can find no system of lexical composition that satisfies his criteria of intentionality and of decomposition into necessary and sufficient conditions (both of which are abandoned in Conceptual Semantics), he decides that the enterprise is impossible, and that lexical concepts must be indissoluble monads. He recognizes two difficulties in this position, having to do with inference and acquisition, and he offers answers. Let me take these up in turn.

The first issue is how inference can be driven by lexical concepts with no internal structure. If one is dealing with inferences such as (P & Q) → P, as Fodor does in most of his discussion, there is little problem, assuming principles of standard logic. But for inferences that involve nonlogical lexical items, such as *John forced Harry to leave* → *Harry left* or *Sue approached the house* → *Sue got closer to the house*, there can be no general principles. Rather, each lexical item must be accompanied by its own specific meaning postulates that determine the entailments of sentences it occurs in. This is the solution Fodor advocates, though he does not propose how it is to be accomplished except perhaps in the most trivial of cases, such as *Rover is a dog* → *Rover is an animal*.

The trouble with such an approach, even if it can succeed observationally, is that it denies the possibility of generalizing among the inferential properties of different lexical items. Each item is a world unto itself. Thus, for instance, consider the entailment relationship between the members of causative-noncausative pairs such as those in (16).

(16) a.   x killed y → y died
      b.   x lifted y → y rose
      c.   x gave z to y → y received z
      d.   x persuaded y that P → y came to believe that P

In a lexical meaning postulate theory, these inferences are totally unrelated. Intuitively, though, they are all instances of a schema stated roughly as (17), where E is an Event.

(17)   x cause E to occur → E occur

In order to invoke a general schema like (17), the left-hand verbs in (16) must have lexical meaning postulates like (18), in which the bracketed expressions are Events.

(18) a.   x kill y → x cause [y die]
      b.   x lift y → x cause [y rise]
      c.   x give z to y → x cause [y receive z]
      d.   x persuade y that P → x cause [y come to believe that P]

But this is a notational variant of the analysis of causative in a lexical decomposition theory: it claims that there is an element *cause* that (1) is mentioned in the analysis (here, the lexical meaning postulates) of many lexical items and (2) gives access to more general-purpose rules of inference.

I suggest that, for fans of lexical meaning postulates, lexical decomposition can be regarded systematically in this light: each element in a lexical decomposition can be regarded as that item's access to more general-purpose rules of inference. The problem of lexical decomposition, then, is to find a vocabulary for decomposition that permits the linguistically significant generalizations of inference patterns to be captured formally in terms of schemas like (17) and rule (12) in section 2.6.2. (See Jackendoff 1976 for a range of such rules of inference.)

I conclude therefore that a lexical meaning postulate approach to inference either misses all generalizations across inferential properties of lexical items or else is essentially equivalent to a decomposition theory. Thus Fodor has correctly identified a problem for his approach but has proposed a nonsolution.

The second difficulty Fodor sees for noncompositional lexical concepts is how one could possibly acquire them. In any computational theory, "learning" can consist only of creating novel combinations of primitives already innately available. This is one of the fundamental arguments of Fodor 1975, and one that I accept unconditionally. However, since for Fodor all lexical concepts are primitive, they cannot be learned as combinations of more primitive vocabulary. It follows that all lexical concepts must be innate, including such exotica as *telephone, spumoni, funicular,* and *soffit,* a conclusion that strains credulity but that Fodor evidently embraces.

Notice how Fodor's position is different from saying that all lexical concepts must be within the innate expressive power of the grammar of conceptual structure, as advocated here. The difference is that in the present approach it is the *potential* of an infinite number of lexical concepts that is inherent in the grammar of conceptual structure—just as the potential for the syntactic structures of all human languages is inherent in Universal Grammar. Lexical acquisition then requires constructing a particular lexical concept and associating it with a syntactic and phonological structure.

Fodor notes of course that not every speaker has a phonological realization of every lexical concept. Since his notion of "realization" cannot include learning, he advocates the idea that somehow the attachment of an innate lexical concept to a phonological structure is "triggered" by relevant experience, perhaps by analogy with the way parameter settings in syntax are said to be triggered. However, the analogy is less than convincing. The setting of syntactic parameters is determined within a highly articulated theory of syntactic structure, where there is a limited number of choices for the setting. The supposed triggering of lexical concepts takes place in a domain where there is by hypothesis *no* relevant structure, and where the choices are grossly underdetermined. As far as I know, then, Fodor has offered no account of lexical concept realization other than a suggestive name. By contrast, real studies of language acquisition have benefited from decompositional theories of lexical concepts (e.g. Landau and Gleitman 1985; Pinker 1989), so the decomposition theory has empirical results on its side in this area as well.

An especially unpleasant consequence of Fodor's position is that, given the finiteness of the brain, there can be only a finite number of possible lexical concepts. This seems highly implausible, since one can coin new names for arbitrary new types of objects and actions ("This is a glarf; now watch me snarf it"), and we have no sense that we will someday run out of names for things. More pointedly, the number of potential category concepts is at least as large as the number of concepts for individuals (tokens), since for every individual X one can form a category of "things just like X" and give it a monomorphemic name. Thus if we can encode only a finite number of categories, we must be able to encode only a finite number of individuals as well. However, it is hard to believe that nature has equipped us with an ability to recognize individual things in the world that is limited to a finite number. So far as I know, Fodor has not addressed this objection. (See Jackendoff 1983, section 5.2, for a more detailed version of this argument.)

From these considerations I conclude that Fodor's theory of lexical concepts cannot deal at all with the creativity of concept formation and with concept acquisition. Nor can any other theory that relies on monadic predicates linked by meaning postulates. By contrast, a compositional theory in principle offers solutions parallel to those for the creativity and acquisition of syntax. (See chapter 3 for more discussion of learnability of concepts.)

2.9   Ending

So what is a concept? I have shown here that for the purpose of understanding the mind, the apposite focus of inquiry is the notion of I-concept, a species of mental information structure. The program of Conceptual Semantics provides a theoretical realization of this notion that unifies it in many ways with a mentalistic theory of the language faculty and with the theories of perception, cognition, and learning. In particular, I have identified the notion of *I-concept* with the formal notion of *conceptual constituent* as developed in Conceptual Semantics. Furthermore, I have sketched a number of the major elements of the internal structure of concepts, showing how the approach accounts for various basic phenomena in the semantics of natural language, and how it meets various well-known objections to theories of lexical decomposition.

In evaluating this approach, I think two things must be borne in mind. First, it does not address what are taken to be some of the standard hurdles for a theory of concepts, for example Putnam's (1975) Twin Earth problem. What must be asked with respect to such problems, though, is whether they are at all relevant to a theory of I-concepts, or whether they are germane only to the theory of E-concepts, as I believe is the case with the Twin Earth problem. If they are problems only for E-conceptual theory, they play no role in evaluating the present approach.

Second, what I find appealing about the present approach is that it leads one into problems of richer and richer articulation: What are the ontological categories, and do they themselves have internal structure? What sorts of fundamental functions are there that create Events, States, Places, and Paths? How are various semantic fields alike in structure, and how do they diverge? How do nondiscrete features interact with each other in phrasal combination? What are the conceptual primitives underlying social cognition and "folk psychology"? How are conceptual systems learnable? And so forth. The fact that Conceptual Semantics begins to provide a formal vocabulary in which such questions can be couched suggests to me that, despite its being at odds with most of the recent philosophical tradition, it is a fruitful framework in which to conduct scientific inquiry.

Chapter 3

Word Meanings and What It Takes to Learn Them: Reflections on the Piaget-Chomsky Debate

Many years after the fact, I finally got around to reading Piattelli-Palmerini 1980, the chronicle of the 1975 debate between Jean Piaget and Noam Chomsky, with the participation of many other interested parties. Being myself a deeply committed Chomskian, though not an altogether orthodox one, I was surprised by the vehemence of the debate. After all, Piaget and Chomsky have a great deal in common. Both believe in complex unconscious mental processing. Both believe that the structure of the world we experience is in large part determined by internal mental constructs of potentially great abstraction. Both are firmly opposed to behaviorism.

As far as I can determine, the major difference between the Piagetian and Chomskian traditions concerns what it takes to learn. Not a small part of the problem in the debate was that Chomsky's argument focused almost exclusively on complex details of the learning of syntax, about which Piaget had virtually nothing to say; likewise, Piaget's ground for argument was conceptual learning, about which Chomsky had virtually nothing to say. So the debate was not carried on in common territory, which led to a certain amount of the mutual misunderstanding and rancor.

Here I am going to try to simplify the problem of learning presented by Chomsky and Fodor in the course of the debate, and see where the main point of disagreement lies. Furthermore, I am going to do it on a ground more recognizable by Piagetians, in the domain of concept learning, as revealed by the child's learning of word meanings. In order to do so, however, I have to present a rather lengthy excursus on what I think concepts and word meanings are.

3.1 The Repertoire of Concepts

How do I conceive of a word meaning? The only reasonable way anyone has been able to conceive of a word meaning within a cognitive theory is

This chapter was prepared for a plenary lecture at the June 1991 meeting of the Jean Piaget Society. I am grateful to John Macnamara for extensive discussion of the issues treated here, and to David Palermo and George Lakoff for useful comments on the original version.

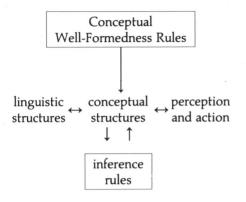

Figure 3.1

in terms of states of a combinatorial system, instantiated either in a system of symbols, or in a system of neurons, or in a system of neuronesque elements such as a connectionist network. Furthermore, the combination of word meanings into phrase and sentence meanings has to be governed by a combinatorial system that in some way more or less parallels the combinatorial properties of the syntax in which the phrases and sentences are expressed. This much has to be essentially unexceptionable.

To make this only slightly more concrete, I think of word meanings as instantiated in large part in a particular subsystem of the brain's combinatorial organization that I call *conceptual structure*. The relation of conceptual structure to mental organization as a whole is diagrammed in figure 3.1. (See chapters 1 and 2 for greater detail.) As in the previous chapters, the arrows in this figure do not stand for psychological processes that take place over time, but just for formal relations of *constraint* among different combinatorial structures. This notion of constraint will become clearer shortly.

The full class of humanly possible concepts (or conceptual structures) is determined by the combinatorial principles of the *Conceptual Well-Formedness Rules*. That is, the Conceptual Well-Formedness Rules characterize the space of possible conceptual states—the resources available in the brain for forming concepts. The set of concepts attained by any particular person will be some subset of these. I am not going to be concerned with how concepts are instantiated by neurons in the brain; crucial as it is, I don't think we have any useful understanding of this issue at the moment. Rather, I want to keep stressing, I am interested in the properties of the combinatorial space available to the brain—what possibilities exist, and what concepts are related to what other concepts in what dimensions. (This way of looking at things so far ought to be fairly comfortable to the Piagetian as well as to the Chomskian tradition.)

What about the other three components in figure 3.1? First look at the *inference rules*. These are relations among conceptual structures, specifying how to pass from one concept to another. So, for instance, if you believe that X *caused Y to take place*, you can infer that Y took place; whereas by contrast if you believe that X *tried to cause Y to take place*, you cannot tell whether Y took place. These differences have to be expressed by the interaction between conceptual structures and the rules of inference. (I include under the term *rules of inference* principles of pragmatics and heuristics; by contrast with much of the philosophical tradition, I don't think there is any serious difference between these and rules of logical inference. See Jackendoff 1983, chapters 6 and 8, for discussion.)

In addition, conceptual structures of course have to be linked by a principled set of *correspondence rules* to the mental representations that serve language: conceptual structures are by hypothesis the form in which the meanings of linguistic expressions must be couched internally. Finally, conceptual structures have to be linked by a different set of correspondence rules to the representations for perception and action, so that perceptual experience can be encoded in a form suitable for linguistic expression.

I should also point out that a combinatorial form like conceptual structure is necessary even for nonlinguistic cognition. For example, there is nothing in a perceptual representation as such that can encode the difference between, say, a particular dog Rover and a generic or stereotypical dog. That is, the difference between a token (or known individual) and a type (or category) is not a *per*ceptual difference, but a *con*ceptual one. (This is discussed in more detail in Jackendoff 1983, chapter 5, and Jackendoff 1987a, chapter 10.) Therefore I conceive of conceptual structure as a meeting ground between concrete perceptual and motor representations and abstract concepts, whether or not they are expressed linguistically.

In short, conceptual structures form a combinatorial space whose possibilities are determined by the Conceptual Well-Formedness Rules; a particular subset of conceptual structure is linked to language; different, possibly overlapping subsets are linked to perceptual and motor representations; and in addition conceptual structures are linked to one another by rules of inference.

3.2   How Words Mean

What is a word meaning, then? Under this view, a word meaning is a fragment of conceptual structure that is linked in long-term memory with a phonological structure (its pronunciation) and a syntactic structure (its part of speech and other syntactic properties such as grammatical gender and case-marking properties). That is, the words one knows consist of stored concepts linked with stored elements of linguistic expression.

So far there should be no great surprises. In particular, I have not ruled out the possibility that word meanings contain stereotypes, lexical extensions, citations of familiar instances, or a host of other possibilities suggested in the literature. All that is required is that *if* such phenomena are part of word meanings, the Conceptual Well-Formedness Rules must make them possible. That is, the expressive possibilities for word meanings, whatever they are, must be encompassed in the Conceptual Well-Formedness Rules. (See sections 2.6–7 for a sampling of the possibilities.)

In this story, a number of factors combine to make a word mean what it does. First is the connection of the concept expressed by the word to perception and action. If the word names an object, for instance, this connection links the concept to what the object looks like, what it tastes like, what it sounds like, and what actions can be performed on it; if the word names an action, this connection specifies what the action looks like, what it is like to perform the action, and so forth. This connection, then, is the present theory's counterpart of what the philosophical tradition calls the *reference* of the word. However, it concerns not the *real-world* counterpart of the concept but the *mental representations* linked to the concept in the perceptual and motor modalities (see chapters 2 and 8). Note that not all words, nor all aspects of any particular word, *are* linked to perceptual or motor components. Many words and parts of word meanings are purely abstract, for instance the token-type distinction just mentioned, which has no perceptual counterpart. So referential linkage is clearly not all there is to word meanings.

A second crucial aspect of word meaning is its interaction with the inference rules. What makes the verb *approach* differ from the verb *reach*, for example? If you *approach* an object, you are going toward it, but you do not necessarily get there. By contrast, if you *reach* an object, you have been going toward it, and you have gotten there. This difference in inference, like the difference between causing and trying described above, follows from a feature of "completiveness" or "boundedness" in conceptual structure interacting with an inference rule that depends on the value of that feature. *Approach* and *try* are noncompletive or unbounded actions, so one cannot infer the final state of the action; whereas *reach* and *cause* are completive or bounded actions, so one can infer the final goal. (See Jackendoff 1991 and references therein for a more precise description.)

A third factor contributing to a word's meaning is its relationship to the rest of the lexicon. For instance, consider the taxonomic relations between *dog* and *animal* in one direction and between *dog* and *poodle* in the other direction. These links within the lexicon form concepts into hierarchies, and they are an important part of our conceptual knowledge; again, they often cannot be specified perceptually. In addition, a well-known phenomenon within these intralexical relations is the tendency of the sisters in a taxonomy to expand their range of applicability to fill gaps between them. For instance, whatever the class of focal color words in a language, each focal color word can be applied to any other colors sufficiently near to the focal color and sufficiently distant from the others (Berlin and Kay 1969; Miller and Johnson-Laird 1976). What this means is that in a language with more focal color words, each of the focal color words automatically has a narrower range of application. This does not follow from any perceptual facts or from any inference rules—it follows from the taxonomic structure of the lexicon.

A fourth aspect of word meanings concerns the interaction of the word with the grammatical patterns of the language. For instance, a number of people (e.g. Anderson 1971; Rappaport and Levin 1985; Tenny 1987; Pinker 1989) have noted that certain verbs vary in completiveness depending on the syntactic pattern in which they appear. A well-known example is the verb *to load*. If I *load a truck with furniture*, the implication is that the truck is full of furniture at the end—that is, the sentence is completive. But if I express a similar action as *loading furniture onto the truck*, there is no necessary implication that the truck is full at the end. A parallel alternation occurs with a wide range of verbs, suggesting that the grammatical pattern itself is carrying an element of meaning that interacts with the meaning of the verb to make the inference possible.

In short, each of the components that constrains conceptual structure—the Conceptual Well-Formedness Rules, the inference rules, and the connections to grammatical expression and to nonlinguistic modalities, as well as the repertoire of related words in the lexicon—has an effect on the meaning of a word, and on how it is used and understood in linguistic and nonlinguistic contexts.

3.3   Learned and Innate Components of Word Meaning

What does this have to do with the debate between Piaget and Chomsky? As I said earlier, I think that the major issue that separates them is the nature of learning. In order for me to address this issue, I have to ask, in the present approach to word meanings, what is entailed in a child's (or an adult's) learning a new word meaning? Very abstractly, we have to think of the child as selecting a conceptual structure for the word and linking it with a linguistic expression (i.e. with a phonological and a syntactic structure). At the same time, if the concept is completely or partially concrete (i.e. has perceptual or motor counterparts), those linkages too must be established in order to achieve competence at using the word.

But what determines the possible concepts that the learner can consider? At bottom, the possibilities are constrained by the Conceptual Well-Formedness Rules, which are by hypothesis the resources that make possible all humanly attainable concepts. Now the point that is crucial to notice here, and the place in the argument where many people get caught, is the question of *where the Conceptual Well-Formedness Rules come from*. The point is that they cannot be learned: *they are the foundation on which learning is based*. This is an argument that in its modern form is due to Jerry Fodor (1975); but its basic idea goes back probably to Kant. What does this mean? In essence, it means that the Conceptual Well-Formedness Rules have to be innate—part of the wiring of the brain. If you like, the Conceptual Well-Formedness Rules specify what kind of a computer the part of the brain is that deals with conceptual structure. In turn, this wiring must be determined by some as yet unknown combination of genetic structure and the principles of neural growth, about which no one has anything useful to say at the moment, as far as I know.

By using the word *innate* I undoubtedly have raised some readers' hackles. Many people, for various reasons, have a strong objection to the idea that brain structure (and therefore mental structure) could be to any significant degree innate. And of course it is Chomsky's contentions about innateness that have enamored—and enraged—different segments of the psychological and philosophical communities. But again, so far I haven't said very much that should be controversial. As Fodor (1975) has pointed out, *everyone* believes in *some* degree of innateness. For the most extreme case, suppose you're an unreconstructed associationist. Then, within this way of describing things, you believe in effect that the Conceptual Well-Formedness Rules encompass the space of possibilities provided by sense-data, plus the combination of elements of that space by the principle of association. But children don't *learn* to have sense-data and they don't learn to form associations; these have to be given as the innate substrate from which learning can proceed.

So the real issue has to be not, Is the space of possible concepts constrained by a set of innate principles? because everyone turns out to believe that it is. Rather, the issue is, How specific and detailed is the set of innate principles, and what are the specifics and details? So it's a matter of degree, not of absolutes, and one can find positions all along the spectrum. At one end, perhaps, fall the unreconstructed associationists. Perhaps at the other end is Jerry Fodor himself, who at least sometimes (Fodor 1975, 1981; Fodor et al. 1980) believes that all word meanings are innate in complete detail, and there is no such thing as word learning. That is, for Fodor, the Conceptual Well-Formedness Rules in effect contain a vast *list* of complete word meanings.

I for one find Fodor's position untenable (see section 2.8 for some reasons). All serious research on lexical organization confirms common sense in suggesting that word meanings are composite—that they are built up from some set of conceptual primitives and principles of combination.

On this view, then, learning a word meaning is to be viewed as *constructing* a structured combination out of the primitives and principles of combination available in the Conceptual Well-Formedness Rules. Word learning is therefore conceived of as an active constructive process, not just a passive process of association—a conception shared by the Piagetian school.

But on the other hand, one must keep bearing in mind that the child can't learn the primitives themselves. Put differently, one can't simultaneously claim both that something is a primitive and that it is learned, for learning entails construction from primitives. If I were to claim that some conceptual unit is a primitive, and it turned out to be learned, I would have no choice but to change my claim and to look for a deeper or more primitive set of basic units from which my unit could be constructed. This is a simple point of the logic of combinatorial systems.

In particular—and this too just follows from the logic of combinatorial systems—a particular set of primitives and principles of combination creates a space of possible concepts. This space is perhaps infinite, but it will have a certain number of inherent dimensions or degrees of freedom that follow from the innate basis (or the axioms, if you like) out of which it is generated. If one wants to add a new degree of freedom to the space, one has to add a new primitive to the innate basis. There is logically no way around this.

So an important empirical issue is, What is a plausible set of innate primitives and principles of combination that on one hand creates the space of concepts possible for adults, and that on the other hand makes this space of concepts learnable for the child?

One of Piaget's important hypotheses is that children acquire their repertoire of concepts in a certain order, starting with basic sensorimotor concepts and gradually progressing from them to more abstract domains, eventually arriving at the most abstract concepts of pure logic. Piaget, as I understand him, claims that this progression or "passage from one stage to another" is a product of a construction or invention that is ultimately based on the original sensorimotor concepts. It is not based on anything "innate," but is just "the result of development" (Piaget 1970, 47). He contests the view of the "nativist or apriorist [who] maintains that the forms of knowledge are predetermined inside the subject and thus . . . , strictly speaking, there can be no novelty" (Piaget 1970, 77).

Notice, by the way, that Piaget somewhat overstates the nativist position, outside of the extreme Fodorian view that all word meanings are innate in toto. If what is innate is a set of Conceptual Well-Formedness Rules, that is, a set of primitives and principles of combination, then this set provides an infinite number of possible concepts, only some finite number of which is attained by any particular human being. This means that within the system there are always new concepts to be constructed that no one has had before. That is, there can be a great amount of novelty in concepts, even if there is none in the potential expressive power of the system.

Interestingly, a view similar to Piaget's has been espoused recently in the work of George Lakoff (Lakoff 1987, 1990; Lakoff and Turner 1989), who claims that abstract concepts are constructed by means of a process of "metaphor" from a basis of concrete perceptual concepts. Lakoff too rejects the need for positing any innate basis for abstract concepts themselves. Although Lakoff does not as far as I know cite Piaget, his theory of metaphor is easily interpreted as one realization of Piaget's theory of genetic epistemology. For example, just like Piaget (1966), he has argued (1987, chapter 20) that mathematical concepts arise from basic sensorimotor or "embodied" operations, and he argues that the process bringing about this evolution is metaphor. So this issue is not confined to the Piagetian school.

I believe Piaget is correct in seeing a connection between sensorimotor concepts and abstract ones (Jackendoff 1976, 1983; see also section 2.6.2). On the other hand, I believe that Piaget, and with him Lakoff, have not examined the process of extension quite closely enough, and that a crucial logical part of the process is being missed. To illustrate this point, I want to look at a particular case in which there is a relation of spatial concepts to another domain, and I want to pick apart very carefully what can be learned and what has to be innate. I will argue that in this case an extension of spatial concepts to this new domain cannot take place unless some aspects of the domain are already made available by the primitives of conceptual structure, that is, unless they are innate. Therefore, even if Piaget and Lakoff are correct in thinking that abstract concepts are built by extending perceptual concepts, they are not correct in claiming that the abstract concepts therefore need no innate basis.

3.4 A Test Case: Concepts of Ownership

That's where the argument is going. To motivate it, we have to look at some facts. The domain we will examine is concepts of *ownership* and especially *change of ownership*. (1) gives some expressions in this domain.

(1) a. Bill gave a book *to* Harry.
         Harry donated the book *to* the library.
     b. Harry received/got a book *from* Bill.
     c. The book was a present/gift *from* Bill *to* Harry.
     d. Harry gave the book *back* to Bill.
         Bill got the book *back* from Harry.
     e. Bill gave the book *away*.

Notice that the italicized words in the examples also appear in sentences about spatial motion:

(2) a. Bill went *to* the store.
          Bill threw the ball *to* Harry.
     b. Harry came *from* the store.
          Bill brought a newspaper *from* the store.
     c. We were on a train *from* Boston *to* Philadelphia.
     d. Then we went *back* to Boston.
          We came *back* from Philadelphia.
     e. Bill pushed the food *away*.

In both cases, there is an entity that undergoes change: in the sentences in (1) the book changes possession; in (2) a variety of things change location. In both cases, the object of the preposition *to* is associated with the final state of the change: the possessor at the end of the events described in (1), the final location of the motions described in (2). Similarly, the object of the preposition *from* is associated with the initial state of the change: the possessor at the beginning of the events described in (1), the starting point of motion in the events described in (2). The use of the adverb *back* in both cases suggests that the change involves a return to an earlier starting point that precedes the described event, either the previous possessor in (1) or the previous location in (2). Finally, the use of *away* indicates a change whose initial point is either possession by the subject of the sentence (1e) or location at or near the subject of the sentence (2e) and whose final point is some other unspecified possessor or location.

The parallelism goes a little further. We can use the verb *go* to describe not only physical motion in space, but also under certain circumstances change of possession, as in (3).

(3) The inheritance went to Philip.

The verb *keep* can be used either to describe causing something to stay in a physical location over a period of time, as in (4a), or to describe deliberate possession over a period of time, as in (4b).

(4) a. Harry kept the book on the shelf.
     b. Harry kept the book.

The verb *be* can be used to indicate either spatial position (5a) or possession (5b).

(5) a. Harry *is* in Camden.
     b. The book *is* Harry's.

In many languages, for example French, this last parallelism is even stronger, in that even the same preposition is used:

(6) a. Harry *est à* Camden.
     b. Le livre *est à* Harry.

What do we make of this linguistic parallelism? Its general outlines are duplicated in language after language, so it doesn't look like just a sheer accident of English grammar or of the history of English. Rather, as many different people have suggested, the grammatical parallelism we observe here is a reflection of a parallelism in the conceptual structure underlying these expressions. The conceptual parallelism proceeds like this:

X is in physical location Y	parallels	X belongs to Y
therefore		
Change in physical location of X	parallels	Change in possessor of X
Initial location of X	parallels	Initial possessor of X
Final location of X	parallels	Final possessor of X
Return to previous location of X	parallels	Return to previous possessor of X
Unspecified different location of X	parallels	Unspecified different possessor of X
Caused stasis in X's location	parallels	Caused stasis in X's owner

That is, the initial conceptual parallelism induces a whole system of parallelisms, which show themselves linguistically as parallelism in use of various verbs, prepositions, and adverbs.

Suppose, then, that there is this conceptual parallelism that accounts for the linguistic parallelism. But *what accounts for the conceptual parallelism*? To start with, observe that spatial location goes roughly under the rubric of a sensorimotor concept, but ownership definitely does not: there is no general way of telling who an object belongs to by looking at it and at its context. That is, ownership is surely an abstract concept. Therefore, according to Piagetian genetic epistemology, one would guess that the child learns the system of concepts surrounding ownership and change in ownership by some suitable extension or abstraction or progression from the understanding of location and motion in space. Similarly, I would assume that Lakoff would want to claim that the domain of spatial location and motion constitutes a metaphor for possession and change of possession. In either case, the idea is that the child, having understood spatial concepts, becomes capable of constructing possessional concepts from spatial concepts by some process of conceptual extension. But possessional concepts are not themselves innate.

Under this assumption, let us (artificially) suppose that a child's learning involves two stages: at Stage 1 the child has acquired spatial concepts but not possessional concepts, and at Stage 2 possessional concepts are present as well. How does the child get from Stage 1 to Stage 2?

Let us suppose further that the child can observe the grammatical parallelisms in the expression of spatial and possessional concepts. Then when the child hears a sentence like *Give the doll to Harry*, not knowing the possessional sense of the word *give*, he or she may guess from the use of the preposition *to* that the speaker wishes him or her to cause the doll to move spatially so that its final position is next to Harry. However, this knowledge will not enable the child to guess that he or she necessarily is supposed to let go of the doll or relinquish control of it, which is part of the meaning conveyed by *give*. (Compare *Give the doll to Harry* to a truly spatial sentence like *Take the doll over to the sofa*, which carries no implications of relinquishing control.) Furthermore, about the only possible concept available to the child in the spatial domain for *The doll is mine* is that the doll is in spatial proximity to me.

Now it is true that spatial proximity is often a physical cue for ownership: *my* clothes are usually on *me*, and *yours* are on *you*, for example. How will the child get the idea that ownership is something different from spatial proximity? Perhaps someone says, *Put the doll down, it's mine, not yours.* The child can infer that his or her own spatial proximity to the doll is not sufficient for ownership, that is, that the concept of ownership is *not spatial*.

What next? With what concept shall the child replace the incorrect spatial interpretation of ownership? Suppose, following Piaget and Lakoff, that no abstract concepts are innate. In the terms that I have stated the problem, this means that the Conceptual Well-Formedness Rules provide no possibilities for abstract concepts. Then the child is in a pickle, for there is no way ever to achieve the concept of possession: the space of possibilities simply does not contain a notion of ownership—*it can't be constructed from any combination of spatial primitives.*[1]

One might try a different explanation: that what is innate is completely general and unstructured, and that possession falls out as a reasonable possibility when spatial location is rejected. There are two problems with this: First, what does "completely general" mean? If possession is not a primitive, out of what completely general primitives is it constructed? Are we back to association again, which we know is inadequate? And second, of all the millions of possible concepts putatively available in a "completely general" system, how does the child manage to pick possession?

Let us see how difficult this concept would be to pick out of a "completely general" system, even if one could be stated. Very roughly, if X owns Y, three things follow:

1. X has a right to use Y.
2. Nobody else has a right to use Y without X's permission.
3. X and only X has the right to assign rights 1 and 2 to another individual, at which point X does not have these rights to Y anymore.

The child must discover a concept with *these very inferences*, from a space of millions of possibilities that by hypothesis has no innate organization. But consider the content of these inferences: the notions of rights and of permission, and of the right to assign rights, are incredibly abstract, and do not follow at all from the spatial parallel. How is the child supposed to discover *them* in an unstructured class of possibilities, just by using extension or metaphor?

In addition, the parallels between physical space and possession are very strictly limited. Physical space is of course 3-dimensional, so an object can move *up*, *down*, *frontward*, *backward*, and *sideways*. By contrast, the possessional parallel has no dimensions: one can't *give* something *upward* or *frontward*. Physical space is continuous: if something moves from point A to point B, it occupies all the intermediate positions between A and B along the way. By contrast, the possessional parallel is discontinuous: there are no intermediate positions that an object traverses between being owned by X and being owned by Y. One can *move* a book *toward* or even *partway toward* Bill; but one cannot *give* a book *toward*, much less *partway toward*, Bill.

If the notion of possession is constructed simply by extending spatial concepts, why are there these striking differences? And if it is constructed by a "general-purpose" system, how does the child happen to construct this particular possibility, with these particular inferences, out of the millions of algebraic possibilities, given that there is no definitive sensory input that picks out this choice?

I would like to suggest an alternative, which flows from what has been called (for reasons that need not concern us here) the *Thematic Relations Hypothesis* or TRH (Jackendoff 1976, 1983; see also section 2.6.2). This hypothesis claims that the parallelism between spatial and possessional concepts is the result of three independent factors. The first is the conception of physical space and of objects being located in it; this is presumably fairly hard-wired and connected to the perceptual system. (It's not clear that Piaget would have accepted even this as innate; but well-known contemporary developmental evidence (e.g. Spelke 1983) suggests that at least a lot of it is.) The second factor is the notion of possession—a relation between a possessed object and a person, the possessor. We will discuss shortly to what degree this might be innate, but fundamentally I think some version of it has to be.

The third and crucial factor involved in the parallelism is an innate abstract organizing system for concepts that elaborates a simple stative relation into a full system of concepts for change over time, beginning points, ending points, stasis, and so forth. This abstract system admits of different realizations, among which are the conceptual systems for space and for possession. This theory is compared very schematically with the theory of spatial extension or spatial metaphor in figure 3.2.

Piaget/Lakoff

spatial concepts → possessional concepts

Thematic Relations Hypothesis

      abstract organizing system

        ↓   ↓

spatial concepts   possessional concepts

     ↑   ↑

notions of object   notions of person

  and location   and possession

Figure 3.2

Let us see how on this story a child might progress from Stage 1, knowing only spatial language, to Stage 2, knowing possessional language as well. At Stage 1, the child understands, for instance, that the object of *from* indicates the initial point of motion and that the object of *to* indicates the final point of motion. The child has presumably constructed this linkage by associating spatial language with perceivable events of location and motion. Now, recall the crucial point when the child receives evidence that *give the doll to Harry* implies something other than spatial movement. At this point, the Conceptual Well-Formedness Rules provide a salient alternative for the relation in question, namely possession. Furthermore, once the child has "discovered" the notion of possession among the innate stock of primitives, the abstract organizing system immediately tells the child how to use known grammatical structures to organize this system, for instance that the object of *from* indicates an initial possessor and the object of *to* indicates a final possessor. That is, given the initial innate "germ" for the system of possession, the spatial parallel permits the child immediately to induce the meaning of the grammatical expressions for possessional concepts.

On the other hand, the child would *not* expect a full parallelism with spatial expressions, because the notion of location in physical space ranges over three continuous orthogonal degrees of freedom, whereas what we might call "possessional space" ranges over the discontinuous unstructured set of individuals.

In short, although at first glance it looks as if the child is learning by a process of "metaphor, " this is not actually the case; the parallelism between the two fields plays a somewhat different role in learning. And, as I have tried to show, the child *cannot* use the parallel to construct a new field unless the Conceptual Well-Formedness Rules make the germ of the new field available.

On the other hand, Piaget may well be right that the child has to understand spatial language before possessional language. Why? The reason is that the referential status of spatial terms allows the child to associate the grammatical patterns of the language with the abstract organizing system, and without this association there is no way to get into the organization of the abstract possessional concepts, where nothing can be observed directly. More generally, this is why sensorimotor concepts provide the anchor for the learning of abstract concepts.

Looking at possession a little more closely, I certainly don't want to claim that the American or European notions of ownership are totally innate; there are certainly wide cultural variations. However, as far as I know, all cultures have a concept of ownership or property rights that can be seen as a variation of ours, varying in what kinds of things you can own, what that entitles you to, and some variants in the exact details of the inferences (for instance whether you have the right to give away your land). I think these variations can probably be learned from observation or instruction. But, as I am continuing to emphasize, the fundamental relation of possession and the fundamental notion of a right cannot be learned from observation or instruction—they have to be available innately in the Conceptual Well-Formedness Rules in order to be on one hand culturally universal and on the other hand culturally modulated. (See chapter 4 for further discussion.)

Some readers may find themselves incredulous at the idea that a concept as abstract and eccentric as possession is innate—hard-wired in the brain. We can understand how a hard-wired set of spatial concepts could have evolved to solve long-standing problems of navigation, but the evolution of a notion of possession seems less inherently plausible. I have three lines of reply. First, the formal analysis of combinatorial systems, with which this chapter began (see also chapters 1 and 2), shows that possessional concepts cannot be derived from spatial concepts alone without adding something else. Second, the way evolution typically works is by innovating some weird little eccentric device, not by innovating big general-purpose systems. So the evolution of an eccentric domain of possession is on evolutionary grounds more plausible than that of a totally mushy general-purpose problem solver, which is in any event likely to be inadequate to the task of learning the notion of possession. Third, the notion of possession is tremendously fundamental to human culture—this abstraction and its inferences constitute one of a very small number of major issues around which each culture constructs its equivalent of a legal system. It is hard even to imagine what a society would be like in which this concept was fundamentally altered—you might even say that Karl Marx tried to imagine such a society, and in practice it didn't exactly work out. So, eccentric and abstract as the concept of possession may be, there are a lot of independent reasons to think it is a basic part of human nature. (See chapter 4 for a broader framework for this argument.)

3.5 Conclusions

This ends my story about the relation of spatial location and possession. The larger point I want to make from this is that the *very same* story has to be true for *any* kind of concept learning. In order for a child to acquire concepts in a new domain, this domain must be within the space of possibilities provided by the Conceptual Well-Formedness Rules. In other words, we must understand Piaget's theory of genetic epistemology via conceptual extension, as well as Lakoff's theory of conceptual learning via metaphorical extension, in a somewhat different way. We have to think of the child as applying an abstract combinatorial system, evoked by the original field, to a previously specified and probably innate "germ" concept for the new field. The process of abstracting away from the original field thus amounts to pulling the combinatorial system off so that it can be applied elsewhere. (See Jackendoff and Aaron 1991 for further discussion of Lakoff's theory of metaphor and its relation to the Thematic Relations Hypothesis.)

Still more generally, I think this is the point Chomsky and Fodor were trying to make in the Piaget-Chomsky debate. Whatever mental processes generalize to new domains, be they association, assimilation and accommodation, inference patterns, or symbolic structure, the domain these processes generalize *to* can't be created out of whole cloth. Rather, one should think in terms of a new domain being, if you like, "discovered"—that is, a previously unsalient or unnoticed possible germ concept is evoked and instantiated in the system of actual concepts, then the existing abstract organizing system is applied to it to construct the entire conceptual domain.

This seems to me a reasonably realistic way to view learning, and one congenial with the overall Piagetian outlook. In particular, like the Piagetian view, it considers conceptual innovation as constructive and even creative. The only part possibly not congenial is the issue of innateness; but much of what I think Piaget objected to in innateness has been drained out. In particular, if we think of conceptual structure as constructed from an innate combinatorial system, a great deal of novelty is indeed possible, since the system provides an infinite number of possibilities, only some small fragment of which are actually realized by any single human being.

To recapitulate, then, I want to stress that the issue ought not to be, How can we account for learning without falling back on innateness? but rather the less prejudged question, How can we account for learning at all, and how much of it relies on an innate basis? From such a standpoint our competing schools of thought can see potential disagreements not as incontestable matters of faith but as matters of degree, hence negotiable. Perhaps this can lead to making some progress together.

Chapter 4

Is There a Faculty of Social Cognition?

The general picture that is emerging from contemporary cognitive science (at least in my interpretation—see chapter 1) is that the mind can be factored into a considerable number of *faculties* or *modules,* each of which specializes in processing a particular form of information and therefore in carrying out particular kinds of perceptual or cognitive tasks. (In turn, I presume that these specializations correspond in some way to specializations of neural connectivity in different areas of the brain; but this is well beyond the scope of the present work.)

This chapter will develop an argument that there is a module or group of modules (a faculty) that is specialized for *social cognition*. In order to present the argument, it is first necessary to explain how I construe issues of modularity.

4.1   Input-Output versus Central Modules

The modules of the mind can be classified along various dimensions. One important dimension for my purposes here is a distinction between *input-output* modules and *central* modules. Examples of input-output modules are those making up the language system (used for both perception and production), the visual system (used for perception), and the motor system (used for output). These modules, very roughly, provide connections between the sensory and motor periphery on one hand and central capacities

This chapter was presented to the Society for Philosophy and Psychology as my Presidential Address in 1991. Discussions with Robert Seyfarth and David Olson were instrumental in helping me begin to think about this topic. I am grateful to the members of the Brandeis Humanities Seminar, for which an earlier version was prepared, for many stimulating remarks. Other important comments came from Noam Chomsky, John Macnamara, Carlos Otero, Alan Fiske, Leda Cosmides, Robert Lange, Janet Randall, Steve Stich, Don Symons, David Murray, Dee Worman, and Nancy Brenner. I have tried to respect their spirit, even if failing in execution. Finally, I apologize in advance for the fact that there are certain to be many relevant references of which I am unaware; this chapter is intended more as an exploratory enterprise than a finished product.

This research was supported in part by NSF Grant IRI 88-08286 to Brandeis University.

on the other. The modules discussed in Fodor's *Modularity of Mind* (1983) are all input modules, but Fodor assumes the existence of output modules as well. (See chapter 1 and Jackendoff 1987a, chapter 12, for discussion and refinement of Fodor's version of the modularity hypothesis.)

Less generally accepted is the possibility that the central capacities are also modular. Fodor (1983), for instance, specifically denies that modularity applies to thought as well as to perception. However, I have argued (Jackendoff 1987a, 1987b) that central capacities too can be divided into domain-specific modules, and that these can be identified by differentiating the forms of representation they process.

According to this view, the function of the central modules is to integrate information provided by disparate input modules into a unified modality-independent conception of the world, and, on the basis of this conception, formulate actions. Within the central capacities, there seem to be at least three major modules (which may well be further subdivided). The first, *conceptual structure*, is concerned with encoding individuals and categories and their combinations into token and type states and events, in both concrete and abstract domains. This level of representation is the central level that is most directly connected to language, and it serves as the level in terms of which linguistic semantics, lexical and phrasal, is encoded (Jackendoff 1983, 1990).

A second central module is that devoted to *spatial cognition*—the construction of a perceived world made of shaped objects moving from place to place and exerting forces on one another (see chapter 6 and Jackendoff 1987b). This module receives input from vision, from the haptic faculty (sense of touch), and even from the system of auditory localization (a sound is heard over to the left, for instance). Spatial representations in turn serve as input for the formulation of action in the world, feeding information to peripheral output (motor) modules. In addition, the spatial cognition module works hand in hand with conceptual structure in the understanding of the physical world; the translation of information encoded in terms of spatial representations into information encoded in terms of conceptual structure provides the key to being able to talk about what we see.

The work of James Lackner and his associates on the body senses such as the semicircular canals and otolithic organs in the ear, touch and pressure sensors in the skin, and muscle spindle receptors (Lackner 1981, 1988; Lackner and DiZio 1984; Lackner and Graybiel 1983) suggests that the information produced by these organs converges on another central module of *body representation*, which keeps track of and calibrates the relative positions and orientation of parts of the body. This faculty is intimately connected with the guidance of movement, and hence with the motor system. It also interacts richly with spatial cognition, since the body is after all one of the objects in the environment. The combination of these two faculties is responsible for the sense of one's own position and motion in space.

Each of these central modules has its own particular expressive power— its own role in the guidance of understanding and action. These differences appear in a formal account as differences in level of representation, at least as distinct as, say, syntactic and phonological representation. Thus both input-output faculties and central faculties appear to support a modular account.

4.2   Issues of Acquisition

A second dimension along which modules can vary is the degree to which differences in the environment influence their development. The visual system develops in essentially the same way in every individual exposed to a relatively normal range of visual stimuli. Spatial cognition develops fairly adequately even in the congenitally blind (Landau and Gleitman 1985); evidently haptic input (and possibly linguistic input) are sufficient to ensure understanding of objects in space.

By contrast, the development of the language faculty is highly dependent on the particular language spoken in the child's environment: children grow up speaking the language or languages they hear around them. Nevertheless, one of the achievements of modern linguistics has been to show that the wide differences among human languages are relatively constrained variations on a theme. Lines of evidence from the structure of numerous languages, from historical changes in languages, from the character of child language acquisition, and from linguistic deficits due to brain damage all converge on the view that there is a highly specified innate basis ("Universal Grammar") from which children develop an adult language capacity during the first ten or twelve years of life. This innate basis is not just a consequence of having a large brain—of "being smarter than animals"; it seems to be a specific brain adaptation, specialized to deal with this particular eccentric form of information we call language.

The musical capacity (Lerdahl and Jackendoff 1983a; chapter 7) also appears to be an independent module (or set of modules) in the human mind. There appears to be no evolutionary justification for such a capacity: unlike language, it is hard to think of convincing reasons why such a capacity should be adaptive. However, the principles and representations organizing the cognition of music are in part peculiar to music, and all of Fodor's criteria for input modules apply to musical perception. Thus it appears that one must acknowledge a separate specialization in this capacity as well.

Music shares with language a culture-dependent component: one must be exposed to the music of one's culture to fully comprehend it. That is, the ability to understand pieces of music is in part acquired. On the other hand, Lerdahl and Jackendoff (1983a) argue that, as in the case of language, a substantial innate basis forms the foundation for culture-specific music cognition. In addition to the culture-dependence found in language acquisition, though, there is a broad variation in competence from one individual to the next, only partly explicable in terms of the individual's past exposure to musical stimuli. People (apparently) differ more widely in musical talent than in linguistic talent.

This exceedingly brief survey should convey the sense in which I think that modularity is widespread both in peripheral and in central systems of the mind, and that the issue of modularity cuts across the problem of acquisition. Modularity does not preclude a culture-specific component, though it does strongly imply an innate basis that constrains culture-dependent variation. (See also chapter 1.)

4.3   First Arguments for a Faculty of Social Cognition

From the perspective given by this overview of "faculty psychology," various kinds of circumstantial evidence suggest there is a module of mind devoted to *social cognition*. As I conceive it, this is a central module, probably a subspecialization of the level of conceptual structure. Its task is to develop an integrated picture of the self in society. Whereas the fundamental units of spatial cognition are physical objects in space, those of social cognition are persons in social interaction. Whereas spatial cognition is concerned with the questions *What is it?* and *Where is it?*, social cognition is concerned with *Who is it?* and *What is this person's relation to me and others?* Here are some of the routes to this conjecture.

4.3.1   Domain Specificity

The concepts of social understanding are incommensurate with those of spatial understanding. Notions crucial to the understanding of social relationships and social actions such as kinship, group membership, and social dominance are not related in any clear way to personal appearance (except where culture codifies it) or to spatial location. Thus conceptual structure must include combinatorial elements related to social organization that have no immediate basis in perception. We will return in section 4.5 to the nature of some of these elements. For the moment, it is just important to observe that social concepts constitute a separate domain from ordinary object perception and categorization. What makes someone an *uncle* or a *boss* or a *comrade* is quite different from what makes something a *dog* or a *table* or *gold*.

4.3.2   Specialized Input Capacities

There are highly specialized input modules (or submodules) devoted to deriving social information. It is well documented that *face recognition* is a separate subspecialty within the visual system, localized in a particular area of the brain, with its own developmental course (Carey 1979; Carey and Diamond 1980). Individuals suffering brain damage in this area can be impaired at recognizing faces (even their own!) without losing general-purpose spatial cognition (Sacks 1985). Furthermore, *voice recognition* is equally specialized in the auditory system, and people can be differentially impaired, so that they do not recognize someone else on sight but only when he or she speaks.

In addition, both the visual and auditory systems are extremely sensitive at detecting *affect*, the facial expression or tone of voice that informs us of a person's emotional state. The physical cues for affect recognition, so far as I know, are not that well understood; but very young children already possess this sensitivity. Language understanding and auditory affect perception can be differentially impaired by brain damage (Sacks 1985, 76–80; Etcoff 1986, 1989), so they evidently invoke distinct mental specializations that process the auditory input in different ways. Moreover, face recognition and visual affect recognition can also be differentially impaired, as can visual and auditory affect recognition; to a certain extent the responsible brain areas can be located (Etcoff 1986, 1989, and references therein).

A striking demonstration of the sensitivity and delicacy of visual affect perception was developed by Heider and Simmel (1944). They produced a 40-second cartoon film in which two triangles and a circle move about the screen. The way they move about is designed to evoke interpretations of these geometric figures as animate characters. And indeed, observers inevitably attribute a plot to the film, with rather precise characterizations and motives being ascribed to all three figures. Furthermore, there is substantial interpersonal agreement among observers. (From personal experience with my children and those of acquaintances, I can attest that even eight-year-olds "get" the film.) On the other hand, when the film is shown backward as a control, there is much less vivid perception of plot and motivation, and less interpersonal agreement. This suggests that there is a subsystem of vision that is acutely sensitive to certain aspects of the character of motion and that interprets these as the product of unseen motivation. Moreover, this subsystem does not require human figures or language to operate: it produces its interpretations even with so primitive an input as Heider and Simmel's triangles and circle.

Though I am generally wary of teleological arguments, it seems apposite to make one here: surely evolution would not have gone to the trouble of developing all this elaborate peripheral apparatus if there were not some important purpose for the information it provides. A central faculty of social cognition, served by the four distinct input modules of face recognition, voice recognition, and visual and auditory affect recognition, would be the right kind of candidate: given its concern with relations to other individuals, it would desperately need accurate information about who one is interacting with and that person's probable state of mind.

4.3.3   Developmental Priority of Social Concepts

Social and cultural knowledge shows considerable variation from culture to culture (and, within cultures, from one individual to another), suggesting that it is all learned. But, following the example of language, perhaps we should be looking for underlying principles that enable a child to learn the culture-specific conventions in which he or she is situated.

Here is a very basic one: Katz, Baker, and Macnamara (1974) found that children as young as 17 months know that proper names, which identify particular individuals, can be applied to person-like objects such as dolls but not to inanimate objects such as boxes. This is many months before they will themselves produce the grammatical constructions that differentiate proper from common nouns (Wug vs. a wug). That is, they seem predisposed to make a cognitive distinction between persons and everything else—the distinction I am claiming is pertinent to social cognition—and they are predisposed as well to find a linguistic distinction that encodes this difference. (Eibl-Eibesfeldt (1989) documents many other examples of complex social behaviors and sensitivities in very young children, in a wide range of cultures.)

4.3.4   Universality of Basic Cultural Parameters

Despite the variation among cultures, there are widespread (and likely universal) aspects of culture, taken for granted, that form a skeleton of issues around which cultures are built. Among these are the concepts mentioned above: kinship, group membership, social dominance. But one also immediately thinks of ownership and property rights, differentiation of social roles, and the existence of elaborate rituals that enhance or instantiate group membership. There is no particular functional reason why human beings have to form cultures this way, but that seems to be the way they are. This parallels the kind of variations on a theme that one finds in the structure of language.

Colleagues in anthropology tell me that much thinking in their field disputes the existence and even the plausibility of cultural universals. This issue is addressed by Brown (1991), who explores the sources of this thinking and finds them wanting in light of more modern evidence, not to mention common sense. Further arguments appear in Eibl-Eibesfeldt 1989. As in the case of languages, the diversity among cultures is obviously more striking and engaging than their uniformity. But one can also learn to appreciate what is *not* noticed—how things are the same—and in the case of language this has proved the more scientifically rewarding inquiry.

4.3.5 *Evolutionary Antecedents*
Unlike the case of language, we have a strong evolutionary reason to believe that there is a faculty of social cognition: the existence of elaborate social structure in many species of mammals, especially primates. The constancy of this structure within members of a species, combined with the variation across species, suggests that there is a substantial innate component to the behaviors underlying these social structures, hence species-specific specializations for social organization.

A particularly pointed discussion of social intelligence has been provided by Cheney and Seyfarth (1985, 1990). In their study of what might be called the social epistemology of vervet monkeys, Cheney and Seyfarth find that monkeys in the wild are sensitive to (and react in complex ways to) such factors as dominance hierarchies, kinship information with respect to self and others, and the expected location of particular monkeys belonging to another band (implying information about group membership). By contrast, they are not at all so sensitive to information of comparable complexity in nonsocial domains, for example the expected location of a hippopotamus or the dangerous significance of fresh python tracks. Cheney and Seyfarth therefore attribute the vervets' social sensitivity to the operation of a specialized faculty, rather than to the application of a general-purpose intelligence in a social context.

If social specializations are so deeply entrenched in other primates, it is only reasonable to suspect that they are present in humans as well. Even if humans have developed greater general-purpose and abstract intelligence, there seems little reason to suppose that evolution would have thrown away preexisting machinery that evidently was so highly adaptive. In fact, Cosmides (1989) demonstrates that certain logical problems that are notoriously difficult for humans can be solved far more reliably if couched in terms of concrete social interactions such as guarding against being cheated. This provides a parallel to Cheney and Seyfarth's observations about vervet monkeys, suggesting a cognitive specialization for social intelligence.

4.4   *A Cognitive Approach to Social Organization*

Let me be somewhat more explicit about what is being proposed. (Similar arguments and proposals have been made by Tooby and Cosmides (1989), Cosmides and Tooby (1989), Premack (1990), Eibl-Eibesfeldt (1989) and Symons (1987, 1991), and I draw freely on their discussion.) The basic premise is that the collective behavior we call "social organization" or "culture" involves the interactions of individuals with each other, and crucially that

each individual's participation in the culture must be supported by cognitive organization in the individual's mind.

More particularly,

the way individuals are capable of acting within a society depends on the way they are capable of internally representing the social context.

It therefore is of interest to ask what this internal representation is like— what principles determine its expressive power, what inferences and heuristics can be performed within it, how it is connected to perception, and how its principles are acquired.

Note how this inquiry parallels the standard Chomskian inquiry into the nature of language, where it is argued that the collective behavior involved in linguistic communication must be supported by a cognitive capacity in the communicating individuals. The investigation of this cognitive capacity is taken to be a significant (perhaps the most significant) aspect of the study of language.

Chomsky (1986) makes the distinction between the study of linguistic communicative behavior and that of the cognitive capacity supporting language by calling the former the study of "externalized language" or "E-language," and the latter the study of "internalized language" or "I-language." The terminology can be adapted here, making a distinction between "E-social organization," the external manifestations of culture, as traditionally studied by anthropologists, and "I-social organization," the human cognitive capacities that support the individual's perceptions and actions in a social context.

The study of I-social organization is situated within psychology, but it must draw a great deal of its evidence from anthropological studies of E-social organization, since the capacity in question is precisely that of engaging in E-social organization. The hope, however, is that many of the universals and parameters of human E-social organization can be eventually attributed to the character of I-social organization, just as many properties of human linguistic communication have been attributed to the mental capacity that constitutes I-language.

4.5   Toward Some Primitives of Social Cognition

My own interest in this material comes from my investigation of a formal theory of human concepts. I am trying to find what formal primitive notions and principles of combination are necessary to describe the meanings of words, phrases, and sentences—not in a lexicographer's or logician's sense of definition, but in a more psychologically adequate framework (chapter 2 and Jackendoff 1983, 1990; other such approaches include Miller and Johnson-Laird 1976, Langacker 1986). Within this work, the concepts for physical space have came together nicely and have begun to interact in an interesting way with research on visual perception (chapter 6 and Jackendoff 1987b). But for other families of concepts, various notions emerge that have no spatial interpretation but do play an evident role in the social domain. Here are some examples.

4.5.1   Persons

Let us start with the notion of a *person* as the fundamental social unit. If there is a separate submodule of conceptual structure dealing with social relations, this means that a person will be represented twice in conceptual structure: in the spatial domain, which encodes physical appearance of the body—but also in the social domain, which encodes personhood. By contrast, tables and chairs will have only spatial representations. (Pets perhaps may be granted some social status.) These linked representations, like the linked phonological content and affect attributed to utterances, function somewhat independently in terms of the knowledge they access and the inferences they license. In particular, one's "folk theory of mind" (including Dennett's (1987) "intentional stance"), is localized in the social domain; it is *persons* to whom we attribute beliefs and desires. Notions of social roles such as kinship relations and social dominance are also stated over the notion of person. One might even hazard a speculation that this formal conceptual dualism—the conceptualization of persons in both spatial and social domains—is the cognitive source for the widespread philosophical and religious belief in mind-body dualism.

4.5.2   Requests versus Orders

Turning to some of the concepts in which the notion of person plays an essential role, consider the concepts expressed by X *requested* Y *to do such-and-such* and X *ordered* Y *to do such-and-such*. Both involve X making some utterance, intended to be heard by Y, which concerns X's wish for Y to perform some action. What is the difference between them? The main difference appears to be that, with *order*, X is in a position of social dominance over Y, and therefore can invoke the authority to impose sanctions on Y if Y does not perform as X desires. In addition, both X and Y have to be aware that this relative position obtains. Something misfires if X issues an order that Y recognizes only as a request, or if X issues a request that Y interprets as an order. In short, an order is something like a request backed up by the conventions of social dominance. Note that the social dominance must be *invoked*: dominant individuals can make requests as well as issue orders. (A similar analysis, with much more comprehensive detail, appears in Bach and Harnish 1979.)

Crucial to this analysis are not only the social dominance hierarchy and awareness of it, but also the consequences: X's authority to issue orders, to expect compliance, and to impose sanctions if not obeyed. As will be seen, this conjunction of factors recurs in a variety of situations, suggesting that it is a basic part of the logic of social cognition.

4.5.3   Transactions

Consider verbs that express transactions, for instance *buy, sell, rent,* and *trade,* widely discussed in the literature (Miller and Johnson-Laird 1976, section 7.2 and references therein; Pinker 1989; Jackendoff 1990). They all share the same basic structure. Take a sentence like *Bill traded his bike to Harry for a horse.* Two actions are taking place: the bike is changing possession from Bill to Harry, and the horse is changing possession in the opposite direction, from Harry to Bill. However, there is a relation between these two actions. Fundamental to their constituting a *trade,* rather than two unrelated changes of possession, is (for a first approximation) that Bill and Harry agree that the bike and the horse are of equivalent value (alternatively, following Cosmides and Tooby (1989), they agree that the bike is worth more to Harry than to Bill, and that the horse is worth more to Bill than to Harry), and that Bill and Harry acknowledge the paired changes of possession as linked by this equivalence.

Almost every part of this, other than the actual physical transfer of the goods, involves a social concept. The notion of agreement—mutual acknowledgment and validation of the other's point of view—is a social, not a physical, transaction. (Bach and Harnish's (1979) notion of "mutual belief" appears to be closely related.) The notion of the value of an object is not a physical attribute but depends heavily on cultural conventions. Moreover, behind the cultural conventions lies a more basic and very abstract conceptualization: the idea that incommensurate objects and actions can be reduced to a linear scale of equivalence along a dimension of value. (See also section 8.5 on the psychological status of the notion of "objective value.")

Nor is the pairing of changes of possession physically necessary for a trade to be concluded. It may still count as a trade if Bill gives his bike to Harry in exchange for a *promise* (or *obligation*) for Harry to turn the horse over to Bill at some later date. What is Harry's promise or obligation in this case? Roughly, it is a granting of authority to Bill to impose sanctions on Harry if Harry does not perform as promised. It is this notion of authority to impose sanctions (again) and Harry's willingness to accept these sanctions that distinguishes a promise from a mere *prediction.* (The logic of exchange is in fact still more complicated, as shown in considerable detail in Cosmides and Tooby 1989; see also Bach and Harnish 1979 on promises versus predictions.)

4.5.4   Ownership

For there to be a change in ownership in a trade, there has to be such a thing as ownership. What does X *owns* Y mean? Very roughly, following Miller and Johnson-Laird (1976) (who in turn quote Snare (1972)), there seem to be three parts: (1) X has the right (or authority) to use Y as he or she wishes. (2) X has the right (or authority) to control anyone else's use of Y, and to impose sanctions for uses other than those he or she permits. (3) X has the right to give away rights (1) and (2).

Note that *lending* something is allowing someone to use it, but receiving in exchange a promise to give it back. That is, lending and borrowing make use of some of the components of owning and some of the components of exchange: more of the same machinery.

It looks as though cultures differ widely in what one is allowed to own (artifacts, land, one's own children, other people, . . .), in what sanctions are imposed for misuse of someone else's possessions, and in how society imposes those sanctions. In addition, some cultures have notions of property rights for certain objects, particularly land, that involve only clauses (1) and (2) above, or only clause (1) alone (Alan Fiske, personal communication): one can use land and perhaps prevent others from using it, but one does not have the right to give it away or sell it. (This difference is one of the major sources of difficulty in Native American land claims.)

But the basic framework is there universally—the child only has to learn what parameters govern ownership or property rights in the local culture. The codification of these parameters (and those connected to kinship, etc.) constitute the basic issues around which a culture constructs its equivalent of a legal system.

4.5.5   Other Schemas for Distributing Goods and Responsibilities

Exchange by virtue of acknowledgment of equal value (including trading, buying, selling, and other related concepts) is of course not the only means by which things change owners. Fiske (1991) distinguishes four basic modes of social interchange: *market pricing* (the cost/benefit assessment found in the exchange transactions we have been discussing), *communal sharing*, *authority ranking*, and *equality matching*. Very roughly, in communal sharing, goods are distributed freely according to need, and labor is contributed freely according to ability. In authority ranking, goods are distributed according to social dominance, while at the same time dominant individuals take some degree of responsibility for their underlings. In equality matching, goods are divided evenly, everyone is expected to take an equal turn, and everyone has an equal vote.

Fiske argues that every society has tacit conventions about which of these modes is appropriate to which circumstances; societies differ in their mix of the four kinds of interaction. In particular, Fiske observes that contemporary Western society is relatively unusual in its stress on the market pricing mode of interaction. (He suggests that this stress in turn has misled Western economic theory into presupposing individuals always to act in self-interest rather than in the interest of a larger community.) He makes the further intriguing claim that these four modes of social interaction exhaust the possibilities, that one can explain all social intercourse through suitable mixtures of these modes. (I am inclined to think that he is close, but that there is at least a fifth mode, which might be called "competition" or "social hostility": we have to see the dark side of society too.)

However the details eventually work out, the basic idea behind Fiske's claims fits attractively into the present framework. He is saying that the skeletal understanding of exchange transactions sketched above is one of a relatively small repertoire of abstract social frames available to a child. "Learning a culture" then consists of fleshing out the particulars of these frames into a culture-particular realization, and creating categories of situations in which to apply the logic of each mode of interaction. A large part of the empirical problem for the study of I-social organization, then, is to partition one's social cognition into those parts that are given in advance—the "Universal Grammar for social cognition"—and those parts that are acquired (and acquirable!) on the basis of environmental evidence.

The story that emerges from these little examples is that even rather simple words of English such as *own, trade, promise, request,* and *order* reveal an underpinning of basic social concepts. Notions like dominance, authority, privilege, right, obligation, value, the imposing of sanctions, and so forth, keep recurring as components of concepts in the social domain, just as the domain of spatial concepts is pervaded by notions like physical object, motion, location, and force. This gives a new kind of evidence for the existence of a faculty of social cognition, and one that gives us some idea not just of its existence but of its content as well.

Note that the putative primitives I am proposing do not appear as such in any particular culture. Rather, the primitives serve as abstract components on which different cultures build different realizations. For example, the fact that the notion of social dominance hierarchy may be a primitive does not determine who is socially dominant in a given culture or how that dominance is established. But without the basic notion of social dominance, all the actions that serve to instantiate a given culture's realization of it would be incomprehensible.

4.6   Ideological Issues

If there is a faculty of social cognition, what would be the implications? I'm not altogether sure, but it seems as though we would have the beginning of a principled answer to total cultural relativism. Despite the differences among cultures, we are all united by the "Universal Grammar" of cultural concepts—and if you like, constrained by it. Our social existence has meaning that is in large part determined by the biological structure of our brains—it is not an arbitrary artifact imposed by the environment. (This point is stressed also by Eibl-Eibesfeldt (1989).)

However, a certain amount of care is necessary in working out and promoting a theory of this sort. Theories about the biological basis of human society, presented in the guise of value-free scientific objectivity, have in fact most often been used to make invidious distinctions among groups in support of racist and sexist policies (as powerfully documented in Gould 1981). It is important to see that the present approach, by contrast, stresses the *universality* of social cognition in the human species, and therefore the essential equality of individuals and groups within this domain.

However, a stress on equality raises an ideological problem in the other direction. Linguists stress that one cannot make value judgments about languages: Black English isn't bad, it's just another language. If we are interested in studying universals of culture, does this place us in the uncomfortable position of not being able to make value judgments about different means of social organization? Are we forced to say that fascism isn't bad, it's just another kind of culture? I think the answer here is this: just because one as a scientist may find that a repressive society provides an interesting source of evidence, that does not exempt one from condemning it *as a human being*. The case is entirely parallel, I believe, to Newport's (1990) study of language acquisition in deaf children whose first exposure to sign has occurred relatively late in life. One does not have to object to the investigation of such cases in order to object to the practices that led to their existence.

Issues like these show how the investigation of human social cognition may easily become highly charged with emotional and ethical overtones. My ideology on such matters is that they should be fully acknowledged and worked through. As in any area of science that potentially impinges on human rights, the utmost sensitivity is called for.

Chapter 5
Unconscious Information in Language and Psychodynamics

Psychodynamic theory is characterized by Horowitz (1988b, 1990) as a descendant of Freudian psychoanalytic theory, the study of the unconscious basis of personality and of personality disorders. The term *psychodynamics* refers to a "play of forces" in the mind between motives to achieve wishes, motives to avoid potential threats, and motives to use control processes such as defenses to prevent threat from occurring. Such motives often come into conflict with one another, and only certain of them appear in conscious awareness.

Horowitz, along with other writers such as Erdelyi (1985), is concerned with developing a rapprochement between psychodynamic theory and cognitive psychology, in particular with providing a stronger empirical basis for the psychodynamic constructs of unconscious mental states and processes. The present chapter is an attempt toward such a rapprochement. I will begin by briefly describing my theoretical biases and the view of the unconscious that they imply. I will then relate this view to the conception of unconscious processes implicit in the psychodynamic approach. Finally, I will suggest an approach to studying phenomena in the dynamic unconscious that grows out of my general methodology.

5.1   Unconscious Knowledge of Language

One of the most important lessons of the last three decades of work in generative grammar is that language does not wear its organization on its sleeve. Rather, one's knowledge of one's native language—one's ability to understand and utter an indefinitely large number of sentences that one has

The original version of this chapter was prepared for a 1984 workshop on Conscious and Unconscious Mental Processes organized by Mardi Horowitz and sponsored by the MacArthur Foundation. It appeared in Mardi Horowitz, ed., *Psychodynamics and Cognition*, 203–220, University of Chicago Press, 1988, and is reprinted by permission of the University of Chicago. I have edited the present version substantially to eliminate overly specific commentaries on other papers in that collection, and to place it in the more general context of the chapters here. I am grateful to Mardi Horowitz for a number of helpful suggestions.

never heard before—is governed by complex principles of which one is not and cannot be consciously aware. Moreover, since adults are not consciously aware of these principles, they cannot pass them down to the next generation of speakers by explicit instruction. Thus language learning—the acquisition of the principles of one's native language—is itself a process of great complexity and subtlety.

Let me give three examples of the sorts of complexities found in English, one each from phonology (the sound system), syntax (the structure of phrases), and semantics (meaning). First, consider the following ten words chosen from different languages, including English.

(1) ptak   thole   hlad   plast   sram
     mgla   vlas   flitch dnom   rtut

This example was devised by Halle (1978, 294), who comments:

> If one were to ask which of the ten words in this list are to be found in the unabridged Webster's, it is likely that readers of these lines would guess that *thole, plast,* and *flitch* are English words, whereas the rest are not English. This evidently gives rise to the question: How does a reader who has never seen any of the words on the list know that some are English and others are not? The answer is that the words judged not English have letter sequences not found in English. This implies that in learning the words of English the normal speaker acquires knowledge about the structure of the words. The curious thing about this knowledge is that it is acquired although it is never taught, for English-speaking parents do not normally draw their children's attention to the fact that consonant sequences that begin English words are subject to certain restrictions that exclude words such as *ptak, sram,* and *rtut,* but allow *thole, flitch,* and *plast.* Nonetheless, in the absence of any overt teaching, speakers somehow acquire this knowledge.

A second example comes from Chomsky 1972. Sentences (2a) and (2b) differ only in the main verb. Yet the difference in sense is striking: in (2a) the boys are to like one another, whereas in (2b) John seems to like the boys.

(2) a. John appealed to each of the boys to like the others.
     b. John appeared to each of the boys to like the others.

Now consider the sentences in (3).

(3) a. John appealed to the boys to like each other.
     b. *John appeared to the boys to like each other.

Notice that (3a) is synonymous with (2a). By analogy, we would expect (3b) to be synonymous with (2b). In fact, however, it is ungrammatical; in some curious way, it is sensed by speakers not to be a sentence of English at all.

Thus the same question arises as with (1): On what grounds do speakers of English judge that (3b) is ungrammatical? It is not its *meaning* that is at fault. It *should* mean the same as (2b). Rather, evidently something is amiss in the use of the reciprocal expression *each other* in this context—something that none of us ever were taught.

The third example comes from Jackendoff 1972. (4a) and (4b) contain exactly the same words and the same intonation pattern, with one exception: the pitch rises slightly at the end of (4a) and falls slightly at the end of (4b). (Capitals indicate stress; the intonation is indicated by the curved line below the sentence.)

(4)   a.   Both John AND Bill didn't go.

      b.   Both John AND Bill didn't go.

The meanings are quite different, though, (4a) means that either John or Bill went; (4b) means that neither went. How does the slight change in intonation at the end of the sentence communicate this difference? Again, this is a fact about English that native speakers will intuitively recognize if it is pointed out to them, but it is clear that it was never taught to us. Like the observations above, it was not even *noticed* until less than thirty years ago. Nevertheless, by virtue of having acquired English by whatever means we did, we have unwittingly acquired the ability to make these judgments.

What we have not acquired, however, is a conscious ability to explain the reasons for these judgments. Rather, we must resort to empirical methods of research to discover the principles behind them. Each of the observations above has played a role in extensive discussion in the literature, involving dozens of other phenomena, in some cases in many languages. Whatever the explanation (or whatever putative explanation readers may come up with on their own), the point is that it is after the fact—it does not play a role in making one's judgments about (1)–(4), which from a conscious point of view are quite direct and immediate.

There is no space here to even begin an analysis of these phenomena, but the overall form of the analysis is a theme song of contemporary linguistics. These particular words and sentences are themselves not part of one's knowledge of language. Rather, one's knowledge of language is internalized as a *rule system* or *grammar*, of which any particular word or sentence is a special case. These rule systems can be applied creatively in understanding and uttering sentences one has never heard before. The content of the rules and the way they apply—and in fact their very existence—are almost entirely hidden to introspection. Only the *results* of their application appear in awareness, as conscious judgments of grammaticality, comprehensibility, similarity and difference of meaning, appropriateness to the situation, and so forth.

Research in linguistics thus seeks to discover the rule systems underlying knowledge of a language. The linguist's exploration is guided, not by direct introspection of the rule systems themselves, but by examination of the conscious by-products of the rule systems, in particular the patterns of grammatical judgments arrived at by speakers of the language. Further evidence often arises from other languages (which insofar as possible we would like to describe by means of rule systems of similar character), from the history of languages, from children's acquisition of language, from experiments on language processing, and from language deficits due to brain damage.

5.2   Linguistic and Psychodynamic Explanation

This mode of linguistic explanation displays an interesting parallel to the mode of psychodynamic explanation described by Shevrin (1988). In attempting to explain the source of a phobia, for example,

> [i]mmediately, we run into a problem inherent in the nature of the symptom: the very experience of it contains a mysterious hiatus—the patient is moved to feel, act, and think with powerful urgency, yet without a rational basis. He can attempt to account for his urgent action afterward and thus to offer his own explanation, but he is in no more privileged position to understand these actions than a naive bystander.... [T]here is a *discontinuity* in his experience and behavior that must be explained.
>
> The model of a psychoanalytic explanation makes several central assumptions. First, the apparent discontinuity in experience ... is really continuous, that is, there are *knowable psychological* causes; second, these knowable psychological causes are *inaccessible* to the patient.... Thus, the psychoanalyst must assume the existence of the psychological unconscious.... The main limitation of the method is its knack for eliciting an embarrassment of riches; even though it can enliven the search for hypotheses, it is an awkward and clumsy means for selecting and testing them. (Shevrin 1988, 120–121)

Let us compare this to the investigation of linguistic knowledge as described above. As in the psychodynamic case, there is an "apparent discontinuity in experience" in the fact that speakers make secure and consistent judgments about examples like (1)–(4), without having any conscious basis for making such judgments, and even though in some cases (such as the disanalogy between (2) and (3)) the judgments seem bizarre from a rational point of view. The linguist, however, assumes that there are *knowable psychological causes* for these judgments, namely the rule systems underlying the organization of language—but that these causes are *inaccessible* to the language user.

This approach is subject to the very limitation that Shevrin envisages, a "knack for eliciting an embarrassment of riches," and one of the principal concerns of linguistic theory is how to appropriately constrain the rule system so as to explain why the observable phenomena come out the way they do and not some other conceivable way. In order to develop appropriate constraints, the linguist often draws on the full arsenal of evidence from other languages and from history, acquisition, psycholinguistic experiments, and brain damage, in an effort to triangulate on a maximally precise and general hypothesis. Although one can hardly claim full success as yet, I have the sense that considerable progress has been made in understanding the principles underlying language in the past thirty-five years. In particular, whatever arguments still rage, there has came to be substantial agreement on the way numerous well-studied phenomena must be integrated into the system as a whole.

5.3   Conscious and Unconscious Information

Let us look in a little more detail at the implications of this approach to language for the general problem of conscious and unconscious processes. A theory of the form that linguists seek to develop—a description of the rule systems governing linguistic behavior—does not fit comfortably into either of the traditional categories for explaining the mind, namely conscious phenomena and neurophysiological phenomena. On one hand, the form of linguistic information and the rules that govern it are certainly not conscious; nor are they assumed to be in any especially close relationship to what is currently known about neurophysiology, either. We haven't the slightest idea, for instance, how something as simple as the speech sound *p* is encoded in the neurons, not to mention the neurophysiological organization underlying more complex linguistic entities such as this sentence.

So what is the psychological status of the rules of language, if they are neither conscious nor physiological? The metatheory assumed by linguists is that they play a role in the *organization of information* in the brain. Just as one can speak of the organization of information in a computer—its programs and database structures—without knowing much at all about the physical and electrical structure in which this information is realized, the assumption is that one can describe the principles governing the structure and processing of mental information, independently of their neurological instantiation. This "functionalist" view of mental information in the "computational mind" is fairly standard in modern-day cognitive science, though there are major ideological splits on how literally to take the computer analogy. (See Dennett 1978, Fodor 1975, and Pylyshyn 1984, as well as chapter 1, for example.)

Although the relationship of the computational mind to neurophysiology finds a strong analogy in the relation of programs and data structures to computer hardware, the relationship of the computational mind to consciousness is far less well understood. In fact, cognitive science has more or less appropriated the term *mind* for "computational mind," leaving no term available for the more traditional phenomenological sense. A reasonable first assumption, however, seems to be the following condition (elaborated in more detail in Jackendoff 1987a):

Correspondence Condition
Every distinction present in consciousness is supported by a corresponding computational distinction.

This condition essentially says that consciousness is not magic—that its content proceeds in a principled way from underlying information structures and the processes that operate on them. Note however that the implication is one way only, in that there may well be computational distinctions that do not appear directly in consciousness, for example the rules of language.

In thinking of the brain as an information-processing device, it is useful to distinguish the *structure* or *form* of the information from the *processes* that give rise to mental information. A great deal of contemporary cognitive psychology has focused on information flow through different kinds of memory and different kinds of processors, on the role of attention in processing information, on constraints on retrieval from memory, and so forth—all considerations of processing. By contrast, there has been relatively little discussion by psychologists of the precise *form* of the information being processed—what the basic elements of mental information are and how they are built up into complex cognitive constructs. However, this seems precisely the right way to construe the principles of linguistic theory: the rule systems underlying language govern the repertoire of possible forms of linguistic information, without necessarily addressing the processes in time by which these forms are developed and used in communication. In the computer analogy, they are descriptions of the data structures on which programs operate.

Other areas of psychology have begun to display a more explicit interest in form. In particular, the theory of vision has taken on new dimensions through research on visual information structure by such investigators as Marr (1982), Shepard and Cooper (1982), and Kosslyn (1980). In the psychology of music, my work with Fred Lerdahl on the forms of information underlying musical cognition (Lerdahl and Jackendoff 1983a) begins to clarify the relationship between issues of traditional music theory and those of experimental work on music perception.

I stress the distinction between form and process because it is crucial to the issue of consciousness. In a widely quoted passage, Lashley (1956) points out that information *processing* per se is always unconscious. For example, one's visual awareness consists of the arrangement of elements in a scene, not of the internal mental processes that give rise to this perceived arrangement. In other words, the most direct support for conscious awareness comes from the information *structures* or *forms* in the computational mind, not from the processes. (Note that one may have dynamic mental representations of *external* processes, say of an object in motion—but one still has no conscious access to the *mental* process by which one constructs such representations.) Thus the correspondence condition can be refined as follows:

Correspondence Condition (revised)
Every distinction present in consciousness is supported by a
corresponding distinction in the information structures present in the
computational mind.

If I wished to be iconoclastic, I might point out that Lashley's observation undercuts the commonly assumed distinction between "conscious processes" and "unconscious processes": if Lashley is right, there *are* no conscious processes. Rather, strictly speaking, one should be asking questions about conscious and unconscious *information structures*. The term *conscious process* might serve, however, as a useful shorthand for "unconscious process that derives or applies to conscious information structures," and when I use it here, I will always mean it in that sense.

Even the term *conscious information structure* is somewhat suspect, in that one is conscious, not of the structure itself, but rather of that aspect of the perceived world that the structure encodes. So I will use the term here as shorthand for "information structure that directly supports the form of awareness." In other words, the view is that the computational mind is all unconscious, but that a certain selected set of the information structures in the computational mind are most directly responsible for the form of our conscious experience. The question I deliberately leave open is *how* these selected structures support awareness. Within my approach, this issue is the locus where the venerable mysteries of the mind-body problem come into play (see Jackendoff 1987a for discussion).

5.4   The Status of the Psychodynamic Unconscious

This notion of the computational mind makes it possible to formulate a fairly explicit position on the kinds of unconscious processes posited in psychodynamic theory. First of all, conscious events such as thoughts, affects, and judgments have to be supported by computational counterparts. But, in addition, the elements of these computational counterparts are also found in information structures that do not necessarily appear in consciousness. That is, it is perfectly appropriate for psychodynamic theory to speak of unconscious assumptions, goals, and judgments that affect conscious experience and behavior.[1]

A second important observation is that unconscious processes participate in complex, variable adaptive behavior, for example as seen in everyday language use. At the same time, they interact richly with conscious processes. For example, one's speech production is governed by largely unconscious processes (Levelt 1989), but it obviously is often a consequence of what utterances one has consciously heard. Moreover, although one does not normally attend to phonological and grammatical details in speaking, one can consciously consider them when writing poetry. Similar possibilities appear in the more general social interactions addressed by psychodynamic theory. For example, one's course of action can be influenced by one's unconscious motives, but it also depends intimately on the details of others' actions, perceived consciously or detected unconsciously. Moreover, one can consciously reflect on one's own motives in planning a course of action.

The case of language also provides evidence against a common misconception, often used against psychodynamic theory, that unconscious processes are temporally earlier and more primitive aspects of information processing than conscious processes. Language use continually involves unconscious processes, both prior to and during conscious phases. So, although same unconscious processes (such as sensory processing) must precede awareness, not all do. In addition, unconscious representations if anything must be *more* highly articulated than those that appear in consciousness, not more "primitive": compare the elaboration of unconscious linguistic structure with the degree of awareness one has of this structure. Moreover, as many have observed, it is likely that unconscious processes involve some degree of parallel computation of multiple representations, only one of which (per modality) appears in consciousness under usual circumstances. Thus it is altogether realistic to expect, by analogy, that unconscious *psychodynamic* processes are very specific and complex—that they rise above the level of general and primitive "drives."

To sum up, the conception of the unconscious as a highly articulated computational system that underlies the form of awareness and behavior is supported by the empirical study of hundreds of linguistic phenomena like those illustrated in section 5.1. In turn, this conception leads to a position essentially in tune with the psychodynamic position.

Why should these parallels between language and psychodynamic phenomena be of interest? The reason, I think, is that language gives one a secure sense both of the rich structure possible in the unconscious and of the precision with which one can study it. It therefore might encourage one to consider psychodynamic theories of comparable abstractness and depth —one is less daunted by complexity known to exist elsewhere—and at the same time to aspire to the higher standards of explanation that can be achieved in a formalized theory.

One important difference between the linguistic and the psychodynamic unconscious should be mentioned. As observed in section 5.1, the principles and most of the structures of language are *never* accessible to consciousness. In order to investigate these principles, one must treat oneself like a black box, seeking the best hypothesis about its inner workings to explain the behavior that emerges in the form of utterances and judgments about utterances. Psychotherapy begins with the same sort of methodology: trying to infer a person's unconscious motives and desires from overt behavior and conscious reports of experience. However, the goal of psychotherapy is not just to explain the black box as it currently exists. Rather, since Freud, it has been a major hypothesis of psychodynamic theory that unconscious motives and desires can be made conscious, and that the process of making them fully conscious can enable a person to come to interact differently with the world. There is no analogue of this further step in linguistic theory. Nevertheless, that should not discourage us from exploring the parallel as far as it goes.

5.5   Toward a Formal Account of Psychodynamic Displacement: Rules of Irrational Inference

Let me give a rough idea of what I have in mind. From my (admittedly limited) acquaintance with the psychodynamic literature, it appears that a wide range of symptoms can be described as underlying conceptual organizations that are the product of *erroneous displacement*, followed by *regularization*.

To explicate these terms, let me start with a phonological analogy—the production of speech errors or "slips of the tongue." In studying speech errors, linguists have concentrated on what they reveal about linguistic structure, not on what unconscious motivations (or "Freudian slips") may have led to their production, and that is what I am going to examine here, very briefly.

Consider the class of speech errors in which a speaker misplaces or exchanges consonants. It has been observed by Fromkin (1971) that the possible positions to which a consonant can be erroneously moved are highly restricted. For example, one might say "tips of the slung" for "slips of the tongue," exchanging the *sl* and *t* at the beginnings of their respective words. But speakers never say something like "slits of the pung," exchanging the initial *t* of "tongue" and penultimate *p* of "slips." That is, sound exchanges invariably involve parallel positions in different words.

Furthermore, when a sound is moved to an incorrect position, it never creates a consonant cluster that violates constraints on possible sound combinations for the language in question. For instance, "slips of the tongue" might be mispronounced as "lips of the stung" by movement of the *s*; but it would never be mispronounced as "sips of the tlung" by movement of the *l*, because *tl* is not a permissible sound combination in English. (Note that *tl* is not in general unpronounceable; it is for instance a permissible combination in the language Tlingit.) In other words, speech errors confirm the existence of those unconscious and untaught principles of English sound structure that we were led to posit in order to account for our judgment of the putative words in (1) above.

Thus speech errors are not completely wild phonologically; there are strong constraints on possible displacements, describable in terms of the phonological structure of words. Such evidence of what occurs and what *never* occurs, drawn from corpora of several thousand speech errors recorded in ordinary conversation, is of great importance in developing theories of speech production (e.g. Garrett 1975, Levelt 1989).

A second altogether predictable effect in speech errors, noted by Fromkin (1971), is that a displacement is invariably compensated by a regularization if necessary. For example, suppose that the *m* in "a monkey's uncle" is erroneously transposed to the second word. The result is always "an unkey's muncle," not "a unkey's muncle." That is, the alternation of *a* and *an*, which depends on whether the following word begins with a consonant or vowel, is sensitive to the removal of the *m*; the article takes the form that is phonologically appropriate for the following nonword "unkey." The upshot of these constraints and regularizations is that an utterance containing a speech error, even if meaningless, is (usually) phonologically acceptable English.

The principles governing psychodynamic displacement of course do not involve phonological structure. Rather, the appropriate form of mental information appears to be *conceptual structure*, which encodes one's understanding of entities in the world, the categories into which they fall, and the relationships among them. Well-known approaches to conceptual structure include the production systems of Anderson (1983), the "scripts" of Schank and Abelson (1975), the prototypes of Rosch (1978), and the idealized cognitive models of Lakoff (1987). Conceptual Semantics, the approach developed in chapter 2 (see also Jackendoff 1983, 1987a, 1990), is, I believe, more attentive than others to the microproblems of finding primitive elements and combinatorial principles, and to the necessity to map perspicuously onto the grammatical structure of language. In particular, psychodynamic phenomena fall primarily in the subsystem of conceptual structure devoted to social cognition (see chapter 4).

Among the important functions of conceptual structure is the ascription of identity to objects and especially to persons in the environment. As is well known, the identity of an object can be independent of changes in its physical appearance over time—a person (or can change radically over the years or even a brief time and still remain the same individual. Jackendoff 1983, chapters 3 and 5, proposes that conceptual structure contains the mental representations that keep track of identity over time and coordinate it with physical appearance and location.

As a first example of psychodynamic displacement, then, consider the not uncommon phenomenon in dreams where a person appears with the face of some acquaintance X, but somehow the dreamer "knows" it is really someone else, Y—without any necessary sense of incongruity. Let us not for the moment inquire into the causes for such a displacement, which may vary from case to case; rather, let us ask how such an anomalous experience could occur at all. In terms of the computational theory, the question is, Is it possible to find an information structure that underlies the experience? Given the little that has already been said about conceptual structure, the beginning of an answer is already at hand: the information specifying the appearance of X has been erroneously linked in short-term memory with the identity Y, temporarily displacing Y's proper link to an appearance. Thus what one knows as Y comes to look like X. Just as in speech errors, then, an anomalous occurrence is caused by the shift of information from its proper place to somewhere else, a simple formal transfer.

A staple of Freudian analysis, of course, is the displacement (or symbolization) of the genitalia in dreams by objects of similar shape. However, Freud also suggests (1900, section III.C) that certain consistent substitutions serve to portray abstract concepts concretely in dreams; for instance, logical connection is represented as simultaneity or temporal proximity, cause and effect as temporal succession, and disjunction as ambiguity or vagueness. Negation and contradiction, he claims, are simply ignored; two individuals or events regarded as similar are often contracted into a single dream-entity, as in the case just discussed. All of these relationships can be captured quite simply in terms of formal substitutions in conceptual structure; more complicated relationships can be described along lines proposed for conscious metaphors by such writers as Lakoff and Johnson (1980).

Another characteristic of conceptual structure is that it is the form of information over which processes of reasoning and inference take place. Such processes are conceived of as formal operations that take one or more conceptual structures ("propositions" or possibly other forms) as input and produce new conceptual structures as output. For instance, the familiar rules of syllogism ("All men are mortal; Socrates is a man; therefore Socrates is mortal") are to be treated as relationships, not among the overt linguistic forms of sentences, but rather among the conceptual structures of sentences, in which the commonalities of syllogistic form are explicit. (Note, though, that the conceptual structures are not themselves directly accessible to consciousness—only the judgments based on them.)

Similarly, another rule of inference might be stated informally as "If X has changed to state Z at time T, X was not in state Z immediately before time T." This principle is in part responsible for the effect of the sentence "Have you stopped beating your wife?" in which a question about the occurrence of a change (to not beating your wife) implies the previous existence of the state from which change took place. Again, this principle applies, not to the overt utterance, but to its conceptual content.

These sorts of principles, studied by logicians and semanticists, are rules of *rational* inference. However, one might conceive of using the same formal organization in rules of "irrational inference." Here is one candidate that seems characteristic of psychodynamic displacement, again stated very informally.

Major premise: "'X has characteristic Z" is bad, to be avoided.

Minor premise: X has characteristic Z.

Conclusion: X does not have characteristic Z—some other person Y does.

In other words, the situation "X has characteristic Z" is flatly denied, but the characteristic Z does not go away: it is displaced onto some other appropriate individual. Within the formal organization of conceptual structure, such an operation seems no harder to state than the displacement of a consonant into the wrong word.

Given such a formulation of displacement, it is possible to ask what constraints exist on it (and they may be different in dreams than in waking life, I suppose). For instance, to what individuals is it possible (or likely) to displace Z, and to what individuals is it *im*possible (or unlikely)? As in phonology—and as in the case of rules of rational inference—such constraints can help reveal unconscious organization of the structures to which the displacement process applies.

In fact, one can begin to infer some of the likely directions of displacement. My impression from the literature with which I am familiar is that "bad" qualities are most frequently displaced from the self onto others, from kin (especially parents) onto nonkin, and perhaps more generally from intimates to nonintimates. In addition, when the source of displacement (X in the rule above) is other than self, the target (Y in the rule above) tends to be someone in a similar social relation to self in terms of gender and dominance—for example, attributes of one's father (dominant to self) are frequently displaced onto one's male boss, teacher, or therapist.

As in phonology, we can see processes of regularization at work. In ordinary (or "rational") circumstances, the conceptual processes of regularization are the logical inferences and hypotheses that one makes to fill in otherwise undetermined information. However, when applied to the results of "irrational inferences," they appear as confabulation. For instance, when one's own aggression is displaced in paranoia, fear of others' aggression is a logical reaction—a confabulated regularization. That is, the reaction is perfectly reasonable, given the (false) premises, in the same way that "an unkey's muncle" is phonologically perfect English. The interesting thing is that a simple formal change can, as a result of regularization, lead to a drastic change in superficial behavior.

Parallel to the phonological case, the applied processes of regularization tend to obscure the damage that has been done to the original information, so that the paranoid's reactions seem to him or her perfectly normal and rational. However, if these processes can be properly separated out and independently explored, they can provide further evidence for the organization of the system as a whole.

5.6   Toward an Analysis of Unconscious Role Schemes

I therefore find myself suggesting an approach to studying psychodynamic phenomena that focuses on their *content* and *formal structure*. By treating these phenomena as richly integrated into one's overall conception of the world, it is hoped that they can be treated as of a piece with the formal system underlying ordinary reasoning, which we are now beginning to learn to study in the rigorous way that phonology and syntax have been studied for some decades. As emphasized in section 5.1, the methodology does not call for direct introspection of the content, which is in general impossible. Rather, one must use whatever fragments of evidence appear in conscious judgments as clues to the underlying unconscious principles of organization.

Horowitz (1988b, 1990) offers a style of analysis that can be construed as a preliminary step in this direction. His approach attempts to characterize an individual's repertoire of "states of mind." Each "state of mind" consists of an affect (for instance those in (5)) associated with a structured relationship schema involving self (for instance those in (6)).

(5)   a.   frightened yearning
       b.   numb immobilization
       c.   explosive rage

(6) a.   self as abandoned child, supplicating other as caregiver, who in
          turn neglects self
     b.   self as wise and strong, showing oneself to wise and strong
          other, who in turn approves of self
     c.   self as righteous assailant, harming failed caregiver, who in turn
          avoids self

Horowitz proposes that the individual's overall pattern of behavior can be characterized in terms of a repertoire of lawful transitions from each of these states of mind to others.

In order to begin making this approach more formally rigorous, one could ask the following sorts of questions:

1. Does one's affect depend systematically on the roles and relationships? Obviously yes, since the affect "frightened yearning" makes intuitive sense associated with role (6a) but seems grossly out of place associated with (6b); similarly, "explosive rage" makes intuitive sense associated with relationship (6c) but not with (6a).

2. Can this dependence be specified formally, so as to *predict* the association of affect with roles and relationships? In order to do so over an indefinitely large range of possible combinations (parallel to predicting linguistic intuitions over novel sentences), it is necessary to decompose the elements of affects, roles, and relationships into the constituents over which the principles governing associations can be formally defined. This does not necessarily mean that these constituents will be available to consciousness per se, any more than the constituents of language are.

3. Is there interdependence between the roles and relationships in these dyads? Intuition suggests again that there is. For example, self in the role of "wise and strong," supplicating other in the role of "abandoned child," seems like a combination close to "ungrammatical," with a bizarre effect not unlike sentence (3b).

4. What are the possible roles and combinations of roles into dyads? Many of the dyads suggested by Horowitz are implicitly relational; for instance, a "failed caretaker" must take care *of someone*, presumably the other member of the dyad, and a "child" stands in implicit relation to a parent. Moreover, a number of relational dyads are variants on the basic relation of social dominance mentioned in the previous section: parents dominate children, mentors dominate students, caretakers dominate their charges, assailants dominate victims. Other roles such as "weak and defective" and "wise and strong" are not inherently relational. Do they function differently from relational roles in psychodynamic states?

5. Some of Horowitz's roles have a great deal of information packed into them. For instance, a "failed caretaker" is someone who *should* have been taking care of someone during some period in the past but has not done so

adequately. Like the sentence "Have you stopped beating your wife?" this role carries an implied history and critical judgment. How do such "loaded" roles add to the complexity of psychodynamic states?

The goal of asking questions like these, with respect to a large number of Horowitz's "states of mind," would be to discover the overall repertoire of unconscious postures available to an individual participating in human relationships, and to elucidate its systematic organization. Such inquiry would lead in two directions. On one hand, it would send one back to the primary data, suggesting new analyses and refinements of previous analyses. On the other hand, broader issues might come to be addressable, for instance the possibility of differentiating personality types, both normal and pathological, in terms of available repertoire of roles, relationships, and state-transitions. Turning back to the "displacements" discussed in the previous section, the formal elements discovered in role analysis might be expected to be as well the sorts of elements over which principles of "irrational inference" operate. On an even more general plane, the goal would be to isolate the basic elements and combinatorial principles common to all psychodynamic phenomena, to find out how they shape social cognition, and through the Correspondence Condition, to discover how they come to shape conscious experience.

In the background all the time is the metatheory borrowed from linguistics: the entities that the theorist manipulates are not merely classificatory devices for expository convenience. They are intended as hypotheses about *psychologically real* elements of the computational mind. Their inaccessibility to awareness is not an argument against their existence, or a proof that their proponents are tilting at windmills: the formal elements of language are unavailable to awareness too. Thus the outlook of linguistic theory not only confirms and refines the psychodynamic view of the unconscious; it also provides an attractive precedent for pursuing and justifying a more fine-grained empirical analysis of the content of psychodynamic states.

I should be clear about the immediate limitations of such an approach. By concentrating on the formal organization of psychodynamic phenomena rather than processing, it offers no direct account of such mechanisms as repression and intrusion, so prominent in these phenomena—it may say at best what material is likely to be repressed or intruded. Similarly, it can say nothing about the processes involved in segregating information into multiple personalities—though it may shed light on what information may cluster together into each personality if such segregation takes place.

Such qualifications may be seen by some as altogether damning, but I think the situation is not so bad. First of all, such an approach does not *exclude* description of process. Rather, as in linguistics, a description of formal organization is to be conceived of as an essential part of a full theory of process. In linguistics, moreover, it has always been the case that developments in the theory of form have inspired more sophisticated theories of processing; one might hope for the same result here. Thus I see a theory of the formal structure of psychodynamic states and inferences, and their relationship to more everyday conceptualization, at the core of an overall theory of these phenomena.

Chapter 6

Spatial Language and Spatial Cognition

Ray Jackendoff and Barbara Landau

Fundamental to spatial knowledge in all species are the representations underlying object recognition, object search, and navigation through space. But what sets humans apart from other species is the ability to use these representations to express our spatial experience: talking about what things are, where they are, and how we might get to them. This chapter addresses two questions crucial to understanding how this is accomplished. First, how does language draw on spatial cognition so that we can manage to talk about what we perceive? Second, how does spatial language thereby provide a window on the nature of spatial cognition?

Our goal will be to explore how language encodes objects and spatial relationships, and to do this in a way that is compatible with constraints on nonlinguistic spatial understanding. At the same time, we will use evidence from language to provide boundary conditions on a satisfactory theory of spatial cognition: our premise is that any aspect of spatial understanding that can be expressed in language must also be present in spatial representations.

We should begin by clarifying the term *spatial representation*. By this we intend a format or level of mental representation devoted to encoding the geometric properties of objects in the world and the relationships among them in space. Because spatial information can be derived from vision, from

This chapter appeared originally in slightly different form in Donna Jo Napoli and Judy Kegl, eds., *Bridges between Psychology and Linguistics: A Swarthmore Festschrift for Lila Gleitman*, L. Erlbaum Assocs., 1991, and is reprinted by permission. A more detailed version is to appear in *Behavioral and Brain Sciences*.

The first author was a graduate of Swarthmore, but did not have the privilege of studying with Lila Gleitman. In order to serve the purposes of the Festschrift, it therefore seemed fitting to complete the gestalt by collaborating with the second author, who did not go to Swarthmore but did study with Lila Gleitman. Both of us are grateful for this opportunity to honor Lila, who through many years of association has been a constant source of inspiration, wisdom, and good jokes.

This research was supported in part by NSF Grant IRI 88-08286 to Brandeis University and by Social and Behavioral Sciences Research Grant 12-214 from the March of Dimes Birth Defects Foundation to Barbara Landau. We are grateful to Edgar Zurif and David Murray for essential references used in this study.

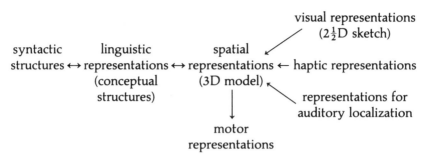

Figure 6.1

auditory localization, and from the haptic (touch) faculty, it demands a format that is not modality-specific. That is, this representation is neither visual nor haptic nor aural, but *spatial*; understanding spatial configurations in the world involves converting or translating modality-specific information into this common format. We also assume that spatial representations must be translatable into a form of representation specific to the motor system, used to initiate and guide behavior: we can touch what we see, look at what we hear, and avoid obstacles as we navigate through space.[1] Finally, in order to account for the language of space, there must be a translation between the spatial format and the representations proprietary to language. Figure 6.1 sketches these relationships among levels of representation; as in previous chapters, the arrows denote translations from one level to another.

Our discussion of spatial language will be in three parts. First, we will discuss language pertaining to object identification and its bearing on some current theories of the encoding of object shape. Second, we will discuss language pertaining to the locations of objects. Differences in these two aspects of language will lead us to the third issue: how the identification and location of objects are integrated in spatial cognition and in language, and why these aspects are so different.

6.1 Talking about Objects

In the vocabulary of an average adult speaker of English, there are on the order of ten to fifteen thousand names for things—count nouns that label different kinds of objects. For a large proportion of object categories, one important criterion for identification is shape (Landau, Smith, and Jones 1988). This means that the spatial representations that are linked to object names must provide enough different shape descriptions, configured in the proper way, to be able to distinguish all the kinds of objects we linguistically categorize on the basis of appearance.

From the nonlinguistic side, a promising approach to the problem of shape description takes object shapes to be represented componentially, as in Marr 1982 and Biederman 1987. In Marr's approach, what corresponds most closely to our notion of spatial representation is the 3D model level, the format in which objects are encoded in object-centered format, independent of viewer's perspective. Even though Marr speaks of the 3D model as part of vision, our framework suggests that it should in fact be capable of accepting input derived from haptic/kinesthetic sources as well, making it non-modality-specific. The representational levels closer to the retinal array, Marr's primal and $2\frac{1}{2}$D sketches, correspond to what figure 6.1 calls specifically visual representations. In addition, Jackendoff 1987a, 1987b has shown that 3D model representations can be translated in part into representations suitable for linguistic expression. Hence the 3D model level, insofar as it can be fleshed out, has the properties with which we have characterized spatial representation.

The primitives for 3D object description in Marr's theory are (1) a set of principles for describing "generalized cones" in terms of an axis and a cross section, and (2) a principle for elaborating a main axis with a subsidiary axis of a particular size and orientation relative to the main axis. Principle (2) applies recursively, so that objects in the 3D model representation are composed of parts, each of which may have a further decomposition. As a result, highly detailed shapes can emerge, making the representations in principle rich enough to support the extensive vocabulary of object names seen in language.

Biederman's (1987) approach to object description can be viewed as an extension of the 3D model system. Like Marr, Biederman proposes that object shapes decompose into parts, but he further suggests that the parts can be represented by a small set of specific generalized cones, 36 in number, which he calls *geons*. Given even a very small set of attachment relationships among the cones—such as "end-to-end" or "top-to-side"—and only a few iterations, Biederman shows that the system can generate at least as many object shapes as there are object names.

Each of these systems is capable of generating a wide range of particular object shapes from primitives. For example, Marr describes schemata for the human figure and various animals, and Biederman additionally describes such objects as airplanes and cameras. In principle, these systems should be able to generate a sufficient number of descriptions to cover all named objects (and, with a suitable similarity metric, could even account for differences among named categories such as *person* versus *gorilla*, whose shapes are quite similar). We believe, however, that evidence from language suggests the need for additional kinds of descriptions.

We therefore would like to make a few elementary observations about spatial and linguistic descriptions of objects that point to gaps in the

Marr-Biederman machinery—aspects of object descriptions that are not a part of their visual representations. In each we will suggest appropriate enrichments of spatial representations that remain within the spirit of the Marr-Biederman approach.

6.1.1   Names for Spatial Parts: Orienting Axes

Many objects can be described as having a *top* and a *bottom*, a *front* and a *back*, and *sides* and/or *ends*. These terms do not describe parts in the same sense as, say, *handle* or *wing*: they are not subsidiary geons tacked onto the object. Rather, they denote regions of the object based on its inherent orientation.[2] How can the use of these terms be derived from a spatial representation?

Aside from language, the orientation of an object is necessary for describing certain relationships among parts, for instance the fact that on the human body the nose, the feet, and the belly button point in the same direction (hence are on the *front* of the body) or that the arms are attached opposite one another and orthogonal to the front (hence are on the *sides*). And relative orientation of parts is clearly crucial in nonlinguistic tasks such as mental rotation, where judgments of object identity often require discriminating right-left reversals of an object (Shepard and Cooper 1982; Parsons 1987). As far as we can determine, neither Marr nor Biederman provides a principled means for encoding such facts of orientation.

One way to express these regularities is to extend the theory of axes in two ways. First, we will call the axis that is expanded into a generalized cone (or geon) the *generating axis*; this is the axis that is central to Marr's and Biederman's account of object shape. Let us impose on the geon up to two further axes, called *orienting axes*, which are orthogonal to the generating axis and to each other. These axes will serve to orient the geon radially. In the case of the human body, the principal generating axis is vertical; it defines the generalized cone of the torso. The two orienting axes determine the front-to-back and the side-to-side directions.

Second, an axis can optionally be marked as intrinsically *directed* or *symmetric*. A *directed* axis indicates inherent regularities that depend on distinguishing one end from the other. For example, the directed front-to-back axis of the human figure establishes the regularity of alignment for the nose, feet, and belly button. A *symmetric* axis indicates regularities that depend on equivalent elaborations at both ends. For example, the side-to-side axis of the human figure establishes the symmetry of the limbs and face parts.

These markings can be carried either by the generating axis of a geon or by its orienting axes. In the human figure, for example, the main generating axis is a directed axis that distinguishes top from bottom. In Biederman's camera, if the long side-to-side dimension is the generating axis for the geon, it is a symmetric generating axis.

Other combinations of generating and orienting axes are also possible. For example, an arrow has a directed generating axis but no significant orienting axes. The human hand has an oriented generating axis (wrist-to-fingers, following Marr) and two directed orienting axes (back-to-palm and pinky-to-thumb).

Retuı ning to the linguistic description of objects, we can use the system of directed and orienting axes to define the terms brought up at the beginning of this section. The *top* and *bottom* of an object are the regions (or parts of the surface) of the object at the ends of whichever axis is vertical in the object's normal orientation. If the object is relatively long and narrow, that is, if it has a horizontal generating axis significantly longer than the other axes, the object can be said to have *ends*—the regions at the termination of this axis. If the object has a horizontal directed axis, one of whose ends normally faces the observer or determines the normal direction of motion, the region determined by that end of the axis is the object's *front*; the opposite end of this axis determines the *back*. Finally, the region determined by the termination of any other horizontal axis can be called a *side*.[3] Thus linguistic and nonlinguistic facts about shape converge in motivating an augmentation of the descriptive machinery available in spatial representation.

6.1.2   Names for Objects Best Described as Surfaces

Consider the spatial representations of sheets of paper, phonograph records, crackers, tabletops, blackboards, rugs, roads, and lakes. What these have in common is that they are principally extended in two dimensions, with a relatively negligible thickness (at least in the relevant context); the linear boundary of this surface can then be defined as its *edge*.

How are such objects to be encoded in spatial representation? It seems intuitively odd to treat a phonograph record as a very fat cylinder with a very short main axis passing through the hole. However, this is the most natural way to formally generate it in the Marr-Biederman framework of volumetric primitives. Furthermore, a lake hardly lends itself at all to such descriptions. For instance, if the lake's generating axis is taken as going from the surface to the bottom, the description is entirely counterintuitive. Alternatively, if its generating axis is taken as parallel to the surface (as it might be if the lake is relatively long and narrow), it seems odd to have the axis fall in the interior of the geon, as Biederman's repertoire would require: that would put the axis underwater.

The problem in these cases is that the Marr-Biederman volumetric primitives require one to directly generate a volume from a linear axis. A more intuitively satisfying analysis of these objects is that they are schematized as *surfaces*, elaborated into a volume by adding a *thickness*. The surface in turn may perhaps be generated by a suitable extension of the theory of generalized cones to the 2-dimensional case, as Biederman suggests in passing. On this analysis, the phonograph record is schematized as basically a disk; the lake is schematized basically as its surface. It seems that an object can be said to have an edge just in case it has such a spatial representation.

In addition to object names for surface-like objects, there are other words that benefit from having such an analysis available in spatial representation. Two classes come to mind: (1) 2-dimensional shape terms like *square, circle, oval*, and *trapezoid*; (2) general terms for "thickened surfaces" such as *slab, sheet, layer, slice, lamina*, and *stratum*. Generalizing beyond nouns, the adjectives *thick* and *thin* can also be seen to place a metric on the elaboration of a surface into a volume, indicating further the general usefulness of this analysis.

6.1.3   Names for "Negative" Object Parts

Some entities may be best conceptualized as *negative parts* of objects, as alluded to by Hoffman and Richards (1984) and Herskovits (1986). Compare a *ridge* and a *groove*. A ridge is conceptualized as a protrusion from the surface of a host object. It has an extended linear generating axis parallel to the surface of the host object, and a directed orienting axis that projects into the surface of the host object, giving the ridge a top and a bottom, plus a (roughly) symmetrical orienting axis that defines its sides. It therefore can be easily described as a part of the host object within the geonic system as elaborated so far.

Now consider a groove. It is conceptualized as a depression in the surface of a host object. It has an extended linear generating axis parallel to the surface of the host object, and a directed orienting axis that projects into the surface of the host object, giving the groove a top and a bottom, plus a (roughly) symmetrical axis that defines its sides. But it cannot be described within the geonic system, because it is not possible to conceive of it as attached to the host object.

A natural way to think of a groove is as a "negative part," a shaped volume scooped out of the object instead of added to it. That is, it is a shape defined by "lack of substance" rather than by the presence of substance, as in the case of normal parts. Other than that, a negative part evidently has shape descriptors—and a linguistic description—essentially parallel to those of ordinary parts. Notice, for example, that a groove not only has a top, bottom, and sides; it can be described as *long* or *short, broad* or *narrow, deep* or *shallow*.

Other negative part names are *hole, pit* (a "negative" *bump*), *notch, slot, scratch, depression, cavity*, and possibly *dent*. Words that name "negative objects" are *ditch, valley, cave, well*, and *door* and *window* (in the sense of 'opening in a wall' rather than the object used to close off such an opening). Thus again a simple enrichment of spatial representation affords revealing analyses for a wide variety of things we can name (though they are not strictly speaking *objects* this time).

6.1.4   Names for Containers and Related Objects

As Miller and Johnson-Laird (1976) point out, English has an extensive set of names for *containers*: objects like cups, bowls, boxes, jars, tanks, and so forth. What is their spatial representation? One possibility, consistent with the system described so far, is that a cup, for instance, is a cylinder out of which a large coaxial negative cylinder has been scooped. However, an alternative with a certain intuitive appeal is that a cup is basically a thickened surface that encloses a cylindrical space—that is, the sides and bottom of the cup are not the residue of extensive scooping but rather basically surfaces.

We are not certain which of these analyses is correct, but there is some evidence that language distinguishes containers from solid objects; roughly, containers are objects that can hold things inside them (see section 6.2.2). In order to encode such a class, we tentatively adopt the second alternative and introduce a distinction between "solid" and "hollow" geons. Solid geons would be encoded as uniformly substantial; hollow geons would be shapes whose substance is distributed only over their surfaces, leaving a shaped empty space inside. (The openings in containers, say the top of a cup, might further be described as negative parts in an otherwise unbroken surface.)

In addition to the containers mentioned above, hollow geons would nicely describe such objects as cars and other closed vehicles, houses and other buildings, stomachs, eggs, balloons, bubbles, violins, and drums. Again, a simple parameter added to spatial representation affords an intuitively natural encoding of a significant new class of objects.

6.1.5   Other Cases

In addition to these factors, spatial representation needs descriptors for surface features like *dots, stripes,* and *marks.* Names for textural features, another aspect of the surface, shade imperceptibly from purely visual terms like *red* and *shiny,* through terms available to both vision and touch like *jagged, bumpy,* and *flat,* to those that seem more specifically haptic, such as *rough, smooth, hard, soft,* and *slippery.* These require further extensions to the theory that will not concern us here.

Beyond our proposed additions to the descriptive power of the Marr-Biederman framework, it remains to be shown that the whole system of decomposition into parts, each composed of a generalized cone, can be adapted to the tolerances necessary for object category discrimination. For instance, descriptions must be potentially fine-grained enough that one can decide which objects are to be named *horse* and which *donkey*, or which *dog* and which *wolf*. On the other hand, they must be potentially indeterminate enough to allow considerable variation in shape within each of these named categories, for example the differences between Dalmatians and Pekinese dogs, and to allow the variation in number, placement, size, and shape of arms on a saguaro cactus. How these tolerances for discrimination are to be formalized is beyond the scope of this study.

In sum, the spatial representation of objects by shape is a rich combinatorial system. It involves as basic units not only generalized cones but also surfaces. These units are schematized in terms of generating axes and orienting axes, which may be directed or symmetric; each of these units may be "solid," "hollow," or "negative." They are combined hierarchically to form complex object descriptions, in the fashion described by Marr and Biederman. In addition, they are detailed in terms of surface and textural features. All of this must be encoded within a framework that can specify tolerances acceptable for category membership.

6.2   Talking about Spatial Relations

The Marr-Biederman framework and all the amplifications we have discussed concern object recognition and categorization, that is, *what* an object is. None of this addresses *where* the object is or, if in motion, its path of movement. But of course that is an essential part of spatial cognition—and an essential part of what we talk about in spatial language.

Here the nonlinguistic side of the investigation is on much less firm ground. We know of no theory of visually based object location that is comparable to Marr's theory of object shape and its relatives, in which one can begin to trace the representational pathways all the way from the retinal array to a multimodal representation that can justifiably be called spatial. So in this section we will rely more heavily on linguistic analysis to suggest what components of spatial representations would need to be encoded in a nonlinguistic theory of spatial location. We draw especially on Talmy 1978, 1983, Jackendoff 1983, 1990, Herskovits 1986, Miller and Johnson-Laird 1976, Bennett 1975, Hawkins 1984, and Clark 1973.

The canonical English expression of a spatial relation between two objects does not relate them directly. Rather, one object (the *reference object*) is used to define a *region* in which the other object (the *figural object* or *figure*) is located. For example, in the sentence *The cat is sitting on the mat*, the prepositional phrase *on the mat* defines a region in terms of the reference object (the mat), and the figure (the cat) is in turn located in that region. Within this complex, the preposition *on* is the linguistic element that expresses the spatial relation, in this case 'contact with the surface of the reference object'. In addition to prepositions, there are many verbs that incorporate spatial relations; these can (almost invariably) be paraphrased by a simpler verb plus a preposition. For instance, *enter* can be paraphrased by *go into*, *approach* by *go toward*, and *cross* by *go across*. (See Jackendoff 1983, 1990 for formalization of these relations.) Here we focus only on spatial prepositions, a fairly complete list of which appears in table 6.1.[4]

One of the most salient facts about prepositions is that there seem to be surprisingly few of them in comparison to the number of names for different kinds of objects. (In fact, there are few enough prepositions that they are usually considered part of the "closed-class" vocabulary, along with auxiliaries, determiners, and inflections.) We can get an idea of the order of magnitude of different spatial relations expressed in English by counting the prepositions (see table 6.1). There are something on the order of 80 to 100, depending on how one counts. Of course, many of these are polysemous, and quite a few are nonspatial (*during*, for instance, is purely temporal), so this count gives us only a ballpark figure. But compare it to the number of count nouns in English—some tens of thousands. Again, many of these are polysemous, and many are not object names, so the count is only rough. But even supposing that the count is drastically biased, there is a difference between the two of approximately two orders of magnitude: for every spatial relation expressible in English, there are perhaps a hundred object names. This qualitative difference is reproduced in every language we know of. (If there were a language with even a thousand prepositions, someone would certainly have raised a big hue and cry about it.)

Given the small number of prepositions, it is not surprising that they exhibit considerable constraints in how they express spatial relationships. The following subsections will present what we believe to be a rather comprehensive enumeration of the factors involved in defining the spatial relations expressed in English. The factors divide rather naturally into four parts. The first, the asymmetry between the figure and reference objects, sets the basic parameters for spatial relations. The remaining three concern the descriptions of the three elements of the spatial relation: the reference object, the figural object, and the region based on the reference object.

6.2.1   Asymmetry between Figure and Reference Object
Due to the distinction between reference object and figure, the standard expression of spatial location is strikingly asymmetrical. To illustrate, we have annotated the figure and reference objects in the sentences in (1).

(1) a.   The book [figure] is lying on the table [reference object].
     b.   The train [figure] reached the station [reference object].
     c.   The star [figure] is inside the circle [reference object].
     d.   The circle [figure] lies around (surrounds) the star [reference object].

Table 6.1
Prepositions of English

Simple transitives	Compound transitives	Prepositions used only nonspatially
about	in back of	ago
above	in between	as
across	in front of	because of
after	in line with	despite
against	on top of	during
along	to the left of	for
alongside	to the right of	like
amid(st)	to the side of	of
among(st)		since
around	*Intransitives*	until
at	afterward(s)	without
atop	apart	
before	away	
behind	backward	
below	downstairs	
beneath	downward	
beside	east	
between	forward	
betwixt	here	
beyond	inward	
by	left	
down	N-ward (homeward,	
from	shoreward, etc.)	
in	north	
inside	outward	
into	right	
near	sideways	
nearby	south	
off	there	
on	together	
onto	upstairs	
opposite	upward	
out	west	
outside		
over		
past		
through		
throughout		
to		
toward		
under		
underneath		
up		
upon		
via		
with		
within		

Note that (1c) and (1d) can describe the very same physical stimulus. However, they organize it differently, exchanging figure and reference object. These different organizations appear to reflect differences in the encoding of the stimulus in spatial representation, corresponding to the reversals of figure and ground shown in classical studies of perception (Hochberg 1978).

As has been noted by Miller and Johnson-Laird (1976) and Talmy (1983), not every pair of objects creates such an ambiguous stimulus: if the objects are unequal in size and/or mobility, the larger and more stable invariably takes the role of reference object. Consider (2), in which the exchange produces an odd-sounding result.

(2)   a.   The book is on the table.
       b.??   The table is under the book.

Even what would seem to be a symmetrical spatial relation—adjacency— is subject to the asymmetry of figure–reference object dyads, as shown in (3).

(3)   a.   The bicycle is next to the house.
       b.??   The house is next to the bicycle.

It does not seem to follow from any fact specifically pertaining to language that the table and the house are more plausible reference objects and the book and the bicycle more plausible figures in this context. Rather, we believe, this asymmetry is more likely to follow from principles of spatial organization, which require that an object be located relative to some other object—presumably, one that will facilitate successful search. Indeed, such an asymmetry has been found in psychological studies of distance estimation between key landmarks and various located objects (e.g. Rosch 1975; Sadalla, Burroughs, and Staplin 1980).

6.2.2   Constraints on the Geometry of the Reference Object
Let us examine how the system of spatial relations makes use of the shapes of the objects being related. Having just discussed the intricate shape descriptions required for object naming, it is worth asking whether the same descriptors can be used when describing an object's place. In fact, they cannot: what proves surprising is how coarsely both the figure and refer- ence objects appear to be represented. This section deals with constraints on the reference object; the even looser constraints on the figure are described in section 6.2.4.

Taking a simple case, there seem to be no prepositions whose figure or reference object must be analyzed in terms of a particular geon. A hypothet- ical example would be the preposition *sprough*, 'reaching from end to end of a cigar-shaped object', appearing in sentences like (4a) but not (4b).

(4) a. The rug extended sprough the airplane.
         The weevil bored sprough the cigar.
         The major axis of an ellipse goes right sprough it.
     b. *The rug extended sprough my dining room.
         *The weevil bored sprough the chair.
         *The major axis of a cup handle goes right sprough it.

Similarly, there are no prepositions that insist on analysis of the figural or reference object into constituent parts. An example might be the hypothetical preposition *betwaft* in (5), which requires the reference object to have a protruding part.

(5) a. The bug crawled betwaft my face.
         'The bug crawled down the junction between my nose and the main body of my face.'
     b. The water ran betwaft the airplane.
         'The water ran down the junction between the wing and the fuselage.'
     c. A stripe extended betwaft the cup.
         'A stripe extended along/down the junction between the body of the cup and the handle.'

Each of these hypothetical words expresses a perfectly plausible spatial relation, but both are perfectly horrible prepositions.

About the most complicated cases we have found—in which some elements of object shape are relevant to the preposition's meaning—are the terms *along* and *across*. *Along* requires its reference object to have a principal axis of significant elongation, so that one can travel *along a road* or *along a beach* but not *along a chair* or *along a round table*. One can travel *along the edge of a round table*, but then the linear edge, not the table as a whole, is serving as reference object. In addition, this principal linear axis must be (more or less) horizontal: a bug can be said to crawl *along a flagpole* only if the flagpole is lying down. (We treat *across* and some further wrinkles in *along* shortly.)

And that is more or less it, in terms of specific shape requirements. However, there do seem to be certain general constraints on the range of geometries exhibited by reference objects. We now describe three such constraints.

6.2.2.1 Volumes, Surfaces, and Lines   The terms *in, on, near,* and *at* require very little in the way of detailed geometry. For something to be *in* X, X must have an interior, but nothing more is necessary. There is no requirement on axes, for example. In other words, the reference object for *in* needs a form descriptor even coarser than Marr's basic cylinder, something like a "lump" (or if a 2-dimensional region, a "blob"). *Near* and *at* require only that the reference object is bounded in extent. *On* requires that its reference object be a line (*on the border*), a surface (*on the square*), or an object whose boundary is a line or a surface (a house *on the lake* or a house *on the hill* respectively).

Inside is somewhat more specific than *in*. It seems to require that its reference object be or contain a bounded enclosure (a negative part or the interior of a hollow geon). Thus, as pointed out by Talmy, one can be either *in* or *inside* a cave or a bottle, but one can be only *in*, not *inside*, a swimming pool or lake, because these are not conceptualized as enclosures or containers.

6.2.2.2   *Axes*   A sizable number of prepositions, such as *on top of*, *in front of*, *in back of*, and *beside*, make reference to an axis. In the case of an object that lacks inherent axes, such as a sphere, these axes are contextually imposed (see section 6.2.3). But these prepositions can also make use of the reference object's inherent axes. *On top of* and *under* project regions from the directed axis that is vertical in the object's normal orientation. *In front of*, *in back of*, and *behind* make use of the directed horizontal front-to-back axis; *beside* and *alongside* make use of a horizontal axis perpendicular to the front-to-back axis. For the purposes of these prepositions, it does not matter whether the axes in question are generating axes or orienting axes.

As mentioned above, *along* requires its reference object to be basically linear and horizontal. Its partner *across* appears to require its reference object to be or to have a surface with sides, so that one can go across, 'from one side to the other'. Just in case the reference object has a significant linear elongation, the *sides* are distinguished from the *ends*: a square table has four sides, but a long rectangular table has two sides and two ends. In such a case, *across* pertains specifically to the sides and not to the ends, so that *across the rectangular table* describes a region that traverses the table's shorter dimension.[5] Nonrectilinear objects in this framework tend to be idealized as though they were rectilinear, so that, with respect to *across*, a round table behaves like a square table and an oval table like a rectangular one.

A further restriction on *across* is that, like *along*, it describes a horizontally oriented region. For instance, one draws a line *across a blackboard* in the horizontal direction, not the vertical. This follows from the stipulation that *across* pertains to the sides of the object, which are normally the boundaries of a horizontal axis.

6.2.2.3   *Quantity of Reference Object*   A different sort of restriction on the reference object appears in the prepositions *between*, *among*, and *amidst*. For *between*, the reference object is not a single object but rather a pair. In the case of *among* and *amidst*, it is an aggregate (or collection of objects), as in *among the people* or *amidst the waves*.

To sum up, the restrictions placed on the form of the reference object by expressions for spatial relations are not at all severe, compared to the potential complexity of objects themselves. At most, these restrictions appeal to the very gross geometry of the coarsest level of representation of the object—whether it is a container, whether it is relatively elongated, whether the elongation is horizontal, and whether it has sides.[6]

We next turn to the description of regions; the few constraints on the geometry of the figure will be easier to state after this discussion.

6.2.3   Constraints on Spatial Relations Defining Regions

The spatial relations expressed in English factor into a number of independent features that combine to produce some of the complexity of the system.

6.2.3.1   Relative Distance   Relative distance concerns how close the figural object is to the reference object. The most salient fact about this encoding is that it is digitized into discrete categories. English has three degrees of distance. The closest possibility is being located in the interior of the reference object (*in, inside*); the next closest is exterior to the reference object but in contact with it (*on, against*); the next is being proximate to the reference object (*near*). Some languages provide additional values for this feature beyond proximate, for instance 'not near but within reach' or 'not near but visible'. One such language is Korean (Soo-Won Kim, personal communication), in which the expressions *yup* and *kiyut* both translate as 'near', but *yup* is confined to more immediately proximate cases. (Other examples are cited by Anderson and Keenan (1985) in connection with systems of spatial deixis corresponding to English *here* and *there*.) On the other hand, some languages have prepositions that collapse two adjacent values of distance in English. For instance, English *in* and *on* can both be translated by Spanish *en*. Thus English represents an intermediate degree of complexity in the distance parameter. To our knowledge, no language encodes more than five or six levels of distance—although, of course, we are able to represent distance at much finer levels for other cognitive purposes.

Each of the degrees of relative distance found in English has a corresponding "negative," which actually means 'farther away from the reference object than'. The three cases are 'farther away than the interior' (*out of, outside*), 'farther away than in contact' (*off of*), and 'farther away than proximate' (*far from*).

The prepositions *among* and *between* also involve the distance feature. As mentioned above, the reference object for *among* is an aggregation of objects, which together define a group or virtual object that contains them all. The figural object is then specified as interior to this virtual object. The case of *between* is similar, except that the virtual object is the minimal space bounded by the pair of reference objects.

6.2.3.2 Direction   Direction of the figural object from the reference object provides a second parameter in specifying spatial relations. For the simplest case, gravitation supplies a vertical orientation necessary to define *over*, *above*, *under*, *below*, and *beneath*.

Orthogonal to gravitation is the horizontal direction that helps define *beside*, *by*, *alongside*, and *next to*. To see that the horizontal is crucial, notice that if a bird is beside, by, alongside, or next to a house, it must not be on the roof or flying overhead: it must be in proximity to the house and no higher than the house. Thus these prepositions designate the relation 'proximate to the reference object in the horizontal direction'. In addition, if the reference object has inherent axes that distinguish front and back from sides, these four prepositions tend to mean 'horizontally proximate to the *sides* of the reference object'. For instance, Bill is not *beside* you if you are facing him.

Similarly, if the reference object has an axis that determines an inherent front and back, *in front of* can mean 'horizontally proximate to the inherent front of the reference object', and *in back of* can mean 'horizontally proximate to the inherent back of the reference object'. However, an alternative interpretation of these prepositions results from *contextually* assigning a front-to-back axis to the reference object: the front is the surface facing the speaker (or addressee), and the back is the surface opposite. In this case *in front of* and *in back of* mean 'horizontally proximate to the contextual front/back of the reference object'. A parallel ambiguity occurs with *on top of*: if a flagpole is lying on its side, one can paint the ball on top of it (referring to the inherent top), or sit on top of it (referring to the contextually determined top, in this case a long horizontal surface).

Not all spatial expressions involving axes leave this choice of reference system open. *On the top of*, by contrast with *on top of*, refers only to the inherent top of the reference object (presumably because it contains the full noun phrase *the top*). *Beyond*, by contrast with *behind*, refers only to the region projected to the contextually determined rear of the reference object. This shows that choice of reference system can be lexically specified, and therefore must be learned.

6.2.3.3 Combinations of Distance and Direction   Distance and direction interact to provide further distinctions among prepositions. For instance, compare *over*, *above*, and *on top of*, all of which specify a region in the upward direction from the reference object. *Over* is indifferent to contact versus noncontact: a cloth may be put over a table (contact), and clouds may fly over a city (noncontact). *Above*, however, specifies noncontact: though clouds may fly above a city, one can only put a cloth above a table by putting it on a higher shelf. Finally, *on top of* strongly favors a contact reading.

In back of and *behind*, which share directionality, also differ in distance. A tree may be *right behind* (proximal), *way behind* (distal), or *right in back of* a house; but *The tree is way in back of the house* sounds odd or colloquial. Evidently the standard use of *in back of* is restricted to proximal distance (and possibly contact), whereas *behind* and colloquial *in back of* are unrestricted.

For a somewhat different case, to move *up* or *down* a mountain, tree, or wall is to move in an upward/downward direction while maintaining contact with (or, marginally, proximity to) the surface of the reference object.

Sergey Avrutin (personal communication) has pointed out that the conceptual features of distance and direction can be used to predict the case-marking pattern of Russian place prepositions. According to his analysis, the two closest grades of distance (interior and contact) assign Prepositional case to their objects; prepositions that involve a direction feature (*over*, *under*, *behind*, etc.) assign Instrumental case; the remaining prepositions (*at*, *near*, *close to*, etc.) assign Genitive case.[7]

6.2.3.4 Visibility and Occlusion   A subsidiary use of some of the directional prepositions invokes the distinction 'visible' versus 'occluded'. A case in English where this distinction is evident is in speaking of paint on a wall being *on top of* or *underneath* the wallpaper. Here *on top of* evidently means 'in contact with visible surface', whatever its orientation, and *underneath* means 'in contact with the surface opposite the visible surface'. (Notice, by the way, that one cannot speak of *the bottom of the wallpaper* in this context; not all the words of vertical orientation generalize to this use.) Vandeloise (1986) argues that occlusion of the reference object is the main relation expressed by French *devant* 'in front of'. Though we would not go quite so far, we believe this criterion does play a secondary role, possibly forming a preference rule system (Jackendoff 1983) with the directional criteria.

6.2.4 Specification of the Geometry of the Figure
The specification of regions now permits us to go back and look at constraints on the geometry of the figural object.

6.2.4.1 Relationships Involving Linear Axis of Figural Object   None of the spatial relations cited so far specify the form of the figural object in any way. However, three prepositions, *along*, *across*, and *around*, express spatial relations between the reference object and the *linear axis* of the figural object. For instance, consider the sense of *along* in *The road is along the river*. This specifies that the main axis of the road is colinear with (as well as horizontally proximate to) the main axis of the river. Similarly, if the figural object is an aggregate, as in *The trees are along the river*, this aggregate is preferentially understood as forming a virtual object whose axis is colinear with the main axis of the river. (On the other hand, if the figural object has no main horizontal axis, as in *The tree is along the river*, the condition of colinearity does not apply. If the figural object is in motion, as in *The dog loped along the river*, the trajectory of the figure rather than the figure itself is colinear with the main axis of the river.) The adjectival form *parallel to* places constraints similar to those of *along*.

Across, as mentioned above, involves a linear region that goes from one side to the other of the reference object. One sense of *across*, seen in *The stick lay across the road* and *The trees extend across the field*, specifies the figure's axis as coaxial with this region. (Other uses, for instance in *Bill ran across the road* and *Bill is across the road from Harry*, locate the figure, viewed as a point, with respect to this region.) The adjectival form *perpendicular to* places constraints similar to *across*.

Around also has a number of variants. Ignoring the one that means roughly *near* (*There are lots of trees around here*), it designates a hollow region whose interior contains the reference object. The figure is specified as occupying the region, either as a linear object surrounding a 2-dimensional reference object (*The road goes around the city*) or as a shell or thickened surface surrounding a 3-dimensional reference object (*There is chocolate around the core of the candy*). A distributed figure object is again acceptable (*There are trees around the house*). A moving figure may either circumnavigate the reference object (*go all the way around*) or *detour around it*.

6.2.4.2 *Distributed Figural Object*   In *along*, *across*, and *around* the figural object may be specified as being linear or (in the case of *around*) a surface. A different class of prepositions requires the figural object to be distributed, either as a substance or as an aggregate. Consider *There was water all over the floor*. *All over* specifies a figural object distributed over and in contact with the entire extent of the surface of the reference object. In *There were raisins throughout the pudding*, *throughout* specifies an aggregate figural object more or less evenly distributed in the volume of the reference object. Thus *all over* and *throughout* are "distributive" forms of the spatial relations normally expressed as *on* and *in* respectively. *All along*, *all around*, and *all across* are similar distributive forms corresponding to the prepositions *along*, *around*, and *across*.

These two kinds of constraints are the only ones we have found on the geometry of the figure; they are thus even coarser than those on the reference object.

6.2.5   Spatial Relations Defining Trajectories

English uses the conceptual category of trajectories or paths to specify the figure's motion (*The bird flew to the house*) or orientation (*The sign points to New York*). There are a few simple ways of constructing trajectories, none of which draw any further on the geometry of the figural or reference objects than we already have.

The simplest class of trajectories are the environmentally oriented directions *up, down, north, south, east,* and *west*. Another class specifies the figure's motion in terms of its own inherent horizontal axes: *frontwards, backwards, sideways*. Another specifies change of the figural object's orientation in terms of its own axes: turn *around*, turn *over*, turn *left*, and turn *right*.

The largest class of trajectories, however, is constructed from the class of regions by attaching one of five operators (Jackendoff 1983). One operator, 'via', creates a trajectory that passes through the region in question. For example, to *run by the house* is to traverse a trajectory that at some point involves being *near the house*; to *walk under a bridge* is to traverse a trajectory that at some point involves being *under the bridge*; to *go through a room* involves a trajectory that at some point is *in the room*. If the region in question is linear, as in *along, across,* and *around*, the 'via' trajectory is coaxial with the region, so that *going along* X involves moving parallel to the axis of X, for instance.

Another kind of trajectory is constructed from a region by attaching the operator 'to', creating a trajectory that terminates at the region in question. For instance, *to* X expresses a trajectory that terminates *at* X. *Into* X and *onto* X express trajectories that terminate *in* X and *on* X respectively. Similarly, the operator 'toward' constructs a trajectory that would terminate at the region if extended, but that does not in fact reach the region. So to *go toward* X is to undergo a motion that if extended would terminate *at* X.

The operator 'from' is just the reverse of 'to': it constructs a trajectory that begins at the region in question. Examples are *The bird emerged from under the table* and *The train came from inside the Soviet Union*. The operator 'away from' is the reverse of 'toward': *Bill ran away from the explosion* describes him as traversing a trajectory that if extended backward would begin at the explosion.[8]

6.2.6   Other Factors

The discussion above has presented not just a sample of the spatial relations expressed by English prepositions; it is essentially all the spatial relations we have been able to find. This section will briefly list some of the complications that remain, none of which involve geometric properties per se.

First, there are uses that involve special situations. Herskovits (1986) points out that to be *at a desk* or *at a sink* usually implies more than being located close to it; one is probably performing characteristic actions, such as writing at the desk or washing at the sink. For another case, to *throw a ball at X* involves more than *throwing it toward X*—roughly an intention to hit X. This difference accounts for the contrasts in (6).

(6)   Bill threw the ball toward/?at Harry without meaning to hit him.
      Bill shot at/?toward Harry.

Other special situations involve conventionalized conceptualization of the reference object. For instance, when traveling, one is *in a bus* or *on a bus* but only *in*, not *on*, *a car*. It seems that in English, large vehicles (buses, yachts, trains, large airplanes) are conceptualized either as containers or as sorts of platforms, but small vehicles (cars, rowboats, small airplanes) are conceptualized only as containers. This is just an idiosyncratic fact of English, as far as we can tell, having nothing to do with principles of spatial representation. For a somewhat different case, a container can be conceptualized either in terms of the volume it surrounds or in terms of the body of its substance, so we can speak of either *the water in the cup* or *the crack in the cup*.

Some special uses appear to involve forces exerted between the figure and the reference object. For example, the preposition *on* is frequently said to involve support by the reference object (Herskovits 1986; Cienki 1988). This is not always the case, since we can speak of *the fly on the ceiling*; but it may be a default interpretation. According to Bowerman (1989), the Dutch preposition *aan* also involves support or attachment, specifically a figural object hanging or projecting from a reference object that is something other than a horizontal surface (for example leaves *aan* a twig, a coathook *aan* a wall, clothes *aan* a line). The English preposition *against*, as in *Bill leaned against the wall* or *The tree fell against the house*, describes contact with exertion of force, usually in a horizontal or oblique direction. Among expressions of path, there is a special reading of *into* found in *The car ran into the pole*, which means not traversal to the interior of the reference object but rather coming into contact with the reference object with considerable force.

Bowerman (1989) cites a further complex case from the verbal system of Korean. It appears that the verb *kki-ta*, roughly 'put in, put together', applies to situations in which the figural object fits fairly tightly into or around the reference object, for instance a ring on a finger, a hand in a glove, a lid on a jar, and a button in a buttonhole. (The English verb *insert* appears to cover part but not all of the same semantic territory.) The verb *ppay-ta* describes the removal of the figure from a reference object with which it has been configured in this fashion. This configuration appears to involve both spatial relations and exertion of force. However, it again makes little reference to the detailed geometry of the figure and the reference object, beyond the fact that there is a match between a positive part of one and a negative part of the other.

Beyond this sort of complication, most of the complexity of English prepositions appears to involve (1) how spatial configurations that are nonstereotypical or ambiguous are forced into the expressions available in the language, (2) how particular prepositions are extended from core place meanings to different sorts of related paths and places (for example the variants of *across* mentioned above), (3) how preposition meanings are extended to nonspatial domains such as time and possession, and (4) how prepositions are used as purely grammatical markers (for instance *Bill believes in capitalism, The letter was received by Bill, a picture of Bill*). Extended discussions appear in Miller and Johnson-Laird 1976, Herskovits 1986, Vandeloise 1986, Brugman 1981, Lakoff 1987, chapter II.2, Cienki 1988, Jackendoff 1983, 1990.[9]

6.2.7 Summary

The descriptions of figures, reference objects, and regions (both places and trajectories) recruit just a few geometric properties and distinctions. The geometry of figure and reference objects specifies at most a single axis of each object. The regions relevant to describing places make further use of the axis, adding qualitative distinctions pertaining to distance and direction of the figure from the reference object. The regions relevant to describing trajectories or object motions then draw on these place descriptions, adding operators that specify the location of the path relative to a given place, and where that path begins and ends. Table 6.2 provides a summary of the factors discussed here.

6.3   Why Is It This Way?

The picture that emerges from this brief overview is that, if we are any-where near being complete (as we believe we are), the geometric descriptions relevant to words describing *what* an object is are much more complex than those describing *where* an object is. This is initially suggested by the fact that spatial prepositions in English are quite few compared to the object names. But more significantly, our investigation has shown that there are severe constraints on the ways in which the meanings of spatial prepositions can invoke object geometries. It is as if the spatial relations expressed by prepositions filter object descriptions, removing much of the detail of object shape and preserving only certain key properties—primarily the boundedness of an object and the axes of its principal geon. Because of this extreme limitation, more complex meanings such as those ascribed to the hypothetical words *sprough* and *betwaft* are simply not available as possible preposition meanings.

Table 6.2
Features of spatial relations (with sample prepositions)

Reference object geometry
Volumes, surfaces, and lines: in, on, near, at, inside
Single axis
    Vertical: on top of
    Horizontal: in front of, in back of, beside, along, across
Quantity: between, among, amidst

Figure object geometry
Single axis: along, across, around
Distributed figure (medium or aggregate): all over, throughout, all along, all around, all
    across

Relation of region to figure object
Relative distance
    Interior: in, inside, throughout
    Contact: on, all over
    Proximal: near, all around
    "Negatives"
        Beyond interior: out of
        Beyond contact: off of
        Beyond proximal: far
Direction
    Vertical: over, above, under, below, beneath
    Horizontal
      Side-to-side: beside, by, alongside, next to
      Front-to-back: in front of, ahead of, in back of, behind, beyond
Choice of axis system:
    Inherent: on (the) top of, in front of, ahead of, behind
    Contextual: on top of, in front of, behind, beyond
Visibility and occlusion: on top of, underneath

Paths (trajectories)
Earth-oriented: up, down, east, west, north, south
Figure object axis-oriented: forward, ahead, backward, sideways, left, right

Operators on regions
    Via: through (= via inside), along (= via along)
    To: to, into (= to in), onto (= to on)
    Toward: toward
    From: from, from under, from inside
    Away from: away, away from

One could stop here and accept this result as an interesting fact about language. But to us it cries out for explanation. We see two possible lines of attack. The first, which we will call the *Design of Language Hypothesis*, claims that the limitation on spatial relations expressible in language is indeed just a fact about language, and that spatial cognition is much richer in the spatial relations it can encode. The other approach, which we will call the *Design of Spatial Representation Hypothesis*, claims that this limitation in language reflects a deeper constraint on how spatial cognition encodes the relations among objects. We will argue that each contributes to the relative scarcity of preposition meanings. Let us take them up in turn.

6.3.1   Design of Language Hypothesis

According to this hypothesis, spatial representation can itself encode a rich range of spatial relations, making use of detailed properties of object shapes. However, most of these are "invisible" to the language faculty and are therefore neutralized or filtered out in the translation into linguistic format.[10]

There is abundant evidence that language does indeed filter representations of spatial relationships. For example, when inserting one's hand through a narrow slot, one must predict the hand's exact angle of orientation relative to the slot in order to be successful. Similarly, throwing a ball to someone involves a sensitive translation of perceived distance and angle into muscular force. And in general, all acts of navigation based on either visual or haptic-kinesthetic perception require delicate judgments of distance and angle. Even two-year-old children appreciate these metric properties or space and can use them in navigating through the world (Landau, Spelke, and Gleitman 1984).

Yet language is crude at expressing such metric information, which plays no role at all in the relationships discussed in the previous sections. To be precise in expressing distances and orientations, one must invoke a culturally stipulated system of measurement, which operates by counting units such as meters or degrees (*go 30 meters, turn 30 degrees*). Such units have no special psychological priority; in fact, it is hard to believe that metrical precision in the human spatial system is accomplished at all in terms of counting up unit measures. Thus the translation from spatial representation to linguistic representation evidently involves a certain amount of filtering, such that significant aspects of spatial relations go unexpressed. (The nonmetric characteristics of spatial language are stressed by Talmy (1978, 1983).)

Could this alone account for the severe limitation in the ways that spatial expressions in language can represent object shape? It appears not, for very similar filtering takes place in translating object shape descriptions into language. One can recognize with great accuracy complicated contours and surface patterns, but they are very hard to describe to someone else. Imagine, for example, trying to describe the Shepard-Metzler objects or the Attneave figures used in visual rotation experiments (Shepard and Cooper 1982)—or the pattern of stripes on a particular zebra, or the shape of a violin, or your mother's chin. These difficulties are augmented by the relative lack of linguistic terms for describing exact sizes of objects, again other than by using a culturally stipulated system of measurement. That is, whatever filtering out of metric information occurs in the expression of spatial relations also occurs in the expression of object shapes.

In short, language indeed does not convey all the representational richness we have for encoding either locations or objects. (That's why a picture is worth a thousand words.) But—this filtering out of metric information does not by itself explain the extreme limitation in the geometric specifications of objects in expressions of spatial relations, since the descriptions of *all* object shapes are subject to the same filtering. We are therefore still left with the puzzle of why objects that are being *named* can be differentiated in relatively complex geometric terms, whereas objects that are being *located* and the regions in which they are located are treated in terms of relatively schematic geometric descriptions. What accounts for this difference?

6.3.2   Design of Spatial Representation Hypothesis: The "What" and "Where" Systems

One possibility is that the disparity is inherent in the spatial representations underlying language. According to this hypothesis, spatial representation itself is relatively rich in its possibilities for describing object shape; but it is relatively limited in the way it can use object shape to encode spatial relations. If this is the case, the disparity observed in language is a fairly accurate reflection of a disparity in the spatial representations that language expresses.

We conjecture that this is indeed the case, and that the disparity in spatial representation is linked to some basic organizational facts about the human brain—in particular that it arises from a functional bifurcation of the system of spatial representation (perhaps into "submodules" in the sense of Fodor 1983 as refined in Jackendoff 1987a, chapter 12). One part of the system is devoted primarily to object shape identification; the other, to locating objects in space relative to each other and to the observer. The expressive power of the system of nouns that categorize objects is linked to the shape identification submodule; the expressive power of the spatial preposition system is linked to the spatial relation submodule.

This conjecture finds an interesting kind of support in neurological evidence that the brain contains separate areas specialized for object identification and object location. Ungerleider and Mishkin (1982) call these areas the *"what"* and *"where" systems* respectively. Building on previous work, they show that damage to inferior temporal cortex in monkeys (the "what" system) produces deficits in pattern and shape recognition, whereas damage to posterior parietal cortex (the "where" system) impairs following routes, reaching for objects, and using landmarks to locate objects.

Farah et al. (1988) document a human case in which bilateral damage to inferior temporal areas (the "what" system) with sparing of parietal regions (the "where" system) produced a deficit in a wide range of tasks involving shape recognition but preserved normal performance in tasks involving object localization and spatial relations.[11] Evidence from Levine, Warach, and Farah (1985) suggests that these same distinctions may even occur in the imagery system. One of their patients could image object shapes, but could not image spatial relationships or object layouts; another could image spatial layouts but the shapes of individual objects.

Computational studies also support this distinction. Rueckl, Cave, and Kosslyn (1988) found that in a parallel distributed processing (PDP) model of a very simple visual system, a certain degree of extra efficiency accrues to a system that strongly separates computation of the "what" and "where" functions, as long as both subsystems have sufficient computational resources. Rueckl, Cave, and Kosslyn studied a model stimulus space containing only nine different shapes, each of which could occur in nine partially overlapping locations. Within this tiny system, it was found that the optimal allocation of resources between the "what" and "where" systems used over three times as many "what" units as "where" units. Though it is hard to know how this case generalizes to a more realistic system, the disparity is reminiscent of that found between the noun system and the preposition system. Rueckl, Cave, and Kosslyn in fact argue that the disparity can only increase as one moves to a more realistic system. Thus our conjecture concerning the design of spatial representation is suggestively supported on computational grounds.

In order to see how these observations bear on the Design of Spatial Representation Hypothesis, let us consider the logic of a representation that separates "what" from "where." What information does the "where" system have to encode? At the very least, it must have a space of possible locations and a way to mark which ones are occupied. But this is obviously not enough. It would not do just for the "what" system to know that one is seeing a cat and a dog, and for the "where" system to know that positions A and B are occupied: is the cat at A and the dog at B, or vice versa? In order to keep track of which objects are where, there must be a liaison between the two representations.

A simple way to accomplish this liaison formally is by coindexing or linking the object representations in the two systems. (A similar proposal is suggested by Kosslyn et al. (1990).) The "where" system could then encode very rudimentary representations of the objects being located, perhaps as simple as 'thing here'. Such extremely schematized objects would place only minimal demands on information-bearing capacity within the "where" system. However, these schematized objects would in addition be linked to or associated with representations in the "what" system that encode the objects' detailed shape. In other words, the "where" system can get by with including just a little object information, as long as it can link its object tokens to those in the "what" system.[12]

An ordinary-life analogy to the situation in the "where" system is the conventionalized representation in maps. What is at issue in a map is how to navigate through a region. A map cannot just specify "wheres": it has to have *something* to stand in for the objects being located. Typically these stand-ins are points and lines, with some conventionalized symbols to distinguish different sorts of objects from each other (big cities vs. small cities, main roads vs. subsidiary roads, churches vs. hospitals, etc.). If a map had to distinguish all the objects by their shape, it would be much more complex and quite possibly unusable. We are not suggesting that the "where" system necessarily encodes something like an internalized map. The point is only that many of the same design criteria are applicable, in particular the need to represent objects as tokens in the representation but to compress their encoding by eliminating most information about their form.

Our guess, then, is that *the relatively simple shape specifications observed in the prepositional system are revealing the extent of detail possible in object descriptions within the "where" system*. These details go somewhat beyond 'thing here', but not much. In particular, as we have seen, the way the system works is not in terms of absolute locations of objects, but rather by locating one object in terms of another. Most of the detail in the system's shape descriptions is concentrated on the reference object, which defines the space in which the figure is located—and even that is highly restricted. The geometry of the figure goes beyond 'thing here' only in the small class of cases in which the issue is its orientation (*along, across, around*) or its distribution through a region (*all over, throughout*).

6.3.3   Directions for Research

This conjecture has suggested two programs of research currently being conducted by one of us (B.L.). The first stems from the asymmetry of spatial relations. According to the linguistic evidence, a spatial relation defines a *region* in terms of a reference object; the figural object is then located in the region. The implication is that regions are in some sense psychologically real—that one can investigate their properties experimentally. Studies currently underway suggest that adults and children as young as three years old make systematic judgments that reveal highly structured regions surrounding reference objects. For example, when asked to make repeated judgments as to whether one object is *near* a reference object, subjects accept all positions within a well-defined region surrounding the reference object. Moreover, the structure (shape) of the region is determined in part by the structure of the reference object: if the reference object is square or round, subjects accept positions within a roughly round region; if the reference object is rectangular, they accept positions within a roughly oblong region. We believe that systematic manipulation of the configuration of the reference object will therefore reveal how people geometrically represent regions, and how they level out particular geometric features from the reference object in doing so.

The second program of research concerns children's acquisition of nouns versus prepositions. According to our approach, a child learning a new object word ought to generalize its use based on properties of the "what" system: the particulars of object shape should matter, but the object's position should not. In contrast, a child learning a new spatial preposition ought to generalize based on properties of the "where" system: the particulars of object shape should not matter, but the object's position should. Landau and Stecker (1990) achieved just this set of results with children as young as three years old.

6.4   Conclusions

We have shown significant constraints on the kinds of spatial relationships that are represented by language. Some of these limits do not appear to be due to absolute limits on the spatial representational system itself; rather, they partially reflect a property of language design: leveling of metric information.

However, we have spent most of our effort here reviewing linguistic evidence that suggests there are very different spatial-representational bases for objects and places. This evidence shows a striking asymmetry between the way object shapes are represented when they are being named and the way they are represented when they play the role of figure or ground object in a locational expression. We have conjectured that these differences in how objects and places are represented reflect a property of neurological design: the independently discovered separation of spatial cognition into "what" and "where." If our conjecture is correct, we have found a bifurcation in the expressive power of language that corresponds to a bifurcation in the functional and anatomical systems of the brain. This is, to our knowledge, the first time within cognitive science that a correlation has been made between a property of grammar and a property of a nonlinguistic part of the brain. What is exciting about this correlation is that, where previous studies have documented the tasks performed by the two systems, linguistic evidence can now provide a window on the actual forms of information the systems encode.

Chapter 7
Musical Parsing and Musical Affect

This chapter explores the issue of what is going on in a listener's mind during the real-time processing of music, such that it is possible to account for the listener's understanding of the music. The issue will be approached through evidence internal to music itself, as well as by analogy with evidence from the processing of language. I will then examine how processing of the sort I propose provides a basis for resolving a long-standing issue in the theory of musical affect.

This examination of musical processing ought to be of more than parochial interest: the issues it raises concerning musical processing bear on larger questions of the brain's overall "style." In particular, I will claim that the parsing of musical inputs is performed by a modular processor that considers many different analyses in parallel. As it happens, the arguments for this claim are more immediately compelling than they are in the case of the language parser, where experimental evidence for parallel processing has accumulated only slowly. Given the similarity of the tasks, the musical case should bolster the argument for parallelism in language processing.

This chapter appeared in slightly different form in *Music Perception* 9, 199–230 (1991) and is reprinted here by permission of the University of California Press. A shorter version has appeared as "Musical Processing and Musical Affect," in M. R. Jones and S. Holleran, eds., *Cognitive Bases of Musical Communication*, American Psychological Association, 1991.

The original version of the chapter was presented at the Conference on Music Perception held at Ohio State University in spring 1990. I am grateful to the participants in the conference for their many useful and encouraging comments. In particular, the chapter was originally intended as part of a larger undertaking in collaboration with Fred Lerdahl; for reasons of geographical distance it proved more convenient to develop our ideas separately. Consequently, I must acknowledge my debt to Fred for his extensive influence and for his detailed commentary on many aspects of the chapter, as well as for the composition of some of the musical examples. I also wish to thank an anonymous reviewer for *Music Perception* for helping me distinguish important from unimportant issues. Finally, I must thank David Rahbee for his help in preparing some of the illustrations.

Readers not conversant with musical notation may find the examples impenetrable. In order to make them accessible, I will furnish a tape of them to readers who send a blank cassette and a return envelope with postage.

More generally, the present proposal can be considered a particular instantiation of Dennett's (1991) "multiple drafts" theory, which claims that the brain is always developing multiple representations and fragments of representations in parallel, with only the most stable alternative(s) appearing in awareness as the "document of record." Furthermore, the phenomena I will be examining present temporal anomalies of the sort discussed by Dennett and Kinsbourne (1992), in which one apparently perceives properties of musical structure some seconds before the evidence for these properties is actually present. This "backward projection" will be seen to follow from the character of the processor.

7.1   What Is Musical Perception?

Following the approach of Lerdahl and Jackendoff 1983a (henceforth *GTTM*), the perception of music parallels the perception of language; it involves the unconscious construction of abstract musical structures, of which the events of the musical surface (the sequence of notes and chords) are the only audible part. The abstract musical structures so constructed are what account for one's musical understanding—they are what make hearing music more than just hearing a sequence of pitch events. A theory of musical perception should therefore contain at least

1. an account of the abstract structures available to the listener,
2. an account of the principles available to the listener to assign abstract structure to pieces of music,
3. an account of how the listener applies these principles in real time to derive abstract structures for a piece as it is being heard, and
4. an account of the facilities in the mind for applying such principles.

The theory of music developed in *GTTM* is intended to serve as parts 1 and 2 of a theory of musical processing. The theory takes the form of a *grammar* of tonal music: a set of principles that (1) define the abstract structures of tonal music that are available to a listener experienced in the tonal idiom, and (2) relate these structures to musical surfaces of pieces in the idiom. To the extent possible given the state of development of the theory, the principles are applied rigorously to a wide range of pieces in the tonal idiom, both preexisting and newly constructed as experimental controls. *GTTM* shows that these principles provide a formal account of many aspects of musical understanding discussed in more traditional musical analysis. (One class of the principles, the rules of grouping, has been experimentally verified and refined by Deliege (1987); another, the principles of time-span reduction, has been tested experimentally by Oura (1991).)

An additional facet of this research is an attempt to divide the principles of musical grammar into three factors. The first factor is the general substrate of auditory processing, the sort of principles involved in what Bregman (1990) calls "auditory scene analysis." Into this factor fall many of the principles of grouping, some of the principles of metrical regularity, aspects of the detection of polyphonic textures, and acoustic aspects of interval tuning. The second factor consists of those principles that are specific to music, but apply to any system of inputs perceived as musical. Into this factor fall the general principles of metrical and tonal systems and of reductions (see section 7.2). Finally, the third factor includes all those principles (or parameters within principles) that are specific to a particular musical idiom such as Western tonal music, for example the details of Western tuning and tonality.

I take it that one of the eventual goals of research in musical cognition ought to be to explain how a novice comes to be able to understand music. By dividing the principles of musical cognition in this way, we can begin to see what aspects of the unconscious principles for understanding music actually have to be acquired by the novice. Presumably, only the factors that differentiate one musical idiom from another have to be learned; the rest can be assumed to be available as part of one's innate psychological makeup. (This parallels familiar arguments from linguistic theory concerning the relation of linguistic universals to the problem of language acquisition; see Jackendoff 1987a, 86–90—or practically anything on language by Chomsky.)

As stressed in *GTTM*, the grammar proposed there is intended as an account of the experienced listener's "final-state" understanding of pieces— the structures that the listener can attain, given full familiarity with the idiom and with the piece, and no limitations of short-term memory or attention. In the case of large, complex pieces, such structures are probably idealizations beyond what most listeners normally attain. Nevertheless they are revealing of the potential to which the inquiring listener or analyst may aspire; they differ from structures of less complex pieces only in degree of embedding and ambiguity, not in their fundamental construction.

A theory of musical perception based on the *GTTM* theory therefore must show how the principles of the listener's internalized musical grammar can be deployed in real time to build musical representations. In particular, it must show that the rules used for idealized "final-state" analyses can actually be used to account for listeners' experience of pieces. The next few sections will work out some aspects of such a processing model.

One could indeed go further and ask how these structures, principles, and facilities are instantiated neurologically in the brain. But since the issue of neural instantiation is beyond the range of speculation in almost every other cognitive domain, it would clearly be premature to attempt to deal

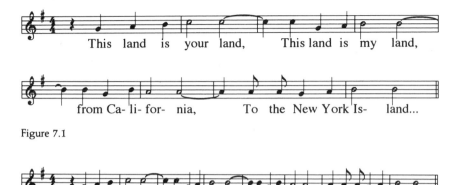

Figure 7.1

Figure 7.2

with it in the case of music. We will therefore be content with a "function-alist" approach in terms of computations over systems of symbols, bearing in mind the hypothesis that these symbol systems and computations are in some way homologous to brain organization and brain events.[1]

7.2   Assumptions about Musical Structure

For present purposes, we can assume that the following aspects of musical structure are essential to musical understanding (see *GTTM* for justification):

1. a *grouping structure* that partitions a piece into motives, phrases, and sections, arranged hierarchically;

2. a *metrical structure* that associates a piece with a hierarchical grid of strong and weak beats;

3. some sort of *reductional structure* that marks events of a piece in a hierarchy of relative importance, such that some are relatively "struc-tural" and some are relatively "ornamental."

To illustrate these structures, consider the beginning of the Woody Guthrie song "This Land Is Your Land," shown in figure 7.1. The *grouping structure* of this melody arranges it into four parallel segments, which in turn pair up into two larger segments, as shown by the bracketing beneath the music in figure 7.2. This bracketing is psychologically real, as can be seen from the difficulty one encounters in trying to deliberately hear the music with alternative bracketings such as those in figure 7.3.

The *metrical structure* of this melody is reflected in the musical notation: it is written in 4/4 time, which means that the first beat of each measure is

Figure 7.3

Figure 7.4

metrically strong, the third beat is of intermediate strength, and the second and fourth beats are metrically weak. Moreover, the melody has a three-note anacrusis (or upbeat), so that the fourth note of the piece receives the first strong beat. Again, this organization is psychologically real: it is virtually impossible to hear this same sequence of notes with other metrical organizations such as those notated in figure 7.4.

The *reductional structure* of the piece is illustrated in figure 7.5. The idea is that it is possible to strip the melody down step by step to its essential structural parts. At each step, relatively ornamental notes are removed, and the result is a melodic contour that both is a coherent melody and also recognizably resembles the previous step. Line *a* in figure 7.5 is the original melody. Line *b* strips it down to a simpler melody consisting only of half notes; yet if one hums the original melody while hearing line *b*, one can hear the similarity. Line *c* simplifies the melody further, to the point where one can see it as an elaboration of the four-note figure C–B–A–B. In turn, line *d* shows that the entire melody can be conceived of basically as a fancy way of getting from the initial "structural" note C to the final "structural" note B.

Since the pioneering work of Schenker (1935), reductional notions of some sort have been an important aspect of contemporary musical analysis. *GTTM* proposes two independent reductional structures: *time-span reduction*, which encodes the importance of events relative to the rhythmic framework provided by grouping and metrical structure, and *prolongational*

Figure 7.5

reduction, which encodes the importance of events in defining domains of tension and relaxation that cut across the rhythmic framework.

In any theory of reduction, the sense of tonality, of "being in a key," plays a crucial role. The reason for this is that a pitch-event's reductional importance is determined primarily by its rhythmic position and its relative "consonance," where consonance is defined by the principles of tonality for the idiom. Different tonal contexts (i.e. different keys) may determine different relative consonance of two pitch-events, resulting in different relative structural importance. For example, the sequence of an A♭ major triad followed by a D♭ major triad is heard as I–IV in A♭ major but as V–I in D♭ major. Other things being equal, a I chord is more consonant relative to the tonality, hence more important in the reductional structure. Hence the A♭ triad is primary on one hearing and the D♭ on the other. In short, a prerequisite to deriving a reductional structure in real time is deriving a sense of tonality. In turn, of course, the tonality must be perceptually determined from the musical surface (the presented sequence of notes).

7.3   A Sample Analysis

To appreciate the intricacies that must be ascribed to a processing model in order to account for even a relatively straightforward piece, let us work through an example, asking how a listener might assign structure to the beginning of a piece as it is heard. The piece we will examine is "Ich bin's, ich sollte büssen" from Bach's *St. Matthew Passion,* the beginning of which is given in figure 7.6. (A full analysis of this piece in *GTTM* terms appears in Lerdahl and Jackendoff 1983b.)

Figure 7.6

Figure 7.7

What the listener hears, of course, is the sequence of pitches with durations; that is, the notated key signature, time signature, bar lines, and beams play no role in the musical surface.

For the moment, I will make two idealizations. First, I will assume, somewhat counterfactually, that the musical surface is presented without any surface accents that would bias interpretations of meter. Such an idealization is probably realized only in computer-generated performances and perhaps performances on the harpsichord or organ, but it is useful for purposes of exposition.

Second, I will assume that, although familiar with the principles of tonal music, the listener is hearing this piece in isolation (i.e. not in the context of the *St. Matthew Passion*) and has never heard it before, so that processing cannot rely at all on contextual expectations or memory of the piece. Thus the listener's task is taken to be comparable to that faced by a speaker of English who has to understand a sentence never heard before; we can think of it as a task of "musical parsing."

Section 7.6 will discuss what might be different when we return to the more realistic case of listening to an accentually inflected performance and to a piece that is to some degree familiar. I will suggest that these additional factors do not materially change the way in which musical parsing takes place.

After hearing just the first event (figure 7.7), the listener has very little information, except that this event is the beginning of a group (or phrase), that it falls on some metrical beat, and that the piece is likely to be in a key whose diatonic collection includes C, A♭, and E♭.

Figure 7.8

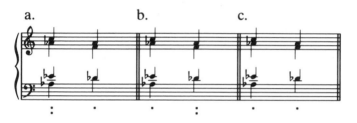

Figure 7.9

Adding the second event (figure 7.8) provides more substantial information. At least three questions must be asked immediately by the listener (not consciously, of course; a better locution would be "by the listener's unconscious musical parser," as will be seen mare clearly in the next section).

1. What is the relative metrical weight of the two events? Using the *GTTM* notation, the three possibilities are given in figure 7.9. In this notation, an event with more dots under it is considered metrically stronger (a strong beat). Hence the first event is stronger in figure 7.9a, and the second in figure 7.9b; alternatively, the two events may be metrically equal, as shown in figure 7.9c.

2. What key are we in? The pitches so far are consistent with the pitch-collections of at least A♭ major, D♭ major, and, much less plausibly, those of their relative minors.[2]

3. Is the first event structurally stronger than the second, or is it weaker —that is, which of these events is more structurally important and which relatively ornamental? We can represent this choice by using the *GTTM* notation for time-span reductions, which encodes relative structural importance as a tree structure. The two possibilities appear in figure 7.10. In figure 7.10a, the branch associated with the second event terminates on the branch associated with the first, so the first event is structurally more important and the second relatively ornamental. This analysis suggests a I–IV progression in A♭. In figure 7.10b the roles of the two events are reversed, suggesting a I–V progression in D♭.

Given just these two events, the answers to all three of these questions are indeterminate. One can hear the initial event as a downbeat or as an

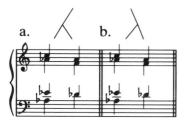

Figure 7.10

Figure 7.11

Figure 7.12

anacrusis to the second event. One can hear the key as A♭ or D♭. Linked with the key, one can hear the harmonic progression in either of the ways suggested in figure 7.10. However, the second possibility is undermined to some degree by the voice-leading of the soprano: as a V–I progression it would have an unresolved leading tone. The V–I interpretation becomes much more salient if the voice-leading is changed to the configuration in figure 7.11. In other words, grammatical principles of voice-leading have an effect on judgment of tonality (see the discussion in Butler 1989 for experiments with similar effects).

To show that the meter and key are at this point indeterminate, we can invent alternative continuations of figure 7.8 that present different possibilities than Bach's. Figure 7.12 presents one in which the first event is heard as a downbeat rather than as an anacrusis (that is, with the metrical structure

Figure 7.13

Figure 7.14

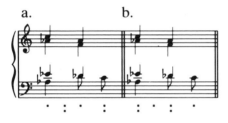

Figure 7.15

shown in figure 7.9a), and in which the key is heard as D♭ instead of A♭. We can also construct a continuation in which the first two events are metrically equal, as in figure 7.9c. Within the constraints imposed by the principles of metrical structure, this can occur only if the two events constitute a two-beat anacrusis in a triple meter. Figure 7.13 illustrates one such possibility.

Now consider what happens when the listener hears the third event of the piece, just an eighth-note C in the bass (figure 7.14). This event must be associated with a beat of metrical structure; the ratios of durations indicate that a smaller-scale layer of beats must be introduced. There are two possibilities: the third event could be on a stronger beat than the first and second beats, or the third event could be weaker (figure 7.15). The structure shown in figure 7.15a implies that the first two events are syncopated, a highly unlikely possibility at the beginning of a piece.[3] The structure shown in figure 7.15b places the third event on the smaller-scale

Figure 7.16

level of beats; this structure is strongly favored by intuition (and by the rules of metrical structure, including Metrical Preference Rules 2, 3, 5, and 6 of *GTTM*;[4] corresponding principles are suggested by Longuet-Higgins (1987)). In turn, the fact that the second beat of the quarter-note level is divided into two events favors interpreting the first event of the piece as a stronger beat (Metrical Preference Rule 5).

The third event can be assumed to be structurally subordinate to the preceding event, because of the dissonance between the bass (C) and the tenor (D♭). However, the overall key of the piece is still indeterminate, as can be seen from figure 7.12, which is identical to figure 7.6 up to and beyond this event.

Even after the fourth and fifth events arrive, the metrical structure is still highly indeterminate. Figure 7.16 gives five possibilities: (a) the first event is the strong beat in a duple meter; (b) the first event is the weak beat in a duple meter; (c) the first event is the strong beat in a triple meter; (d) the first event is the second weak beat in a triple meter; (e) the first event is the first weak beat in a triple meter. All of these possibilities can be realized with fairly plausible music. Consider figure 7.17, in which the dashed bar lines indicate the point up to which the passages are identical. Structure 16a is the most likely interpretation of figure 7.17a; structure 16b is of course Bach's choice (figures 7.6 and 7.17b); structure 16c is the most likely interpretation of figure 7.17c; structure 16d is most likely for figure 7.17d (whose musical surface is moreover identical to figure 7.17a except that the final event probably receives less stress); structure 16e appears in figure 7.17e. Of these five, only the last is relatively hard to hear.

The metrical uncertainty can even be continued a few events further into the piece. Figure 7.18 is identical to the musical surface of the Bach chorale up to the dashed bar line, at the eighth event of the piece.

What finally settles the meter in the Bach chorale is a combination of factors that have accumulated up to this point:

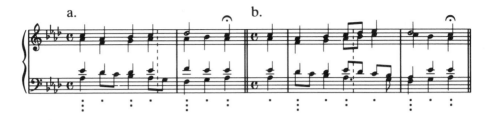

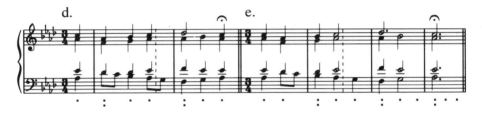

Figure 7.17

1. the dotted quarter note A♭ in the bass should begin on a strong beat (Metrical Preference Rules 5 and 6);

2. the suspension in the soprano and alto in measure 2 should begin on a strong beat (Metrical Preference Rule 8);[5]

3. the long soprano D♭ in measure 2 should begin on a strong beat (Metrical Preference Rule 5).

These factors determine that strong beats should fall two beats apart, requiring a duple meter. Projecting backward through the piece to the beginning, the first strong beat must fall on the second event. By contrast, in figure 7.18 the suspension and long soprano D♭ are displaced one beat to the right. This forces a distance of three beats between strong beats, hence a triple meter. Projecting this meter backward results in the first event falling on a strong beat.

Next consider the tonality (or key) of the piece. This cannot be determined with certainty without taking into account complex factors. Looking again at figure 7.12, the pitch collection (or total set of presented pitches)

Figure 7.18

in the first measure would strongly bias the listener toward an interpretation of A♭ major. However, the cadence in the second measure fixes the key as D♭ and forces the G natural in the first measure to be heard in retrospect as a chromatic alteration. (Section 7.7 will discuss what I mean by "in retrospect.") In the actual Bach chorale, the tonality is fixed by the continuing consistency of the presented pitch collection with completely diatonic A♭ major, and by the full cadence in A♭ at the end of the phrase.[6]

This exercise of analyzing the information available to the listener at any point in time, though exhausting, has hardly been exhaustive. And I have dealt only with the briefest portion of a relatively simple piece, for which the listener has no sense of any processing complexity. What is the point of going through all this trouble? We will now examine the implications of this exercise for a theory of musical parsing.

7.4   Three Models of Parsing

Section 7.1 claimed that the processing of a piece of music as it is heard amounts essentially to deriving the abstract structure of the piece in real time. We have just seen that one of the fundamental problems facing the processor is the indeterminacy of the analysis at many points—an indeterminacy that sometimes cannot be resolved until considerably later in the music. I will propose three models of increasing complexity that attempt to do justice to these observations.

The first model might be called a *serial single-choice* parser. Such a processor computes only one analysis at a time for a piece. Confronted with a potential indeterminacy among multiple analyses, it chooses the most likely alternative as the one to continue with. If what is chosen at one point as the most likely analysis proves later on not to be viable, the parser must back up to the choice point, choose the next most likely possibility, and pursue that as far as possible. If the parser can reach the end of the piece, the resulting analysis is selected as the correct one. This basic mode of operation is a feature of one popular breed of linguistic parser (for example the augmented transition network (ATN) parser described in Wanner and Maratsos 1978), so it is worth considering for music parsing as well.

There are at least two serious problems with this model. The first is in deciding which of a set of alternative analyses should be tried. In order to choose among alternative possibilities, all of them must first be formulated. Consider, for instance, the point after the second event of the Bach chorale (figure 7.8), where the parser must decide which single metrical structure to pursue. Should it assign the second event a metrical weight greater than, less than, or equal to that of the first event? In order to make this decision on other than an arbitrary basis, all three alternatives must be formulated and tested on the evidence of the music up to this point. Similar choices with respect to both meter and key arise at every point in the music up to at least the fifth and possibly even the eighth event. Therefore, at each of these points, the parser must have access to the available choices and their relative likelihood, in order to be able to decide which single analysis it will try first. Thus there is a basic logical difficulty in the conception of this processing model: in order to compute only the single most likely analysis, it must first compute at least fragments of all possible analyses.

A second difficulty with this model has to do with the way it putatively recovers from incorrect analyses. If at some point it is forced to backtrack, it must pass through and reanalyze all the music between the choice point and the most recent event, while at the same time new events are occurring inexorably as the piece goes on. Given the amount of indeterminacy we have seen in a very short passage, one would expect that this sort of parser would spend a great deal of its time backtracking. For example, in the Bach chorale, it would likely begin by trying a downbeat-first analysis after the second event, since, according to the musical grammar, this structure is inherently most stable (Metrical Preference Rule 2; see note 4). After the fourth event it would probably choose a duple meter (Metrical Preference Rule 10),[7] resulting in the structure in figure 7.17a. But this possibility would be disconfirmed three events later by the A♭ in the bass continuing beneath the eighth notes. It would then go back to the fourth event and try a triple meter, as in the structure in figure 7.17c; this would be disconfirmed by the suspension in the soprano and alto five events later (Metrical Preference Rule 8; see note 5). Having tried successively the two possibilities with an initial downbeat, it would erase everything it had done and backtrack again to the second event, assigning it a strong beat this time. At the fifth event a decision would have to be made between a strong beat (implying duple meter) and a weak beat (triple meter). We can suppose that it would choose the duple meter (Metrical Preference Rule 10) and finally come up with the correct analysis. However, if the input were figure 7.17e instead of figure 7.17b, it would have to backtrack once more before hitting on the correct meter.

In order for the parser to accomplish all this backtracking in real time without a sense of effort or loss of information, one must attribute to it considerable speed in comparison to the speed of the music. The parser will often have to perform many analyses one after another, fast enough to keep up with the flow of the musical surface in real time. In the present example, all the backtracking must be done after the eighth event of the music has been heard, and while successive events are still being taken in. In short, the processing load imposed by the music must be borne by increasing speed of the parser.

Let us next consider what might be called a *serial indeterministic* model. The basic characteristic of this model, like the previous model, is that it computes only a single analysis at a time for a piece. However, when confronted with an indeterminacy, it does not make a commitment as the previous model does; rather, it bides its time and collects evidence, without making a decision until such time as a unique analysis can be settled on. The idea behind this sort of parser appears in linguistic parsers such as those developed by Marcus (1980)[8] and Frazier and Fodor (1978). Such parsers compute preliminary analyses of local parts of a sentence but do not connect them up into a global analysis until a single correct structure can be determined for the whole.

This sort of parser avoids the onerous backtracking of the serial single-choice model. But it does not escape the basic logical difficulty. In order to decide when it is appropriate to commit itself to an analysis, the parser must have available to it all the candidate analyses among which it could decide, plus an evaluation of the evidence that would decide among them. So, for example, in the Bach chorale, we have seen that the metrical structure cannot be settled for certain until the resolution of the suspension in the second measure. However, it is precisely the defining characteristic of such a parser that it does *not* have the analyses available: it has put off any analysis until it can make a decision.

It is only wishful thinking to assume that the correct analysis can some-how miraculously "emerge" when enough evidence has accumulated. If we want to explain the principles by which the correct analysis is developed, in information-processing terms, it is necessary to have the parser formulate candidate analyses from which the correct one can be selected. Otherwise we are claiming that the mind does it in essence by magic—that is, we deny rational explanation.

A second problem with this sort of parser is that it makes the wrong sort of prediction about musical experience; it suggests that up to the eighth event of the Bach chorale we should have no experience of metrical structure at all, since none has been adopted by the parser. But this is patently wrong: we clearly have metrical intuitions long before the definitive evidence arrives.

As long as both serial models have entailed the computation of multiple analyses, we might as well bite the bullet and propose a *parallel multiple-analysis* model, in the spirit of Dennett's (1991) "multiple drafts" theory of cognition. The idea behind this model is that when the parser encounters a choice point among competing analyses, processing splits into simultaneous branches, each computing an analysis for one of the possibilities. When a particular branch drops below some threshold of plausibility, it is abandoned. Whatever branches remain at the end of the piece then contain viable structures for the piece as a whole. Language parsers with this organization are discussed by Bever, Garrett, and Hurtig (1973), Hickok (1991), and Berwick and Weinberg (1984) (though the last authors do not end up endorsing such a model).

In the Bach chorale, such a parser would develop three concurrent metrical analyses after the second event is heard, corresponding to the three possible distinctions in metrical weight shown in figure 7.9. After the fourth event, two of these analyses would branch further; hence five analyses would be active at once, corresponding to the five structures in figure 7.16. As observed in the previous section, the long A♭ in the bass is inconsistent with three of these (16a,d,e), so the parser will abandon them when the A♭ is heard. Of the remaining two, only 16b puts the suspension on a strong beat, so 16c will be abandoned upon resolution of the suspension, leaving only one viable metrical structure. In short, this parser proceeds more or less in the same manner as our informal analysis in the previous section.

A parser of this sort overcomes the logical problem of the other two: alternative hypotheses are always formulated and available to be compared with one another. It also overcomes the problem of backtracking in the serial single-choice model. In the parallel model, increased complexity in the music requires increased numbers of analyses proceeding in parallel; hence processing load demands not more speed but more space. It is hard to evaluate this trade-off, as we know little about space limitations in the brain. However, the speed required for backtracking in the serial model does seem implausible.

One important difficulty in developing a parallel multiple-analysis model lies essentially in data management: how many hypotheses can the processor entertain at once, and how long does it let a "wrong" hypothesis continue before abandoning it? If this model is on the right track (and, inasmuch as the other models prove not to be even logically coherent, this is our only candidate at the moment), these questions should be susceptible to experimental techniques such as memory load tasks and priming tasks. Not being an experimentalist, I do not intend to address them here, except to point out that the complexity of the Bach analysis puts a surprisingly large lower bound on the number of hypotheses the parser must be able to entertain at once without appreciable stress. Fred Lerdahl has suggested (personal communication) that cadenced group boundaries are points where less stable analyses are "pruned," a hypothesis that should be experimentally testable.

Another difficulty with the parallel model as stated so far lies in its prediction about musical experience. If indeed five analyses are being pursued simultaneously after five events of the chorale, why don't we experience all five at once? Such a prediction is clearly at odds with intuition. Rather, as in other cognitive domains, it is generally the case that we perceive only one interpretation at a time. This observation lies behind the appeal of the single-analysis models of musical processing. However, it is not inconsistent with a parallel model either, given the proper interpretation of the phenomenology. It is true that we are *conscious of* only one analysis at a time, or that we *can attend to* only one analysis at a time. But this leaves open the possibility that other analyses are present unconsciously, inaccessible to attention. This is the position I will adopt.

To flesh this position out slightly, I propose that the processor contains a *selection function*, a device that continuously evaluates the currently active analyses for relative plausibility and designates one of them as the currently most salient. This selected analysis will be the single one that appears in awareness as *the* structure of the music at this point. With the addition of the selection function, a parallel model can be made more compatible with the basic intuitions of musical experience.[9]

However, the addition of a selection function still does not completely solve the problem of musical experience. How can it be that, although the parser cannot determine the meter and key of the chorale until the eighth event, we seem to hear the meter and key immediately? This would appear to be a temporal anomaly: we seem to have an experience of meter and key about three seconds before our brain has the information that can determine them.

This situation is reminiscent of the temporal anomalies of the "color phi phenomenon" and the "cutaneous rabbit" discussed by Dennett (1991) and Dennett and Kinsbourne (1992), in which visual and tactile experiences apparently precede the stimulation that could give rise to them. Dennett and Kinsbourne's analysis of these phenomena is apt here: it is crucial to distinguish between the *experienced time of a percept* and the *time at which a percept is computed*. They argue that the temporal organization of percepts is as much a product of mental representation as their spatial organization and therefore that, within certain temporal limits, it is possible to compute properties of the represented sequence of events in a different temporal order than they are represented as taking place. It is as though our experience has a window of "perceptual present" that views a moving belt of ordered events, and the brain can arrange and rearrange elements within this window in any order before they move off into the "past."

In the musical case, this approach allows us to explain the "retrospective" perception of meter and key. After the eighth event of the Bach chorale, the selection function can choose a single analysis. But since this analysis contains a meter and a key all the way from the first to the eighth event, and since all eight events are (evidently) within the temporal window of "perceptual present," we experience this structure as having been "the" structure of the music all along.

Returning to the comparison of the parallel model with the serial models, it may seem at first blush as if the parallel model invokes a great deal of objectionable machinery. However, more careful consideration suggests that all the information it uses is used in a similar way in the serial models. Each model uses the rules of musical grammar to generate possible analyses, and each model must use exactly the same evidence in the music and exactly the same criteria from the grammar to decide which of the possible analyses is the most plausible one.

The only major difference between the parallel model and the serial ones is in how they decide among competing analyses. In the serial single-choice model, the decision is made before exploring the implications of each possibility—on a hunch, as it were. In the serial indeterministic model, the decision is made before committing to any analysis in particular (a notion that proves computationally incoherent). In the parallel model, the selection function chooses among analyses as they are being derived. In fact, the parallel model is in a sense the simplest of the three in this respect: the problem never arises of deciding when to commit to a particular analysis, or when to give up on a particular analysis and backtrack, or which analysis to backtrack to. Rather, all analyses are undertaken, and they are abandoned independently of each other, leaving the field to whatever analyses remain active.

We will next discuss some psycholinguistic evidence that a parallel model is necessary for the language processor as well. This will bolster the plausibility of the parallel model for musical processing.

7.5   Evidence for a Parallel Multiple-Analysis Model of Language Processing

Consider the problem of how a listener accesses words in memory as they are heard. The problem for word access is in many respects similar to that of musical perception: many words have multiple meanings, yet the listener must select the correct meaning for the context of the sentence in which the word occurs. This selection goes on without any conscious effort, and in fact people do not usually even notice that alternative meanings are possible.

A widely cited program of experimental research in psycholinguistics (Swinney 1979, 1982; Tanenhaus, Leiman, and Seidenberg 1979) has shown that, for a brief time after a word is heard in a spoken sentence, all of its meanings are active, regardless of preceding semantic and syntactic context. In a typical experiment of this sort reported by Onifer and Swinney (1981), the subjects heard either sentence (1a) or sentence (1b).

(1)　a.　All the cash that was kept in the safe at the bank [1] was [2] stolen last [3] week when two masked men broke in.
　　 b.　A large piece of driftwood that had been washed up onto the bank [1] by the [2] last storm stood [3] as a reminder of how high the water had actually risen.

While auditory presentation of the sentence continued uninterrupted, the subjects were presented with a lexical decision task: they saw a sequence of letters such as MONEY, STUDY, RIVER, TWELVE, or a nonsense syllable flash on a screen, and were asked to decide whether it was a word or not. (The subjects in general had no idea that there was any relation between the tasks of listening to the sentences and responding to the visually presented sequences.)

The interest of the experiment lies in the way the word *bank* primed (sped up recognition of) certain of the presented sequences. With the letter sequences STUDY, TWELVE, and the nonsense syllable it had no effect. When the lexical decision task was presented at point 3 in the examples, the sequence MONEY was primed in sentence (1a) and the sequence RIVER was primed in sentence (1b), as would be expected from the semantic relation between these sequences and the meaning of the word *bank* appropriate to the example. However, when the lexical decision task was presented closer in time to the actual occurrence of the word *bank*, at points 1 or 2 in the examples, *both* MONEY and RIVER were primed in both examples. That is, even though only the financial sense of *bank* is appropriate in (1a) and only the topographical sense in (1b), the priming results show that shortly after the word is heard, both senses are unconsciously accessed by the listener.

The hypothesis suggested by these results is that the language processor must access all senses of a word in order to determine which is appropriate to the context. In fact, just as with the musical parser, it makes little sense to claim that the correct meaning will somehow emerge without a choice being available. On the other hand, in the time it takes to utter a few more syllables, that is, by point 3 in the examples, the processor has been able to choose a contextually correct sense and abandon the other, so only the correct sense primes any more.

One further complication in the story. The examples above place the word *bank* in a context where the preceding part of the sentence determines the appropriate sense; even so, both senses are accessed. What happens when the context of the sentence does not determine which meaning is to be chosen? Sentence (2) would be such an example.

(2)   We went down to the bank to meet some friends we hadn't seen for a while.

In this case, priming by both senses of *bank* continues a bit longer in the sentence than it does in (1); but at some point priming eventually comes to be restricted to a single sense, usually the more common one (Hudson and Tanenhaus 1984). Thus the language processor evidently finds it necessary to choose a single interpretation as "the" interpretation, even when the contextual evidence does not warrant a choice.

The relevance of these experiments for a theory of music parsing should be clear. The previous section claimed that the most plausible model for music processing is one that develops all possible analyses for a piece as it is heard, then abandons analyses as they became disconfirmed by succeeding evidence. These experiments show that something similar, and perhaps even more extreme, goes on in language processing: each word of a heard sentence is assigned all possible analyses, and then the processor culls out those that are disconfirmed by surrounding (preceding and following) context; but the listener is unaware of any of these meanings other than the one eventually chosen as appropriate for the context. Insofar as such a model is experimentally supported in the case of language, it lends stronger plausibility to the claim that the brain solves the problem of parsing musical structure in a similar fashion.

A second line of evidence from language is even simpler to describe. Sentence (3) is a case of a "garden path" sentence (so called because the listener is seduced or "led down the garden path" into an incorrect analysis; see Marcus 1980 for discussion).

(3)   The horse raced past the barn fell.

Many speakers of English find this sentence unintelligible until it is pointed out to them that it is a reduced form of (4a): it is related to (4a) in exactly the way that (4b) is related to (4c).

(4)   a.   The horse that was raced past the barn fell.
       b.   The picture painted by Bill was beautiful.
       c.   The picture that was painted by Bill was beautiful.

Evidently, what goes wrong in (3) is that the listener interprets *raced* as the main verb of the sentence because of its contextual plausibility, and is then unable to reanalyze it as a past participle when the real main verb *fell* is heard. (4a) does not present this difficulty, because the intervening words *that was* explicitly mark *raced* as a past participle; hence the listener knows the main verb is yet to come. (4b) also does not raise this difficulty, because in the context it is much less likely for *painted* to be interpreted as a main verb: horses race, but pictures don't paint.

This well-known example is frequently cited as a demonstration that the language parser settles on a single interpretation for an utterance long before the utterance is complete, and that if this single interpretation is disconfirmed, the parser finds it difficult or impossible to "backtrack" for an alternative. What is not usually asked, though, is at what point the parser has abandoned alternative lines of analysis. The sentences in (5) bear on this question.

(5)   a.   The horse led a long way down the road fell.
      b.   The horse led a long line of wagons down the road.

Neither of these has the phenomenological shock value of (3), yet the proper interpretation of the word *led* cannot be determined until the choice between *way* and *line* has been evaluated, three syllables later. This suggests that, for at least this long, multiple readings are under consideration in these examples, and the subsequent context can be used to choose one and abandon the other.

This case is analogous to that encountered in the Bach chorale: there, metrical evidence is inconclusive at the beginning, yet no sense of surprise ensues when the necessary evidence arrives. In both cases, we have concluded that alternative analyses are simultaneously available to the parser, and that a selection function evaluates the relative viability of the alternatives. Moreover, we have seen in the cases of (2) and (3) that the selection function for language does not wait forever to make its decision; after a while, if the evidence does not decide between analyses, it chooses one over the other on the basis of frequency or plausibility or structural simplicity—whatever extracontextual factors may be at its disposal.

As a further point of similarity, Bever, Garrett, and Hurtig (1973) and Hickok (1991) give experimental evidence that the language parser computes multiple syntactic analyses in parallel. In particular, Bever, Garrett, and Hurtig argue that the clause boundary is the point at which all but the most salient analysis are discarded. This parallels Lerdahl's suggestion, mentioned in the previous section, that cadenced group boundaries are points where the musical parser takes stock and eliminates implausible analyses. (Further discussion of this model of language processing appears in Jackendoff 1987a, chapters 6, 11, and 12.)

7.6   Toward a More Realistic Model

The model of musical parsing discussed so far has proceeded under two idealizations of the task: (1) that the musical signal is presented bereft of accentuation that would help determine the meter, and (2) that the piece presented is not familiar to the listener, so that musical memory cannot help determine the structure. I now want to ask briefly how much the story changes if these idealizations are removed.

Consider the issue of accentuation. Is our account of processing unrealistic because accents that mark strong beats have been ignored? Couldn't meter be determined more straightforwardly by attending to accents in the musical surface? Two kinds of evidence converge on the conclusion that such a story is too simple.

First, we can function quite well in the absence of accentual cues. Performances on the organ and harpsichord lack distinctions of attack and dynamics, for example. Much worse musically are those primitive computer-synthesized performances that wipe out all "microstructural" distinctions of note length and timing between attacks. Although we may experience the latter as mechanical and unmusical, we do not encounter any conscious difficulty in determining their meter. This suggests that accentual cues are not essential to the process of determining meter. And when they are absent, the information available for determining meter must be essentially as described in the previous sections.

Are we to assume that the machinery that makes use of nonaccentual cues is held in reserve just in case accents are not present? A more reasonable assumption, consistent with perceptual processes in general, is that this machinery is always operating, interacting with the detection of accents. If so, our account has not complicated the process by idealizing the input—it has simplified it.

A second reason the parser cannot just use accentual cues as a shortcut is that it would be misled by any passage in the musical surface that had accents on weak beats. In order to function properly in such situations, the parser must rely on independent principles of metrical organization that can function in perceptual rivalry with accentuation, for example patterns of articulation, harmonic rhythm, and above all (in the eighteenth- and nineteenth-century idiom) the assumption that metrical regularity persists throughout a piece. Of course, insistent cross-accentuation can throw the listener's sense of meter off, but this is an extreme case.

We see therefore that accentuation is neither a necessary nor a sufficient condition for a metrical strong beat. In the *GTTM* theory, this situation is described by making accentuation just one of a number of interacting criteria that collectively determine metrical structure.[10] (Section 4.2 of *GTTM* shows this interaction, demonstrating the complete parity between accentuation and these other factors.)

The upshot in terms of the parser is this: The parser cannot use accentuation as a shortcut for determining metrical strength of a beat. Rather, the most that can happen is that an accent will change the relative stability of parallel analyses, placing relatively more weight on analyses in which the accent falls an a strong beat. Otherwise, the logic of the parser is unchanged. In short, our idealization is justified, and our model is easily augmented to include distinctions of accent.

Turning to the second idealization, what difference does it make to the parser if we factor in the listener's familiarity with the piece? Notice, of course, that the parser has to be prepared to deal with novel pieces, so our idealization is a special case of the more general situation. This means that all the machinery we have posited for the novel case must be present and available when listening to a familiar piece as well. How much is it used?

It is conceivable that memory of a piece completely supplants the operation of the parser—that it enables the listener to infer the correct structure immediately, without the parser having to follow along concurrent blind alleys. If this were true, one could conceive of the parser as essentially switching off for a familiar piece.

However, consider that in hearing a familiar piece, one must verify (unconsciously, perhaps) that one is indeed hearing the piece stored in long-term memory. The musical surface being presented might diverge at any instant from what is remembered, and the attentive listener would notice the difference immediately. In order to make this comparison, the processor has to be actively comparing the presented surface to the recalled structure.

For a more complex case, consider listening to a piece that is not altogether identical to a remembered piece—say a variation on a known theme or a new arrangement of a popular song. Here the musical surfaces may differ considerably; even the meter and mode of the variation may differ from those of the theme. In order to recognize the relation between the heard piece and the remembered one, then, the processor must be comparing not just musical surfaces but the abstract structures of the two pieces, in particular the reductions. This means that perception must invoke the parsing process, deriving all the musical structure for the input, computing structures that can be compared with the remembered ones. Hence it is performing essentially the same computations whether listening to a totally novel piece or to a variation on a known one.

Why, then, should the parser switch off just in the single case when the piece being heard is altogether familiar? Such a hypothesis actually makes the processor more complex rather than less, since it has to decide when a piece is familiar enough to switch off the part of perception concerned with parsing. It seems reasonable, therefore, to suppose that the parser is fully active even when musical memory is engaged, and that all structures of the piece, including erroneous analyses, are computed in essentially the manner described above. In other words, our second idealization does not in any substantial way distort the theory of the processor.

Notice that language processing is subject to similar conditions. Consider again the "garden path" sentence *The horse raced past the barn fell*. Even after one has had the sentence explained—and even after many years of acquaintance with it—it still sounds odd, considerably worse than *The horse that was raced past the barn fell*. Evidently, memory for the proper structure of the sentence does not entirely prevent one's language parser from unconsciously constructing an erroneous structure, although memory may mitigate one's sense of shock.

More generally, the idea is that the music processor, like the language and visual processors, is a *module* in the sense of Fodor 1983. As such, it is "informationally encapsulated" from long-term memory of pieces: it has only the rules of musical grammar at its disposal to develop an analysis. Moreover, its operation is obligatory: in response to any plausibly musical signal, it tries its best to develop a musical structure. (This point is suggested also by Bharucha (1987).)

7.7   Implications and Realizations in the Processor

An intuition shared by many people (musicians and nonmusicians alike) is that understanding or appreciating music has something to do with expectation. To put this intuition very roughly, each fragment of music, as it is heard, builds in the listener expectations of what is to come. Either these expectations are fulfilled by the succeeding music, with an accompanying positive affect or satisfaction in the listener, or else they are not fulfilled, with an accompanying negative affect such as surprise or disappointment.

This intuition becomes more fully fleshed out in the "implication-realization" approach of Leonard Meyer (1956, 1967a, 1967b, 1973) and Eugene Narmour (1977), developed as a theory of melody. (Experimental work based on this theory includes Rosner and Meyer 1986 and Schmuckler 1989.) Its basic premise is that particular melodic elements set up expectations or implications (Meyer changes from the former term to the latter over the years) about the melody's completion. For instance, a melodic leap, or gap, near the beginning of a phrase implies that it will be filled in stepwise in the course of the phrase. An upward stepwise progression implies an eventual continuation up to the tonic (or dominant, whichever is closer); a downward stepwise progression implies continuation down to the tonic (or dominant). Similarly, an upward arpeggiation of a chord implies an eventual arpeggiated continuation upward to the tonic (or dominant), and likewise for a downward arpeggiation. Meyer shows that such "musical implications" are not just superficial associations to past experience but rather the product of musical cognition—the construction of abstract musical structures by the listener on the basis of a multitude of internalized principles of musical form.

A difficulty with this theory from the point of view of *GTTM* is that it does not provide a rich enough treatment of the final outcome of musical processing, that is, what there is for fragments of music to imply. However, the basic insights of the Meyer-Narmour approach can be applied to the more complex and abstract musical structures posited in *GTTM*.

The theory of musical parsing sketched in sections 7.3 and 7.4 makes possible an explicit notion of musical expectation or implication, or what might be called *prospective hearing*. The theory claims that the parser uses the principles of musical grammar to assign multiple possible analyses to the fragment of music heard thus far. Among these principles, there are many that can project structure for parts of the music that have not yet been heard. For example, one of the principles of grouping[11] creates a preference for symmetrical organization. When a single group is heard, this principle leads the processor to create a potential structure in which this group is balanced by a second group of the same length—that is, there is an "expectation" that the music will continue in a way that fills in a symmetrical structure. Similarly, the strong preference for a constant meter[12] projects the existing metrical structure beyond the portion of the musical surface that has already been heard; and the principles of cadences[13] project closed harmonic patterns at the (projected) ends of phrases. Notice that these rules need not anticipate exactly what notes will appear in the musical surface. Rather, they project only the abstract structures that are to be associated with the actual notes of the musical surface as they occur.

These projections or anticipations of abstract structure, then, are parallel to the sorts of syntactic anticipations exploited by most theories of language processing. For instance, a syntactic parser encountering the word *the* will engage a structural schema for a noun phrase, the syntactic unit whose beginning is signaled reliably by *the*. However, this schema is abstract, in that it makes no prediction about the actual words of the anticipated noun phrase. The same goes for many "expectations," "implications," or "anticipations" in music. (This is not to say that very specific events in the musical surface may not be anticipated as well, for example the resolution of a suspension.)

In addition to prospective hearing, the model permits us to describe a phenomenon that may be called *retrospective hearing*. This accounts for various sorts of "satisfaction," "shock," or "surprise" associated with the hearing of music. Here are three representative cases.

1. The processor is computing multiple analyses in parallel, but settles the indeterminacy among them before the point in time when the selection function makes a forced choice. This results in the listener hearing the music with the proper structure, and "projecting this structure backward," in the sense described in section 7.4. This is the case we encountered in the Bach

chorale; phenomenologically, this case is experienced as "hearing the music without effort."

2. The processor is computing multiple analyses in parallel, and enough evidence has accumulated for one of these to be chosen as most plausible by the selection function. However, subsequent events in the musical surface lead to a relative reweighting of the analyses being computed by the processor. The selection function thereby "changes horses in midstream," jumping to a different analysis. The phenomenological effect of such an occurrence will be a "retrospective reanalysis" of the passage as it is heard. Instances of this case might include figure 7.12, where a phrase initially heard as being in A♭ is suddenly heard as being in D♭, as well as similar reanalyses of tonality in the beginnings of the finale of Beethoven's 4th Piano Concerto (where initial C major is replaced by G), the finale of Beethoven's E minor Quartet, Op. 59, No. 2 (C major becomes E minor) and the third movement of Brahms's F minor Clarinet Sonata, Op. 120, No. 1 (E♭ becomes A♭).

3. The processor is computing multiple analyses in parallel, and subsequent events are not consistent with *any* of the existing analyses. All must be abandoned and the processor must start over. This case is experienced as a sense of bewilderment, "losing one's bearings" musically. An instance of this might be the passage for which Mozart's "Dissonant" Quartet is named: the beginning of the piece creates a sensation of A♭ major or some closely related key, but the entry of the first violin on A natural and the way the other parts resolve create a sense of tonal disorientation.

Such cases could be constructed in further variety, to deal with metrical structures, grouping structures, and reductions as well as tonality. However, these three seem fairly representative of the ways in which a parallel multiple-analysis model with a selection function might respond to an incoming musical surface. At the same time, they allow for an enriched notion of musical "implication" and "realization" or "nonrealization."

7.8   Memory and the Expectation Theory of Affect

As mentioned at the beginning of the last section, an important intuitive attraction of the "implication-realization" theory of musical understanding lies in its potential connection to musical affect, a link suggested particularly strongly in Meyer's earlier discussions of the theory. However, there is a fundamental difficulty with basing a theory of musical affect on the standard intuitive notion of expectation. If one is listening to a piece one knows very well, one knows exactly how the music is going to continue. There should hence be no occasion whatsoever for shock, surprise, or disappointment at the way the piece turns out (unless the performer on this occasion happens to make a mistake), and therefore no possibilities for distinctions of affect.

In short, according to this approach, the affect evoked by a piece of music should diminish to the vanishing point with increasing familiarity.

In fact quite the opposite is the case, at least for what we call "good music"—music that we (or the culture as a whole) come to consider as of lasting value. Such music continues to engage us more deeply as we get to know it better. This would seem to be a fatal flaw in an expectation-based theory of affect.

To push this point home, consider also the experience of "musical imagery," in particular replaying a familiar piece in one's head. In this case nothing can be unexpected, since everything experienced comes from one's own memory. Again, this appears to rule out any possibility of surprise or shock. Yet it is certainly possible to derive considerable affect from such experiences.

The alert reader will no doubt suspect how I will propose to overcome this problem. But first, in order to make the problem clearer, I would like to review Meyer's discussion of it in his essay "On Rehearing Music" (1967a). Meyer gives six arguments why it would be possible to enjoy a piece on repeated hearings in spite of the consequences of an intuitive theory of affect based on expectation. I will argue that they all fail (and Meyer himself does not give the sense of being entirely convinced).

Argument 1: A complex piece of music may require a number of hearings before one can understand the implications of its events. As these implications are worked out by the listener, enjoyment increases.

Reply: Although repeated hearings do often increase musical understanding, this does not affect the force of the objection: once one knows a piece well enough to know *exactly* what events are coming next, there is no uncertainty that can lead to shock or surprise. One's expectations at any moment in the piece are that a certain continuation will occur with probability 1.

Argument 2: Memory is not perfect; one tends to misremember or forget the less well structured (or less predictable) parts of a piece. Thus these parts will tend to remain unexpected on repeated hearings, and "musical experience maintains its vitality longer than would otherwise be the case" (Meyer 1967a, 47).

Reply: Although this point is likely valid, the opposite can also be the case. Everyone has had the experience of thinking "Here comes that beautiful place!"—enjoying it in full knowledge of exactly what it is going to sound like, with both memory and affect fully engaged. One can enjoy a perfectly remembered turn of the phrase, predictable or not, and the experience need not lack vitality.

Argument 3: One enjoys a familiar piece by virtue of the "aesthetic illusion": one "suspends knowledge" of the music, in effect deliberately ignoring memory and hearing the piece "as if altogether new."

Reply: although one does sometimes have such experiences, whether by accident or design, these are not the typical cases of reexperiencing a familiar piece. The experience related in the preceding reply is probably more common. The problem with both of these arguments is that they attempt to conflate enjoying a piece with not remembering how it goes.

Argument 4: One's expectations are tempered by one's knowledge of the musical style of the piece—and conversely, new musical experiences alter one's expectations about the style as a whole. As a result, the "internalized probability system" is constantly undergoing subtle change. Therefore the effect of one's knowledge of style on the hearing of a piece is never the same, and consequently one's expectations differ, even if slightly, on successive rehearings of the piece.

Reply: This point too has some validity: one's accumulation of musical experience undeniably changes the way one hears pieces one has known for a long time. Yet this is not a necessary prerequisite for enjoying a piece on rehearing it; one may just like hearing it again, even if no further knowledge has accumulated about its style. Moreover, this argument, couched by Meyer in terms of "probabilities" of what the next events will be, again ignores the fact that, in a piece one knows well, the probabilities will remain essentially in the neighborhood of 1, whatever one's knowledge of style.

Argument 5: One's enjoyment of repeated rehearings may come from the differences between individual performances, in how different performers shape expectations about how events will take place.

Reply: I again agree that this is a possible source of delight in rehearing (or dismay, in the case of a poor performance!). But, as Meyer himself admits, the experience of rehearing a well-known recording, where everything is exactly the same, can occasion enjoyment too.

Argument 6: Finally, Meyer essentially grants all the counterarguments just produced, and asks, Given a listener who knows a piece and its style so well that expectations are not any different than the last time, "will the listener find rehearing the work a rewarding experience?" (p. 49). Meyer says that if the listener can be shown to enjoy the work "as much as he ever did" (p. 49), then the expectation theory can be considered disproven. Since "listeners do in fact tend to tire of music with which they become very familiar" (p. 49), Meyer considers the theory to remain viable.

Reply: The relevant test case for the expectation theory is not whether a listener continues to enjoy a familiar piece to the same degree, but rather whether he or she can enjoy it—to derive affect from it—*at all*. As already belabored too many times, familiarity should lead to total loss of surprise, shock, or disappointment at events of the piece. In order to save his theory, Meyer insists on too strong a criterion for abandoning it.

To be sure, overexposure to any piece of music, no matter how great, will lead to loss of attention, then irritation, then disgust—just like overexposure to chocolate sundaes. But just as appropriately spaced chocolate sundaes can be a recurring source of delight, so can appropriately spaced hearings of a piece of music one knows very well. Whatever sense of fatigue may occur in the capacity for attention or aesthetic pleasure is therefore extraneous to the issue of what brings about the aesthetic pleasure in the first place.

In short, then, none of these arguments, even if true, succeed in blunting the basic objection to the expectation theory of affect. Knowing a piece well does not reduce its affect to zero or nearly so, as the expectation theory seems to imply. Moreover, Meyer's arguments, with the possible exception of argument 3, completely fail to address the question of how one could derive affect from musical imagery, where one's expectations determine precisely what musical events are going to be heard.

7.9 Rescuing the Expectation Theory

Still, there is a germ of insight in the expectation theory of affect, which can be recovered and built upon in terms of the approach to musical processing proposed here. The solution comes in a number of parts.

The first, and most obvious, is that we should not require expectation to bear the entire burden of deriving affect. Certain aspects of affect, for instance, come from very local sources in the musical surface. For example, it is a long-standing (even ancient) observation that tempo affects the musical response. Other things being equal, fast music will tend to be exciting and slow music will tend to be soothing. Sheer volume too has an effect. More interesting perhaps is the evidence about the "shape of the beat" discussed by Clynes and Nettheim (1982) and Clynes and Walker (1982), who show experimentally that manipulation of the attack and release envelopes of individual notes can be correlated with strong differentiation in listeners' emotional responses. These factors are especially interesting because they are notated at best crudely in printed music, yet are highly controlled (even if unconsciously) by good musicians as an integral part of their performance.

Returning to issues involving the parser, musical affect is produced not just by hearing (and predicting) the musical surface of a piece, but by the activity of deriving in real time all the details of abstract musical structure. The musical structure has intrinsic points of instability or tension, which require resolution and therefore result in affect. In addition, since alternative analyses are being processed concurrently, the points of tension in each individual analysis may or may not coincide with those of its cohorts. This tension among the conflicting analyses may also surface in the listener's experience as affect, even though only one of the analyses is experienced at the moment as "the" structure of the music.

As Meyer notes, determining the structure of any reasonably complicated piece of music involves too many details and too many large-scale considerations for a limited-capacity processor to accommodate all possibilities on a single hearing. Repeated hearing aided by memory is likely necessary before all the events of the piece can be integrated into the structure. It is this full integration of every event into the course of processing that makes the experience of "good" music richer on repeated hearings.

Now let us turn back to the question of why familiarity with a piece need not diminish its affect. The answer has to do with the character of the processor. If, as suggested in section 7.6, the parser is modular and informationally encapsulated from musical memory, it does not care whether the piece is familiar or not; it goes through pretty much the same motions regardless.

Under this conception, even if the listener consciously knows that, say, a deceptive cadence is coming, the processor itself is innocent of this knowledge. The selection function therefore projects as most salient the stablest continuation of the current musical surface: a full cadence, in which the conclusion of the phrase is a harmonic relaxation. As a result, when the deceptive cadence actually arrives, the selection function has to reevaluate the relative salience of its analyses, creating a retrospective reanalysis in which the conclusion of the phrase tenses away from the dominant.[14] Listeners are not consciously surprised or shocked by this resolution (as they might be on first hearing), because they know the piece. But musical affect is still evoked, because the listener experiences (1) the increase in tension at the end of the phrase and hence the relative instability of even the most stable analysis of the musical surface, and (2) the temporary instability of the selection function at the moment when it changes its choice of most salient structure. Because the parser is independent from conscious memory, it will be taken in every time by a deceptive cadence, which will therefore produce its characteristic affect, as long as one is attending to the music.

Because of the obligatory operation of the parser, it will apply even to music that is being imaged, that is, being "heard in one's head." Whatever musical structure is retrieved from memory in the course of producing a musical image, the processor goes dumbly to work on it, recreating the structure already being stored in and retrieved from long-term memory. Hence the music can potentially be experienced as though one is hearing it externally.

To sum up, the expectation theory of musical affect does not make much sense if we think in terms of *conscious* expectations or a parser that has full access to one's musical memory. But it *does* make sense if the processor is conceived of as parallel to that for language, using the rules of musical grammar to construct abstract structures that analyze the musical surface, and operating autonomously with at best limited access to musical memory. No matter how well one knows a piece, expectation, suspense, satisfaction, and surprise still occur *within the parser*. In essence, the parser is always hearing the piece for the first time—and that is why affect remains intact.

Chapter 8
The Problem of Reality

We see [the world] as being outside ourselves, although it is only a mental representation of what we experience inside ourselves.... Time and space thus lose that unrefined meaning which is the only one everyday experience takes into account.
René Magritte
(Scutenaire, René Magritte)

8.1 Introduction

Underlying the practice of cognitive science is a basic tension in its goals that to me has much the flavor of a paradigm split in the sense of Kuhn. The tension has to do with how one phrases the fundamental question for a theory of mind. I have been trying to articulate this split for some time, at least since Jackendoff 1983, but its history certainly goes back much further than that.

For convenience, I will call the two competing versions of this fundamental question the "philosophical" version and the "psychological" version, although they are hardly the exclusive property of philosophers and psychologists respectively—hence the scare quotes.[1] The "philosophical" version grows out of questions of epistemology, and might be stated something like this:

This chapter was originally prepared as the second of my Nijmegen Lectures at the Max-Planck Institut für Psycholinguistik in Nijmegen, and I wish to express my gratitude for the opportunity to present my ideas there and discuss them with so many interested people. In particular, Pim Levelt provided valuable advice on the form of the argument. Thanks are also due to William Rapaport and Dan Dennett for important comments.

The chapter has appeared also in *Noûs* 25 (1991) and is reprinted here by permission of the editor. Figure 8.2 is reproduced from J. R. Lackner and P. DiZio, "Visual Stimulation Affects the Perception of Voluntary Leg Movements during Walking," *Perception* 17 (1988), and appears here by permission of the editor. This research was supported in part by NSF Grant IRI 90-46528 to Brandeis University.

"Philosophical" version: What is the relationship of the mind to the world, such that we can have knowledge of reality, such that we can have beliefs and desires about things in the world, and such that our sentences can be true or false?

The "psychological" version grows out of issues in perception. It might be phrased something like this:

"Psychological" version: How does the brain function as a physical device, such that the world seems to us the way it does, and such that we can behave effectively in the world?

These two approaches to the mind look *very* close, particularly in a case like visual perception. The "philosophical" approach might ask, "If something out there in the world is red, how do I come to know it is red?"; the "psychological" approach, "What leads me to the conviction that something out there is red?" These ways of phrasing the question seem nearly indistinguishable, but I think in fact there is a major gulf between them. This chapter will be devoted to demonstrating the existence of such a gulf and assessing the prospects of the two approaches.

By way of introduction, it is revealing to examine some quotations from Jerry Fodor, who embodies in a single person *both* sides of the paradigm split. Fodor, with feet firmly planted in both the philosophical and psychological traditions, proves to be deeply conflicted in the presuppositions he makes about the goals of cognitive science. Consider first the following, from *Psychosemantics* (Fodor 1987, 133):

> The advantage of making an innate theory true is that, quite generally, true theories license more reliable predictions than false theories do. God gave the male stickleback the idea that whatever is red is a rival. Because this idea is *false*, the stickleback's innate psychological theory mediates only stereotyped behavioral coordinations, and those only while adventitious ecological regularities obtain. God gave us such—rather more complicated—ideas as that if x wants that P, and x believes that not-P unless Q, and x believes that x can bring it about that Q, then ceteris paribus x tries to bring it about that Q. Because this idea is *true*, our innate psychological theory mediates vastly more flexible behavioral coordinations than the stickleback's, and will continue to do so as long as human nature doesn't change. That is one reason why we wrote *Hamlet* and the stickleback didn't.

This passage illustrates the conflict vividly. On one hand, Fodor wants to be a psychologist: he insists that an organism's behavior is determined by its mental representations, over which formal manipulations take place. Moreover, some of these representations and principles are innate. On the other hand, he is holding on very hard to his roots as a philosopher, in his use of the terms *true* and *false* with respect to mental representations. As a result, this passage comes down clearly on the philosophical side of the divide.

By contrast, consider Fodor's paper "Methodological Solipsism Considered as a Research Strategy in Cognitive Psychology." Here he argues that a computational psychology has to be stated in terms of the mind as a purely syntactic engine—that behavior has to be determined purely in terms of mind-internal notions. He concludes (Fodor 1980a, 71):

> ... truth, reference, and the rest of the semantic notions aren't psychological categories. What they are is: they're modes of *Dasein*. I don't know what *Dasein* is, but I'm sure that there's lots of it around, and I'm sure that you and I and Cincinnati have all got it. What more do you want?

In this passage Fodor seems to be coming down on the psychological side and rejecting "truth, reference, and the rest of the semantic notions" as part of the theory. (At least I *think* this is what he has in mind—I can't make any other sense of the jokes.)

Another such passage occurs in Fodor's discussion of Putnam in the volume on the Piaget-Chomsky debate (Fodor 1980b, 333):

> The reasonable assumption ... is that human beings have an ethology, just as other species do; that the morphology of our cognitive capacities reflects our specific ... modes of adaptation. Of course, we are in some respects badly situated to elucidate its structure.... *From in here* it looks as though we're fit to think whatever thoughts there are to think.... It *would*, of course, precisely because we *are* in here. But there is surely good reason to suppose that this is hubris bred of an epistemological illusion. No doubt spiders think that webs exhaust the options.

This is clearly within the world view of the "psychological" version of cognitive science: the world looks the way it does *to us* because of the way we're built.

The position I want to advocate here is closest to the last of these quotations: Whatever the nature of *real* reality, the way reality can look *to us* is determined and constrained by the nature of our internal mental representations. Such a "constructivist" view can be traced back at least to Kant; in modern times it has been strongly advocated by the Gestalt school. For instance, Koffka (1935) emphasizes the distinction between the "geographical environment," the world as it "really is," and the "behavioral environment," the world as it is construed by the organism. He argues at length that the organism's behavior can be understood only in terms of the latter. Similarly, Michotte (1954) and especially Michotte et al. (1962) stress the notion of "phenomenal reality," the sense of reality-in-the-world experienced by the organism, showing how this sense is itself a mental construct. The arguments to be presented here follow in the same tradition.

8.2   What Mental Representations Are Supposed to Be

I am using the term *mental representation* with some trepidation here, for lack of any more appropriate English term. Let me try to be more precise about what I have in mind.

As proposed in chapter 1, I am taking a mind very abstractly to be a combinatorial space of possible states, instantiated in a brain. This space has an inherent organization—many independent degrees of freedom, each with an inherent discrete or continuous range of possibilities. A particular mental representation R can be thought of as a location or region in the total space of possibilities. What makes R what it is is simply its relationship to other possibilities in the space—how it is distinct from other possibilities, what possibilities are close to it in what dimensions, and so forth. When we as theorists use symbols to state a theory of mental representations, it is not the symbols themselves that are significant, but rather the range of distinctions possible in the system of symbols we adopt: these distinctions are claimed to be homologous to the organization of the relevant subsystem of brain states.

I am trying, therefore, to take the notion of *representation* as an entirely nonintentional notion. A representation is not necessarily *about* anything; if you like, it does not strictly speaking *represent* anything. (Hence my hesitation in using the term except as a rigid designator for what cognitive scientists believe the mind has in it.) The point of this notion of representation is that it can in principle be instantiated in a purely combinatorial device like the brain as I understand it, without resort to any miraculous biological powers of intentionality such as Searle (1980) wishes to ascribe to the brain.[2] I return to the status of intentionality in section 8.4.

To say that we perceive the world in the terms provided by our mental representations—Koffka's behavioral environment—does not deny the existence of a physical reality; I am certainly not advocating a radical idealism. But then, how does the *real* real world—Koffka's geographical environment—affect mental representations? Barring magic or divine intervention, the only mechanism available is this: Physical stimuli (photons, sound waves, pressure on the skin, chemicals in the air, etc.) act mechanically on sensory neurons. The sensory neurons, acting as transducers in Pylyshyn's (1984) sense, set up peripheral levels of representation such as retinal arrays and whatever acoustic analysis the ear derives. In turn, the peripheral representations stimulate the construction of more central levels of representation, leading eventually to the construction of representations in central formats such as the 3D model level (Marr 1982) and conceptual structure (Jackendoff 1983), which encode our understanding of the world. The connection from the world to these central representations, then, involves no intentionality—just the syntactic transformation of states within one combinatorial system (or module) into states in another combinatorial system, through principles of correspondence. (If there is feedback in perception, as I believe, the relationship is more properly described as mutual interaction between combinatorial systems.) Thus the central representations have *no* direct access to the real world. This, I take it, is the main point of Fodor's (1980a) "methodological solipsism"; as Sprague (1960) puts it, the brain is deaf, dumb, and blind.

A crucial boundary condition on this central encoding is that it is impossible to place *every* distinction in the world in correspondence with a distinction in the brain—otherwise the brain would have to be a literal copy of the world down to every detail. Hence some distinctions in the world—in fact probably *most* distinctions in the world—are inevitably left out of mental representation. In addition, the encoding of the world in terms of a central format of representation is conditioned not only by the input from more peripheral levels (and ultimately from physical stimuli), but also by the organization of the states available in the central format itself. That is, the representation of the world in the mind is constrained by the expressive power of the mind's combinatorial repertoire, in particular by the "grain" of this repertoire—the structure of similarities within the space of representations.

The position emerging from this approach seems paradoxical. Why, if our understanding has no direct access to the real world, aren't we always bumping into things? Why does the visual system, for example, seem to give us a true picture of reality? To address this issue, I have to split it into two parts.

1. Why does the visual system work effectively in guiding behavior? Because it has evolved so that the organism works. An organism that detects obstacles, predators, food, and conspecifics in an ecologically general way is better off than an organism that bumps into things, can't evade predators, can't find food, and can't find other folks to mate with. That is, evolution has given us a visual system that incorporates an *ecologically viable* system of representation, one that has enough of the right distinctions in it, connected to enough distinctions among stimuli, to enable us to function as we do.[3]

2. Another angle on the question is an adaptation of Fodor's answer: *From in here* it seems as though we can see all there is to see. There is nothing to contradict our conviction that we can trust our visual experience. That is, from the psychological point of view, the conviction of a "true

picture of reality" is itself a psychological artifact, a function of our inherently limited frame of reference.

I want to push this latter argument very hard, taking a broad look at our experience of reality. I want to show that in case after case, the "philosophical" approach leads to uncomfortable metaphysical problems (most but not all of them well known), whereas the "psychological" approach permits—at least in principle—a revealing account of the phenomena.

8.3   Examples

I want to consider three kinds of cases, crossed with a range of six psychological domains.

Case 1:   The simplest are cases of *underrepresentation*, where there are parts of the "true" picture of the world that we simply don't have.

Case 2:   *Illusions* are situations in which, from the point of view of an "outside observer," the "true situation" is one thing, but the person involved experiences another. Sometimes the "outside observer" and the "inside observer" are the same person, so that one has "anomalous experiences"—belief and immediate experience are at odds.

Case 3:   *Constructions* are situations where there is *nothing* in the physical stimulus that remotely corresponds to the character of the experience. Here the question of what is a "true picture of the world" is extremely cloudy.

We find one or more of these cases in pretty much any psychological domain.

8.3.1   Vision

Let's start with the visual system. It is obvious that our visual system underrepresents the "true picture." For example, our representations don't contain any distinctions corresponding to ultraviolet or infrared light. This is not a necessary fact about the visual system: there are organisms that are sensitive to these wavelengths. Do we thereby have a *false* picture of reality and these other organisms have a *true* picture? This seems like an extreme conclusion. Better to adopt the "psychological" approach and be content to say that different organisms are just sensitive to different environmental distinctions.

Turning to illusions, how do we account for the experience of the Müller-Lyer illusion or the Ames room? Following the "psychological" approach, the organism is using its normal unconscious computational techniques to arrive at representations that in these cases happen not to agree with representations arrived at from most other points of view. That is, these illusions are products of the visual system operating in normal fashion.

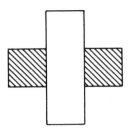

Figure 8.1

However, from the "philosophical" point of view of the first Fodor quotation cited above, the salient fact about these illusions is that one's mental representations while experiencing them are *false*—they do not properly represent their real-world content. The difficulty with this is that mental computations, in Fodor's view, are supposed to preserve semantic content (Fodor 1983; Pylyshyn 1984). If one has arrived at a false representation through normal computational routes, then these procedures must suddenly have failed to preserve content, without having changed their functional properties at all. But then, we have no way of knowing when they are *ever* content-preserving, except after the fact. How can we be so sure that what we take to be *normal* perception is giving us true representations? In short, focusing on the truth or falsity of representations doesn't really help us understand the distinction between visual illusions and normal perception.

Consider next visual constructions, such as one experiences in viewing something as elementary as figure 8.1. Here one vividly sees the shaded portions of the figure as a unified object, partly occluded by a rectangle in front of it. Michotte, Thinès, and Crabbé (1964) call the hidden part of the shaded object the "amodal complement of a perceptual structure": it is contributed by the perceptual system, not by the physical world.

Now what is the status of this "amodal complement" in the "philosophical" approach? The point is that *it's just a picture*—the "truth of the matter" is that such a unified object doesn't exist. Do we want to say then that our mental representations of figure 8.1 are *false*? I don't think so: we probably want to reserve the term *falsity* for cases such as seeing figure 8.1 as, say, a picture of Jerry Fodor.

Note also that appealing to the "derived intentionality" of a picture, that is, what the creator of the picture *intended* it to be a picture of, may help sometimes in determining a "true" reading of the picture. But not this time: as it happens, I had nothing in particular in mind when I drew figure 8.1. Maybe I was just doodling and it popped out. Does that change the truth or falsity of your perception of it? The issue simply makes no sense.[4]

By contrast, on the "psychological" view, the stimuli in pictures lead to visual representations by normal routes. One can speak easily of the "amodal complement" as a constructed part of a representation, derivable from the stimulus by normal processes. These processes, moreover, are ecologically viable: they have evolved so that we can see objects occluded by other objects.

Of course, the way we investigate vision empirically is to fool around with stimuli to see what illusions and constructions we can evoke. In terms of the "philosophical" approach, this isn't addressing the issue of how our representations come to be true; but from the "psychological" point of view, it *is* investigating how they come to be ecologically viable. It is only under the assumption that the machinery has a consistent manner of response to input (not "sometimes true and sometimes false") that a standard psychological manipulation makes sense.

8.3.2 Language

Language, as far as I can tell, is *all* construction. For example, what reality is there to the word *dog*—as a word? Its physical manifestations are a series of sound waves or a series of marks on paper that are taken by the perceiver to be tokens of the word. But what makes them tokens of the word? Essentially, their ability to evoke the perceiver's construction of the phonological representation /d/ followed by /ɔ/ followed by /g/, collected together as a unit. Moreover, at least under normal conditions, this sequence of sounds must be understood to be intended by its producer to evoke the English word *dog*; there is something deviant about treating a parrot's or a speech synthesizer's production of the noise *dog* as an utterance of the *word*. Even considering just these mild subtleties, it begins to be difficult to see how the predicates *true* and *false* apply to one's phonological representations in response to an incoming stimulus. Am I hearing a "true" utterance of *dog* when the parrot makes the noise? One can make a policy decision about how to treat it, but as in the case of the visual construction in figure 8.1, there doesn't seem to be a real fact of the matter. And again, it seems to make more sense to reserve the term "false interpretation" for the case in which one mishears what someone else has said—quite a different matter.

By contrast, on the "psychological" view, everything goes through nicely. The word *dog* is real for us, despite its variable and fleeting physical manifestations, because we have phonological representations embedded within a grammar and lexicon of English; these confer upon the word an individuality within our computational scheme.

Note that it is also a part of the modular perception of language that a semantic intention is invariably attributed to the source of the language—this is just the way linguistic signals are normally processed. Thus, when an input arrives that is of the proper form to set off linguistic processing, semantic intention is attributed even if the source is a mindless parrot or computer.

The problems of reality get even worse when we think about syntactic structure. Is a syntactic structure real, something in the world? There is no such thing as an NP, a VP, or an Adjective in the environment.[5] Thus the issue of the truth of our NP-representations doesn't make much sense. Neither, for that matter, does the notion of phonological or syntactic entities as objects of propositional attitudes. Speakers don't believe (or believe in) NPs or phonological distinctive features or rules of aspiration (even if linguistic theorists do).

8.3.3 Music

Let's now think about the perception and cognition of music. Again, the whole domain is, as far as I can tell, pervaded with construction. What is the "objective reality" of the *Eroica* Symphony or "Stardust"? It seems to me that these pieces are best considered to be abstractions that can be realized in performances or scores, of wildly varying physical characteristics (it is possible, though appalling, to conceive of the *Eroica* played by a quartet of marimbas; and of course a popular song like "Stardust" can be subjected to endless arrangements). But the abstraction that unifies different performances of a piece of music is precisely captured in the mental representation of music—the mental structures that performances evoke. That is, the constancy and reality of a piece of music are purely mental.

In addition, it hardly makes sense to say that the representations one constructs in response to hearing a performance of the *Eroica* are true or false. Nor does it make sense to claim one has propositional attitudes toward musical representations, which aren't, as far as I can tell, propositions. The whole story becomes even more absurd if we think of the process of composition. Presumably, Beethoven wrote the symphony by virtue of creating mental representations (imaging music) that he wanted the written notes to evoke—in the absence of any overt musical signal. Were his representations false until he wrote the symphony down? Did they suddenly acquire a truth-value when the score was written or the first performance took place? I can't make any sense of such questions—they entirely misconstrue the character of musical perception and experience.

In short, I find it difficult to see how the "philosophical" framing of the issue of musical cognition can lead into any serious investigation. By contrast, the "psychological" approach leads again to an inquiry into rules and representations—a structured combinatorial space—that enable us to internally construct our musical experience and have the conviction that it is part of reality. This is the basis of the approach to musical cognition developed in Lerdahl and Jackendoff 1983a (see also chapter 7), which parallels generative linguistics in its outlook on the psychological reality of musical structure.

8.3.4   Social Cognition

For a change of pace, consider the concepts involved in social cognition (chapter 4), a domain about which cognitive science and the attendant philosophical literature have had virtually nothing to say. Again there is a vast amount of construction going on. Concepts like marriage, group membership, academic tenure, and debt have a vast number of possible physical manifestations in "objective reality." What holds them together is not a "tendency to behave in certain ways"—such tendencies are just the symptoms. Rather, these concepts are stipulations or organizing principles that guide or force choices among an infinite range of possible actions. Though they are purely abstract, they are absolutely real to us. We can speak of the truth or falsity of whether X is married to Y, but certainly not of whether belief in the institution of marriage is true. Marriage isn't just a mass illusion!

Sometimes these aspects of reality are said to be "socially constructed." But accepting such a view *tout court* is to be satisfied too easily. Just as in the case of visual or linguistic perception, what is the brain's causal access to social reality? To be sure, external social relations are necessary to induce social cognition, but on the other hand there can be no conventions of society unless the members of society mentally encode them. And the causal access to external social relations has to be through the same channels as ordinary perception: the good old sense organs. So barring telepathy, the physical evidence for social concepts is only indirectly related to the concepts themselves.

The "psychological" approach here leads us to ask what social concepts are like as formal entities—in what combinatorial space they are embedded and how this space is linked to the perception and formulation of concrete actions. We can investigate the acquisition of such concepts, their cross-cultural realizations, and their evolutionary antecedents in primate societies (Cheney and Seyfarth 1990), and we can ask how they contribute to the way the world seems to us. If only a dream for the future, this is clearly a viable enterprise for research.

8.3.5   Our Bodies

Closer to home and more concretely, consider the experienced reality of our own bodies. Though we take this experience so much for granted that it seems beneath notice, it parallels visual experience in many respects. We certainly have propositional beliefs in the existence and position and size of our bodies (if asked). But there are lots of gaps, illusions, and constructions that occur under various conditions.

Consider first gaps, or underrepresentations. One doesn't have perceptual experience of the state of one's liver, the growth of one's toenails, one's saccadic eye movements, or the change in tension in the numerous muscles involved in breathing or in tongue movements during speech. Does that mean we have a *false* mental representation of our bodies? No, just incomplete.

Turning to illusions, a good first case is the "phantom limb" phenomenon. Amputees who certainly have a propositional belief that they have lost a leg often nevertheless *feel the leg is there*: it has a position, and it may be subject to pains or itches. There is nothing wrong with the brain—it is operating normally, and evidently receiving enough input from the nerve ends in the stump to project what it should (under normal inputs) project. In fact, according to Sacks (1985, 64), the existence of a phantom leg is essential for the successful use of a prosthesis; the amputee must invest the prosthetic limb with the "feel" of the phantom in order to walk satisfactorily.

Sacks also discusses (1985, 42–52) the case of a woman who through inflammation of the proprioceptive nerves lost all body position sense, and described herself as feeling literally disembodied. It was possible for her to guide her movements visually but not by feel. This disability certainly is not a defect in propositional belief. Rather, it is the proprioceptive equivalent of blindness: the brain simply is receiving no proprioceptive information.

A third case, this time one involving brain rather than body damage, is the phenomenon of neglect. In the wake of a stroke, a patient may claim, for instance, that someone has left this revolting leg in his bed, and for some reason he can't understand he can't toss it out. When asked where his own leg is, he suddenly realizes he can't find it; then, to his horror, he discovers that this other leg is attached to him! Here, then, there seem to be elements of propositional belief produced as a by-product of malfunction in the mind's representation of the body. The patient's conviction of the truth of these propositions is as strong as your conviction or mine that the sky is blue; it does not succumb to reason (Sacks 1985, 53–55). This case as well as the previous two show that the sense of reality of one's own body is not as self-evident as one might want to think. Like vision, it is a kind of understanding, the product of processing internal to the mind.

These three cases have all involved pathologies of one sort or another. But body illusions can be produced in normal people as well. Here's one example of many explored by James Lackner and his associates (this one from Lackner and DiZio 1988). A subject is placed in the setup pictured in figure 8.2, walking on a circular treadmill while holding a stationary horizontal bar. The floor is rotating backward, so the subject has to step forward in order to hold the bar. The wall around the treadmill has vertical stripes on it and can rotate independently.

Figure 8.2

Lackner and DiZio explore four cases. (1) If the wall rotates at the same rate as the floor, subjects experience themselves as in motion and the enclosure as stationary. (2) If the wall is stationary, subjects still experience themselves in motion, but for some strange reason the wall is moving along with them. (3) If the wall rotates in the same direction as the floor but faster, the visual cues for self-motion are faster than those provided by the stepping motion. This conflict is unified in the subject's experience in a variety of possible ways. The most interesting one for our purposes is that some subjects experience their legs as growing longer at the extension of each step, so that they feel as though they are "Elastic Man"—the body representation comes to be deformed. (4) The final condition is when the wall rotates in the opposite direction from the floor, so that the visual cues for self-motion indicate *backward* motion. Under this condition, some subjects experience themselves as voluntarily stepping backward, even though they are actually stepping forward. Hence there is a drastic deformation of the experience of the body and even—crucially—of volition.

What makes this happen? As in the case of vision, if we place the organism in an environment to which the organism's normal processes and representations are not ecologically adapted, the organism produces representations that are strictly speaking false, but still strangely consistent. Just as in experiments involving visual illusions, these body illusions are used as clues for how the normal processes work in a normal environment. But then, are our representations *true* in a normal environment?

Not always. Lackner points out the following case: If you stand on one foot, it is physically bearing twice the weight it would in a normal stance.

But it certainly doesn't feel that way; one feels little if any change in pressure on the right foot upon lifting the left off the ground. Lackner observes that this is a function of the body representation's adaptation to normal gravitational force. In an artificially produced gravitational field of 2G, if one shifts from a normal stance to a single foot, the experienced change in pressure is *enormous*.

The point of this example is that the mental representation of body experience is, even under normal conditions, not a *true* representation in the "philosophical" sense. More specifically, these cases show that one's sense of the body's reality is in many respects a construction, produced by automatic and more or less modular subcomponents of the mind. Again, the investigation of these problems can be pursued only under the "psychological" version of the fundamental issue. It is not so obvious that one can even formulate them within the presuppositions of the "philosophical" version.

8.3.6   Our Selves

The most dramatic case, presaged in the fourth condition of Lackner and DiZio's experiment, is the conception of the self. We certainly can't find anything physical corresponding to the self, nothing to point to, but it is as real to us as anything. The self too appears to be a conceptual construction; Dennett (1988) calls it a "center of narrative gravity," an abstract entity to which one's history is attributed. The constructive nature of the self is especially evident in the dissociation of multiple personality disorder (Kluft 1984; Humphrey and Dennett 1989), in which people behave as though they have numerous distinct selves, as being different people in succession. Some of the selves are even aware of other selves and yet experience the multiple personality as nonanomalous. There are a lot of fearsomely complicated issues here that I have no desire to discuss. For present purposes the point is that in this context the "philosophical" approach to the mind, "How does our representation of the self come to be true?", seems to me clearly beside the point; whereas the question "How does the mind work such that it generates an ecologically viable self-concept that on occasion dissociates?" is one that can be pursued productively. (It is perhaps worth speculating that the self is one's own representation in the subdomain of social cognition, whereas the body is one's own representation in the spatial domain—see section 4.5.1.)

8.4   The Status of Beliefs, Truth, and Intentionality

Now, where does all this leave ordinary language terms like *truth* and *belief* (in the propositional attitude sense)—more generally, all the terms that invoke intentionality? We could take an approach like that of Stich (1983) or Churchland (1981), and just say that the idea that there can be truth and beliefs is *simply wrong*. One might even fantasize that if people came to talk more scientifically, these terms would drop out of the language. But I find such a resolution too brittle. For one thing, the discovery of the facts about the rotation of the earth has not in the course of some centuries stopped people from talking about the sunrise, nor has it made sentences about sunrises "simply wrong." For instance, *Sunrise is at 6:40 a.m. today* does not have the curious status of a sentence containing a false presupposition, such as *The present king of France is bald*.

I prefer a story in which *truth* and *belief* have a status similar to *sunrise*: they are words of English that express human concepts, and they ought to be subject to semantic analysis, just like *dog, cat, run, throw*, and *from*.

On this view, if we want to achieve Tarski's and Davidson's goal of a theory of truth, we have to ask, What human concept does this word pick out? What abstract construal of the world does it evoke? To answer these questions, we have to embed these terms in a general theory of concepts—not, as the philosophical tradition has done, take them as the *basis* for defining concepts. That is, in some sense we have to turn the philosophical enterprise inside out.

Here is a case that helps show what I have in mind. Suppose we are studying plants, and we decide we want a scientific theory of fruits and vegetables. As it turns out, there is no biological property that corresponds exactly to everyday usage. So there is a mismatch between everyday concepts and science. At this point, then, the course of investigation splits in two.

1. What are the biological properties of plants? Within this enterprise, the terms *fruit* and *vegetable* either drop out or come to be used in a technical, noneveryday sense. In particular, the biological sense of *fruit* includes things like tomatoes and cucumbers and maybe even things like pine cones; there probably is no biological term corresponding even roughly to *vegetable* at all. Does this mean the terms *fruit* and *vegetable* are simply wrong, and there is no such thing? No. Rather,

2. We can investigate the psychological characteristics that lead us or license us to have concepts like fruit and vegetable in the everyday sense, involving not only form and biological function but also taste and human use.

Now by analogy: Suppose we are studying psychology and we want to know how sentences, represented mentally, can be true of the real physical world. As shown above, there seems to be no psychological property that corresponds to everyday usage. Thus there is a mismatch between everyday concepts and science. The course of investigation splits in two.

1. What are the psychological properties of people such that they function in the physical world? (That is, How do we formulate a materialistic psychology?) Terms like *truth* and *belief* either drop out or come to be used

in a technical, noneveryday sense. In particular, there has to be some nonintentional term that takes the place of evaluative terms like *true* and *false*, perhaps something having to do with the syntactic congruence of representations coming from independent sources in perception and/or memory.

2. But in addition, we can ask, What psychological properties of human beings lead us or license us to have concepts like truth and belief in the everyday sense? This is the approach I'm advocating for the intentional terms. The only difference between this and the fruit-vegetable case is that here both aspects of the investigation are within psychology, so we have to be very careful not to get them confused.

What would the latter theory look like? That is, what concepts do the words *true* and *belief* express? An approach to the conceptual analysis of *belief* is proposed in Jackendoff 1975, 1980, 1983, chapter 11, based on linguistic evidence not widely noted in the philosophical literature. As it turns out, all the well-known referential and inferential difficulties of belief-contexts (e.g. the invalidity of existential inferences into belief-contexts, and Quine's (1956) phenomenon of referential opacity) can be completely duplicated in sentences that describe pictures. To give just one example among many, adapted from Russell (1905): a sentence like (1a), contradictory in isolation, is perfectly sensical as a complement of *believe* (1b) and describes (on one reading) a mistaken belief. An entirely parallel case appears in picture-descriptions (1c,d). (Note that there is no embedded clause in (1c,d), so a traditional solution in terms of quantifier scope won't work.)[6]

(1) a. The blue-eyed girl has brown eyes.
    b. Ralph believes that the blue-eyed girl has brown eyes.
    c. In Ralph's picture, the blue-eyed girl has brown eyes.
    d. Ralph painted the blue-eyed girl with brown eyes.

Notice also that the verb *picture*, as in *Bill pictured Mary as pretty*, is ambiguous between pictorial representation, verbal description, and belief.

These parallels in grammatical, lexical, and inferential patterns suggest that the underlying logic of pictures and beliefs is pretty much the same— in particular that the ordinary language concept of belief is cognitively modeled on that of pictures. This is perhaps not surprising, given the intuition that many beliefs are experienced in part as mental images or "pictures in the head."[7]

Beginning with Wimmer and Perner (1983), there has been a series of experiments showing that children under about the age of four have difficulty correctly reporting someone else's false belief. The conclusion usually drawn from these experiments is that young children do not have a fully developed theory of other minds. However, Zaitchik (1989) shows that children under four have similar difficulty describing a photograph of some previous situation that no longer obtains. (The child has seen the photograph taken but has not seen the photograph itself.) Zaitchik conjectures that children's difficulties with false beliefs and with incorrect photographs stem from a common difficulty with representations of any sort—photographic or mental. If so, this brings developmental evidence in line with the grammatical and inferential evidence for the conceptual analysis of belief as a sort of mental picture.

What makes a design on a piece of paper count as a picture? Basically, in a picture there is some relation perceived, intended, or projected between it and other parts of the world; it is said to be a "faithful depiction" or a "true picture" just in case it can be mapped onto the intended aspects of the world under appropriate representational conventions. By analogy, a belief is faithful or true (it gives a "true picture of reality") in case it maps appropriately onto reality. That is, the notion of correspondence between a belief and the world parallels (even lexically) that between a picture and the world.

Let us now consider the status of intentionality in the context of this analysis. As far as I can see, this relation of correspondence between "mental pictures" and the world is precisely what the term *intentionality* is supposed to denote. In other words, the notion of intentionality of mental representations arises as part of an exegesis of the ordinary-language concept of belief—if you like, as a component of the theory of folk psychology. As such, the fact that intentionality turns out to be problematic or even inexplicable is no problem: folk psychology is full of all kinds of crazy things. But as part of a scientific theory of how the mind works, *intentionality* turns out to be a technical term like *phlogiston* or *the ether*—a theoretical entity that arises from a fundamental misconstrual of the problem.

Of course, the *behavioral* reality of other minds and of propositional attitudes is beyond doubt, whatever their *geographical* reality. Moreover, whatever "the truth of the matter," this aspect of behavioral reality is clearly ecologically viable. As Dennett (1987) puts it, we inherently adopt the "intentional stance" in our dealings with other human beings (and to a lesser extent with other organisms, including computers); we have evolved to adopt it because it works, at least most of the time.

Fodor (1987), however, goes one step farther and maintains that, because the intentional stance works, it must be scientifically true—that is, he argues that the folk psychological view is the correct "philosophical" theory of the mind as well. But this is like claiming that the ordinary language notion of vegetable must constitute a true natural kind. By this point I think we can see why this further move is both unnecessary and misguided.

8.5   Why Would One Want to Maintain the "Philosophical" Position?

The overall story emerging is that an account of how we experience the world—how the world is to us—seems tractable within a theory of nonintentional mental representations. Not easy, but susceptible to research. By contrast, the issue of how our representations come to be true leads over and over into blind alleys, metaphysical puzzles, and internal contradictions, difficulties that seem to me the mark of a wrong approach.

Nevertheless, a lot of people seem unwilling to give up the "philosophical" approach for the "psychological" or "constructivist" program in the face of these problems. Why?

A basic reason, I think, is that the constructivist view goes violently against common sense: it apparently makes everything we experience subjective. The theory does not permit a sense of reality, but only *reality for so-and-so.*

This objection can be decomposed into two threads, one from language and one from more general intuition.

1. *If reality is observer-relative, how is it that we manage to understand one another?* (This objection is essentially Quine's (1960) "indeterminacy of radical translation," now applied at the level of the single individual.)

Two answers. The first, from Katz (1966), in his earlier mentalistic incarnation, appeals to innateness. The organization of our thoughts and perception—and their relation to the world—is biologically constrained enough that our conceptual commitments are bound to be pretty similar. To use Quine's example, everybody is going to see a rabbit rather than a collection of rabbit parts because of the way visual cognition is built to work. More generally, evolution took a long time to get a working visual/navigational system; but as a result, it is pretty reliable within certain tolerances.

The second answer to this objection is that we *don't* always understand each other, even when we think we do. This is particularly evident in the case of abstract concepts. Quine's indeterminacy of radical translation in a sense does apply when we are dealing with world views in areas like politics, religion, aesthetics, science, and, I guess, semantics. These are domains of discourse in which the construction of a combinatorial space of concepts is underdetermined by linguistic and sensory evidence, and innateness does not rush in to the rescue.[8]

2. *But dammit, I know the world is out there!* There *is* a reality, independent of my perception, and I can see it! (And kick it, too!)

The answer to this objection has to be more or less Kantian: That's what we are built to think! Such an answer sounds on the face of it question-begging, but in light of the numerous phenomena cited above, it makes somewhat more sense. To use Dennett's (1987) term, realism is a *stance* that we are built to adopt. Skepticism is possible for scientific purposes, but not for ordinary life. Again, the claim is that our natural realism, the idea that the world is pretty much as we experience it, may not be *true*, but it is certainly ecologically viable.

As further incentive to reconsider the status of what seems like external reality, I want to revert once more to my training as a linguist. There are circumstances where language gives us an opportunity to vacillate between describing a characteristic as part of the external world and describing it as part of the mind of the perceiver. Compare the following sentences:

(2)   a.   This book bores me.
       b.   This book is boring to me.
       c.   I am bored with this book.
       d.   This book is boring.
       e.   I am bored.

(3)   a.   These ideas are valuable to me.
       b.   These ideas are valuable.
       c.   I value these ideas.

(4)   a.   I like ice cream.
       b.   Ice cream is nice.

Who does the boredom belong to? In (2a), (2b), and (2c) the boredom is described as the result of an interaction between me and the book, with perhaps more responsibility being attributed to the book in (2a) and (2b) and a little more being attributed to me in (2c). In (2d) the observer plays no role: boringness is a property of the external object alone. In (2e) the reaction of boredom is attributed solely to me, with no necessary external stimulus for the boredom. For our purposes here, the interesting case is (2d), where the book's capacity to induce boredom is taken as observer-independent, just like its length in *The book is 182 pages long*. Similar shifts occur in (3) and (4). What we see in these cases (which are quite numerous in English) is our ability to externalize experiential properties and then experience them as really out there. How can something be objectively boring, delightful, valuable, or worthless without someone who is bored or delighted or who values it? Yet we speak this way all the time. The fact that in these cases we can so easily drop the observer's contribution to the perception and project it onto the percept makes it more plausible that we do the same thing for other "objective" properties as well.

8.6   *Learning to Live with Constructivism*

Still, even if one intellectually accepts the constructivist argument that our sense of reality is the product of a stance, one may well be left with a sinking feeling. How can we live with this view of ourselves? In particular, how can we do science, which supposedly is seeking the truth about the world, if we don't believe in truth as a scientifically viable concept? Do we have to (and can we) purge our language of all its intentional terms in order to be properly scientific?

I don't think so. The metalanguage for science has to be ordinary language and has to presuppose the ordinary realist stance. Consider the practice in quantum physics, which says the world is physically very different from the way we naturally understand it. Physicists don't (and can't) change their language, and in particular they continue to describe in nonquantum terms the very instruments with which they make quantum-theoretic measurements. I am told (Hugh Pendleton, personal communication) that there is considerable informal discussion in the field about how to draw a pragmatic boundary around the domain that is described in quantum terms, leaving the context to be understood within the ordinary stance.

I think the same sort of approach has to be pursued in psychology. The theory must be stated in constructivist terms; but at some remove from the phenomena under description, one has to revert to the ordinary-language stance of realism. I don't see any problem in principle about this; it is just that one has to be explicit and sensitive about what one is doing. The goal, in any event, is not to find some sort of Absolute Truth, but to arrive at a humanly comprehensible understanding of the world we experience.

Does the constructivist stance make reality go away, or make our reality seem less real? No: we still will go on living our lives for the most part within our natural realist stance. Knowing the biology of reproduction does not have to make sex less fun—though it does present the risk of viewing sex just as a grotesque piece of natural engineering (Kundera 1981, 213–214). I submit that most of us have learned to live with that risk pretty easily. Similarly, seeing ourselves as devices constructed to have a realist stance about the world and an intentionalist stance about our fellow humans does not prevent us from freely adopting these stances. On the other hand, we have lost our innocence: realism now carries an element of existential choice that was not there before.

I suspect that, at bottom, people find constructivisim threatening because it removes the last remaining bastion of human privilege in the natural world. The Copernican revolution denied us a position at the physical center of the universe; the Darwinian revolution placed us as just another step in the biological continuum. This leaves us in a precarious position, with only our minds to distinguish us from the rest of nature.[9] Recall our initial quotation from Fodor: it is our mind's ability to have true representations that makes us special; "that's why we wrote Hamlet and the stickleback didn't." Hubris indeed.

I don't think Fodor is alone in this feeling: many of us have a deep-seated (if unspoken) need for a sense of transcendent superiority over the rest of nature. This need fuels a basic emotional resistance to constructivist psychology, which says on the contrary that even our much-prized minds are just natural devices. But what purpose does this sense of superiority serve? At this point in the history of humanity, maybe a little bit more humility about our place in the natural order wouldn't be such a bad thing.

Notes

Chapter 2

1. My interpretation here is confirmed by Dennett's (1987, 288) revealing anecdote, in which Fodor explicitly endorses Searle's position on the "intrinsic intentionality" of mental states.

2. Generative Semantics used this observation as motivation for assimilating semantics to syntactic principles. The central program of the theory was to reduce *all* semantic compositionality to syntax. As more and more was discovered about semantic structure, it became clear that this program was not feasible. For at least some generative semanticists, the conclusion was that syntax should be abandoned altogether. As seen in figure 2.1, the approach here is to retain syntax for its proper traditional purposes, but to invest semantic expressivity in a different component with appropriate expressive power: conceptual structure.

3. A point of notation: I will use angle brackets ⟨ ⟩ to enclose an optional constituent in a formal expression, the traditional parentheses being reserved to notate arguments of a function.

4. See Jackendoff 1983, sections 10.3–5, for further discussion of the Thematic Relations Hypothesis, and why it justifies the approach of Conceptual semantics as opposed to model-theoretic (E-)semantics. These sections also implicitly answer Dowty's (1988) charge that the "metaphorical extension" of thematic relations to nonspatial fields is incoherent. Basically, the cross-field generation of thematic relations probably only makes sense in terms of I-semantics, but Dowty is seeking an explication based on E-semantics.

   Lakoff and Johnson (1980) and Lakoff (1990) subsume the facts accounted for by the Thematic Relations Hypothesis under a theory of "metaphor." In particular, Lakoff (1990) deals with almost exactly the same facts as Jackendoff 1983, chapter 10, without attribution; his "Invariance Hypothesis" appears quite close in its specifics to the Thematic Relations Hypothesis. However, Jackendoff and Aaron (1991) show that thematic parallelism is quite distinct from metaphor as traditionally conceived, and that Lakoff and Johnson's extended sense of the term glosses over important differences.

5. This analysis of *climb* was to my knowledge first proposed in Fillmore 1982; a formal treatment in terms of preference rules appears in Jackendoff 1985a.

6. This analysis of *see* is adapted from Miller and Johnson-Laird 1976 and appears in more detail in Jackendoff 1983, chapter 8.

7. Actually, he finds evidence but disregards it; see Jackendoff 1983, 125–127 and 256, note 8.

Chapter 3

1. Lakoff (personal communication) has suggested that the relevant physical basis for possession is not spatial proximity but rather holding or grasping, and that the notion

of physical control generalizes or extends to social control, of which possession is one particular form. But the very same problem arises: social control simply *is not* physical control; some new abstract notion must be introduced that makes this concept available. In addition, the expressions of holding and grasping do not display the grammatical and lexical parallels to possession seen in (2), so the child would have no linguistic basis for a "metaphorical" extension, as is possible in the present analysis.

Chapter 5

1. At the same time, neurophysiological description is of course not ruled out. Neurophysiological events underlie all mental processing, conscious and unconscious, and the relation of these events to computational events must be worked out. This is crucial, for instance, in order to describe the effect of chemical changes due to drugs or hormone imbalances on the operation of the computational mind and thereby on awareness.

Chapter 6

1. Our assumptions here may be oversimplified. For example, there is good reason to suspect that visual, haptic, and auditory information will have to connect with more than one motor system (e.g. one that guides reaching and another that guides locomotion). In addition, there may be cases where visual information may be directly translatable into motor commands, without being translated into amodal spatial terms (e.g. control of some eye movements). Nevertheless, translation into a common format is necessary in order to explain a large variety of tasks, including how language is readily learned and used by individuals whose modality of experience differs from the norm (e.g. see Landau and Gleitman 1985).
2. We are speaking here specifically of *inherent* top, bottom, front, back, and sides, based on the object's shape. There are also contextually imposed uses of these terms; see section 6.2.3.
3. These criteria are stated fairly carefully; they interact in interesting ways depending on the shape and function of the object. For instance, a house normally has a *front*, a *back*, and *sides*—but no *ends*, since it is not long and narrow. A wide but shallow office building may be said to have a *front*, a *back*, and two *ends* (a left end and a right end); the axis defining front-back is orthogonal to that defining ends. Therefore there are no axes left over to define sides. By contrast, a bus has a *front end*, a *back* (*rear*) *end*, and two *sides*; here the criteria for *front/back* and *end* project onto the same horizontal axis, and the orthogonal axis remains to define sides. Finally, a rectangular carton may be said to have two sides and two ends—but no front and back, since its axes are symmetric.
4. Within table 6.1, *compound* prepositions are combinations of words that function grammatically as a single preposition, more or less parallel to compound nouns such as *garbage man* and *big top*. *Intransitive* prepositions, often classified as adverbs in traditional grammar, are locational and directional words that occur in all the usual grammatical positions for prepositional phrases but need not be followed by a noun phrase. Many of them, such as *outward* and *upstairs*, contain a preposition as a constituent. In addition, many standard prepositions such as *below*, *nearby*, and *through* can occur with or without an object. By analogy with the familiar distinction between transitive and intransitive verbs, then, these uses of prepositions with and without objects have been termed *transitive* and *intransitive* respectively. (See Jackendoff 1973 for more detail.)
5. Going across a bridge is a special case, in that one goes from one *end* of the bridge to the other. Presumably this is motivated by the fact that the bridge itself extends from one side to the other of something else, such as a road or a river.

6. There are a few exceptions to this overall generalization. Nautical terms like *port* and *starboard* require a boat as reference object. *Upstairs* and *downstairs* involve levels in a building (though not necessarily *stairs*, since one can go upstairs in a building with only elevators). And the compounds with *-ward* such as *homeward* and *shoreward* involve reference to the object named by the initial noun. We assume that the meaning of these terms goes outside the spatial relation system proper, involving an interaction with the object shape (or category) system.

7. In Avrutin's data, the prepositions that take Prepositional case include *na* 'on' and *v* 'in, inside'. Those that take Instrumental include *za* 'behind', *nad* 'above, over', *pered* 'in front of', *pod* 'under', and *mezdu/sredi* 'between, among'. Those that take Genitive include *u* 'at, very close to' and *okolo/vozle* 'near, not far from, close to'. The one problematic example he has provided is *mezdu/sredi* 'between, among', which we have analyzed as 'interior to' and which therefore should take Prepositional case. It will take further research to decide whether this is truly exceptional or whether our feature analysis must be modified.

8. 'Toward' and 'away from' are more restricted than 'to' and 'from', in that the region they are constructed from is always 'at X'. There are no expressions *toward on X* or *away from under X*, parallel to *onto X* and *from under X*, for instance.

9. Pinxten, van Dooren, and Harvey (1983) make an exhaustive exploration of Navajo spatial terms. Though they emphasize how different the Navajo spatial framework is from that of English, there are few surprises with respect to the parameters discussed here (insofar as we can follow their discussion without competence in Navajo). About the only case that involves a shape descriptor for an object, the issue with which we are most concerned, is *biniká*, a postposition meaning roughly 'passing through a hole', as in the eye of a needle. Interestingly, the French verb *enfiler* implies a similar geometry of something slipping through a narrow aperture (Jacques Mehler, personal communication). Thus, although we do not want to claim that English exhausts the spatial relations expressible in language, it does appear to provide a substantial and representative sampling.

10. One might attempt to explain this filtering in functional terms: perhaps, for example, people can manage to communicate effectively despite expressing only a small range of spatial relations, so language has evolved (biologically and/or diachronically) to have no more such expressions than necessary. We are suspicious of such explanations, which seem to beg the question, given the proliferation of vocabulary in so many other domains. Why are there, for instance, so many verbs of manner of movement and verbs of emotional reaction but so few prepositions? Why do we coin new specialized color words but never new specialized prepositions? It is not a satisfactory answer to say that we just don't need more elaborate spatial relations to make ourselves understood: we could make ourselves understood without lots of the words in our vocabulary.

11. Farah et al. call the difference one between "visual" and "spatial" capacities. One of us (R.J.) has a somewhat different interpretation: that we should think of both as subsystems of the multimodal spatial capacity. Since all the tasks tested by Farah et al. were exclusively visual—there were no haptic or motor tasks—the evidence so far does not distinguish the two possible interpretations.

12. Of course, formal indexing does not answer the psychological or neurological question of how the link is effected. But this is altogether parallel to the well-known problem within language of how multiple representations are psychologically or neurologically linked—for example, what it means neurologically for the representation of the sound of a word to be linked to the encoding of its meaning.

Chapter 7

1. Current neural network or connectionist theories of computation (e.g. McClelland and Rumelhart 1986) invoke massively parallel processing in a way partly congenial with the model to be advocated here, and claim to be more closely modeled on neural mechanisms. Such networks have in fact been proposed for music processing by Bharucha (1987) and Gjerdingen (1990). On the other hand, neural network technology is as yet far from being able to encode the kinds of structures necessary to implement anything remotely resembling the *GTTM* theory; even simple structures such as meter and serial order are not without difficulties. Given this situation, one would hope that the insights of structural theories (including traditional theory as well as that of *GTTM*) would not be rejected simply because the technology is not up to stating them. Rather, it should be a goal of a "microstructural" theory to explain why the traditional generalizations about structure emerge at the higher level of organization.

2. Mentioning actual keys such as A♭ and D♭ is psychologically unrealistic for the majority of listeners, who lack perfect pitch. A more apt way of putting this might be "The pitches so far are consistent with the pitch-collections of (a) the major key in which the soprano of the first event of figure 7.8 forms the third degree, (b) the major key in which the soprano of the first event of figure 7.8 forms the leading tone, (c) much less plausibly, the minor keys in which the soprano of the first event forms the fifth and second degrees." That is, key-finding is to be conceived of as imposing a grid of scale degrees on a sequence of pitch-events, not as identifying an absolute name for the key. My use in the text of key names should therefore be consistently construed as an abbreviation for this psychologically more appropriate characterization.

3. However, this possibility does occur occasionally, for instance in Schumann's song "Dein Bildnis wunderselig" from the Op. 39 *Liederkreis*.

4. These rules are stated as followed (*GTTM*, 76, 84, 88):

Metrical Preference Rule 2
Weakly prefer a metrical structure in which the strongest beat in a group appears relatively early in the group.

Metrical Preference Rule 3
Prefer a metrical structure in which beats of level L_i that coincide with the inception of pitch-events are strong beats of L_i.

Metrical Preference Rule 5
Prefer a metrical structure in which a relatively strong beat occurs at the inception of
a.   a relatively long pitch-event
     (plus five other cases)

Metrical Preference Rule 6
Prefer a metrically stable bass.

5. This rule is stated as follows (*GTTM*, 89):

Metrical Preference Rule 8
Strongly prefer a metrical structure in which a suspension is on a stronger beat than its resolution.

6. I assume that, in determining the key of a piece, the listener makes use of as much relevant information as is available in the musical surface: the total distribution of pitches and rhythms can be taken into account. The simplest case is when the pitches presented

in the surface are consistent with only a single key, and the cadential formulas correspond to that key. By the end of the first phrase, our Bach chorale satisfies this condition.

However, if the available pitch classes present in the musical surface do not completely determine a key, criterial intervals such as semitones and tritones (Brown 1988; Butler 1989) will play a prominent role; as shown above, voice-leading considerations also may play a role. Conversely, when the total set of pitch classes creates a conflict (for example if a chromatic alteration is present), grammatical factors such as harmonic progression, temporal ordering, and rhythmic status play a role. (Longuet-Higgins's (1987) "semitone rule" is an example of this sort of rule.)

The limiting case of underdetermination of key is when the musical surface contains only a single pitch or at best a single triad. As suggested by Butler (1989), this pitch or triad is by default taken to determine the most likely tonic; a slightly more general form of this observation appears as Longuet-Higgins's "tonic-dominant preference rule." This default rule is motivated by the fact that pieces conventionally begin on the tonic or with a tonic triad. (In turn, this fact explains the finding reported by Krumhansl (1990) that one can pretty successfully determine the key of preludes by Bach, Chopin, and Shostakovich from just the first four pitches of each piece: most of them, particularly those by Bach, begin with a tonic triad or arpeggio that includes at least three pitches. One does not need Krumhansl's statistical techniques to do this well.)

7. This rule is stated as follows (*GTTM*, 101):

Metrical Preference Rule 10
Prefer metrical structures in which every other beat is strong.

8. Marcus (1980) calls his parser a "deterministic parser," because it does not backtrack. However, in the sense intended here, it is indeterministic: it manages to fend off a final decision on analysis by using a "lookahead function" that contains a limited number of items whose analysis is held open.

9. See Jackendoff 1987a for discussion and justification of a selection function in the faculties of linguistic and visual processing. The "Darwin machine" of Calvin (1989) suggests a possible implementation of a selection function: the patterns for each analysis are duplicated many times over in the brain, and the more stable ones recruit active memory away from less stable ones until the latter are wiped out. A similar idea appears in "winner-take-all" connectionist networks (McClelland and Rumelhart 1986).

10. This rule is stated as follows (*GTTM*, 79):

Metrical Preference Rule 4
Prefer a metrical structure in which beats of level L_i that are stressed are strong beats of L_i.

11. This rule is stated as follows (*GTTM*, 49):

Grouping Preference Rule 5
Prefer grouping analyses that most closely approach the ideal subdivision of groups into two parts of equal length.

12. This rule is stated as follows (*GTTM*, 72):

Metrical Well-Formedness Rule 4
The tactus and immediately larger metrical levels must consist of beats equally spaced throughout the piece.

This is a well-formedness rule in classical tonal music, but in universal musical grammar only a strong preference. See *GTTM*, sections 4.4 and 4.5, for some discussion.

13. Time-Span Reduction Well-Formedness Rules 3d and 4 (*GTTM*, 159) and Time-Span Reduction Preference Rule 7 (*GTTM*, 170). The statements of these rules are too technical to quote out of context here.

14. The fact that the parser may project abstract structures rather than actual notes accounts for the fact that many different chords can serve as the final element of a deceptive cadence, as long as they preserve proper voice-leading relations to the preceding dominant. The parser need not project each of these possibilities as a distinct analysis, though perhaps the most common resolution, that to *vi*, is projected.

Chapter 8

1. Readers who find my terminology offensive are free to substitute their own. Dan Dennett (personal communication) has suggested "Cartesian" versus "Quinean," though I am not sure I would endorse the latter: my sense is that Quine does not address psychological mechanisms enough to be a good exemplar of the approach I have in mind.

2. Note that, should such miraculous powers turn out to exist, the purely combinatorial properties of the brain still need to be studied. If one wishes to reserve the term *mental representation* for brain-states-with-intentionality, I have no objection to introducing a new term, say *mental distinctions*, for the nonintentional states that I am calling mental representations here. Readers with such predilections should feel free to make the substitution throughout.

3. Dennett (1987) describes this situation in terms of the brain being a "syntactic engine" that mimics a "semantic engine": by virtue of its evolutionary history, it acts for the most part as though it is making genuine contact with properties of the physical world.

4. This point was made earlier by Koffka (1935, 657):

> The best examples for our argument are perhaps certain trick films after the pattern of Mickey Mouse, for here there is objectively neither motion nor emotion, but a mere sequence of strange drawings. But this sequence gives rise to objects in the behavioral world of the observers which move, and are agile or clumsy, exuberant or dejected, and so forth. The merit of this example lies in the fact that here all these characters are *only* in the behavioral objects and entirely absent in the geographical ones. The "meanings" which those forms and motions possess for us are therefore most clearly aspects or results of the psychophysical organizations produced by the stimuli.

It bears adding that the "derived intentionality" of cartoons, that is, the cartoonist's intent to portray something, is for naught unless the draftsmanship is good enough to produce the requisite psychophysical organization. Are we understanding a poorly drawn cartoon *falsely* if we fail to perceive it as the cartoonist intended? Again this seems to be an inept term for the situation.

5. If one wants to be a Platonist after the manner of Katz (1981), one may claim that these things are in the environment as "abstract objects." I then strengthen my statement: There is no such thing as an NP in the *perceivable* environment—that is, there is no way a mind can gain causal access to such things as abstract NPs.

6. Jackendoff 1985b shows that parallel phenomena appear in sentences about intentions to act; Fauconnier (1985) extends aspects of the parallelism to a wide variety of cases, including contexts involving tense logic, counterfactuals, and quantification.

7. One might think of this analysis as claiming that the notion of belief is in some sense metaphorical, following for instance Lakoff and Johnson (1980) and Lakoff (1987). However, I find such a construal an unreasonable stretch of the notion of metaphor. In the standard cases, a metaphor involves an arbitrary extension of a semantic field to a new domain, acknowledged by the speaker to be "rationally" anomalous, for the purpose of

creating some colorful or artistic effect. The concept of a belief as a mental picture is not metaphorical in this sense. Rather, the parallelism to pictures is a deep cognitive extension without which we would have no way at all to think or speak about beliefs (outside scientific theories, perhaps). (See Jackendoff 1983, 209–210, and Jackendoff and Aaron 1991 for further discussion of similar cases.)

8. This reply appears in Rapaport 1988 and Jackendoff 1983, independently.

9. Freud (in a quotation I am now unable to locate) said something like this too. In fact, some of the early Darwinians sensed this crisis from the start, in some cases with disastrous personal consequences (Gruber 1960).

References

Anderson, J. R. (1983). *The Architecture of Cognition*. Cambridge, Mass.: Harvard University Press.

Anderson, S. (1971). "On the Role of Deep Structure in Semantic Interpretation." *Foundations of Language* 6, 387–396.

Anderson, S., and E. Keenan (1985). "Deixis." In T. Shopen, ed., *Language Typology and Syntactic Description*. Cambridge: Cambridge University Press.

Armstrong, S. L., L. R. Gleitman, and H. Gleitman (1983). "On What Some Concepts Might Not Be." *Cognition* 13, 263–308.

Bach, E. (1986a). "Natural Language Metaphysics." In R. Barcan-Marcus, G. Dorn, and P. Weingartner, eds., *Logic, Methodology, and Philosophy of Science*, 573–595. Amsterdam: North-Holland.

Bach, E. (1986b). "The Algebra of Events." *Linguistics and Philosophy* 9, 5–16.

Bach, K., and R. M. Harnish (1979). *Linguistic Communication and Speech Acts*. Cambridge, Mass.: MIT Press.

Bennett, D. (1975). *Spatial and Temporal Uses of English Prepositions: An Essay in Stratificational Semantics*. New York: Longman Press.

Berlin, B., and P. Kay (1969). *Basic Color Terms: Their Universality and Evolution*. Berkeley and Los Angeles: University of California Press.

Berwick, R., and A. Weinberg (1984). *The Grammatical Basis of Linguistic Performance*. Cambridge, Mass.: MIT Press.

Bever, T. G., M. F. Garrett, and R. Hurtig (1973). "The Interaction of Perceptual Processes and Ambiguous Sentences." *Memory and Cognition* 1, 277–286.

Bharucha, J. (1987). "Music Cognition and Perceptual Facilitation: A Connectionist Framework." *Music Perception* 5, 1–30.

Biederman, I. (1987). "Recognition-by-Components: A Theory of Human Image Understanding." *Psychological Review* 94 (2), 115–147.

Bolinger, D. (1965). "The Atomization of Meaning." *Language* 41, 555–573.

Bowerman, M. (1989). "Learning a Semantic System: What Role Do Cognitive Predispositions Play? In M. L. Rice and R. C. Schiefenbusch, eds., *The Teachability of Language*. Baltimore, Md.: Paul H. Brooks.

Bregman, A. S. (1990). *Auditory Scene Analysis*. Cambridge, Mass.: MIT Press.

Brown, D. E. (1991). *Human Universals*. New York: McGraw-Hill.

Brown, H. (1988). "The Interplay of Set Content and Temporal Context in a Functional Theory of Tonality Perception." *Music Perception* 5, 219–250.

Brugman, C. (1981). "Story of *Over*." Bloomington, Ind.: Indiana University Linguistics Club.

Butler, D. (1989). "Describing the Perception of Tonality in Music: A Critique of the Tonal Hierarchy Theory and a Proposal for a Theory of Intervallic Rivalry." *Music Perception* 6, 219–242.

Calvin, W. H. (1989). *The Cerebral Symphony*. New York: Bantam Books.

Carey, S. (1979). "A Case Study: Face Recognition." In E. Walker, ed., *Explorations in the Biology of Language*, 175–202. Cambridge, Mass.: MIT Press.

Carey, S., and R. Diamond (1980). "Maturational Determination of the Developmental Course of Face Encoding." In D. Caplan, ed., *Biological Studies of Mental Processes*, 60–93. Cambridge, Mass.: MIT Press.

Cheney, D., and R. Seyfarth (1985). "Social and Non-Social Knowledge in Vervet Monkeys." *Phil. Trans. R. Soc. Lond.* B 308, 187–201.

Cheney, D., and R. Seyfarth (1990). *How Monkeys See the World.* Chicago: University of Chicago Press.

Chomsky, N. (1965). *Aspects of the Theory of Syntax.* Cambridge, Mass.: MIT Press.

Chomsky, N. (1972). *Language and Mind.* New York: Harcourt Brace Jovanovich.

Chomsky, N. (1975). *Reflections on Language.* New York: Pantheon.

Chomsky, N. (1986). *Knowledge of Language.* New York: Praeger.

Churchland, P. M. (1981). "Eliminative Materialism and the Propositional Attitudes." *Journal of Philosophy* 78, 67–90.

Cienki, A. (1988). "Spatial Cognition and the Semantics of Prepositions in English, Polish, and Russian." Ph.D. dissertation, Brown University.

Clark, H. (1973). "Space, Time, Semantics, and the Child." In T. E. Moore, ed., *Cognitive Development and the Acquisition of Language*, 27–64. New York: Academic Press.

Clynes, M., and N. Nettheim (1982). "The Living Quality of Music: Neurobiologic Basis of Communicating Feeling." In M. Clynes, ed., *Music, Mind, and Brain: The Neuropsychology of Music*, 47–82. New York: Plenum.

Clynes, M., and J. Walker (1982). "Neurobiological Functions of Rhythm, Time, and Pulse in Music." In M. Clynes, ed., *Music, Mind, and Brain: The Neuropsychology of Music*, 171–216. New York: Plenum.

Cosmides, L. (1989). "The Logic of Social Exchange: Has Natural Selection Shaped How Humans Reason? Studies with the Wason Selection Task." *Cognition* 31, 187–276.

Cosmides, L., and J. Tooby (1989). "Evolutionary Psychology and the Generation of Culture, Part II." *Ethology and Sociobiology* 10, 51–97.

Declerck, R. (1979). "Aspect and the Bounded/Unbounded (Telic/Atelic) Distinction." *Linguistics* 17, 761–794.

Deliege, I. (1987). "Grouping Conditions in Listening to Music: An Approach to Lerdahl & Jackendoff's Grouping Preference Rules." *Music Perception* 4, 325–360.

Dennett, D. C. (1978). *Brainstorms: Philosophical Essays on Mind and Psychology.* Cambridge, Mass.: MIT Press.

Dennett, D. C. (1987). *The Intentional Stance.* Cambridge, Mass.: MIT Press.

Dennett, D. C. (1988). "Why Everyone Is a Novelist." *Times Literary Supplement*, Sept. 16–22, 1988.

Dennett, D. (1991). *Consciousness Explained.* Boston: Little, Brown.

Dennett, D., and M. Kinsbourne (1992). "Time and the Observer: The Where and When of Consciousness in the Brain." *Behavioral and Brain Science* 15.

Dowty, D. (1979). *Word Meaning and Montague Grammar.* Dordrecht: Reidel.

Dowty, D. (1988). "On the Semantic Content of the Notion 'Thematic Role'." In G. Chierchia, B. Partee, and D. Turner, eds., *Properties, Types, and Meaning.* Vol. 2: *Semantic Issues*, 69–130. Dordrecht: Kluwer.

Eibl-Eibesfeldt, I. (1989). *Human Ethology.* New York: Aldine de Gruyter.

Erdelyi, M. H. (1985). *Psychoanalysis: Freud's Cognitive Psychology.* San Francisco: Freeman.

Etcoff, N. L. (1986). "The Neuropsychology of Emotional Expression." In G. Goldstein and R. E. Tarter, eds., *Advances in Clinical Neuropsychology*, vol. 3. New York: Plenum.

Etcoff, N. L. (1989). "Asymmetries in Recognition of Emotion." In F. Boller and J. Grafman, eds., *Handbook of Neuropsychology*, vol. 3, 363–382. New York: Elsevier Science Publishers.

Farah, M., K. Hammond, D. Levine, and R. Calvanio (1988). Visual and Spatial Mental Imagery: Dissociable Systems of Representation." *Cognitive Psychology* 20, 439–462.

Fauconnier, G. (1985). *Mental Spaces*. Cambridge, Mass., MIT Press.

Fillmore, C. (1982). "Towards a Descriptive Framework for Spatial Deixis." In R. Jarvella and W. Klein, eds., *Speech, Place, and Action*, 31–59. New York: Wiley.

Fiske, A. (1991). *Structures of Social Life: The Four Elementary Forms of Human Relations*. New York: The Free Press.

Fodor, J. A. (1970). "Three Reasons for Not Deriving 'Kill' from 'Cause to Die'." *Linguistic Inquiry* 1, 429–438.

Fodor, J. A. (1975). *The Language of Thought*. Cambridge, Mass.: Harvard University Press.

Fodor, J. A. (1980a). "Methodological Solipsism Considered as a Research Strategy in Cognitive Psychology." *Behavioral and Brain Sciences* 3, 63–73.

Fodor, J. A. (1980b). "Reply to Putnam." In Piattelli-Palmerini (1980), 325–334.

Fodor, J. A. (1981). "The Present Status of the Innateness Controversy." In *Representations*, 257–316. Cambridge, Mass.: MIT Press.

Fodor, J. A. (1983). *Modularity of Mind*. Cambridge, Mass.: MIT Press.

Fodor, J. A. (1987). *Psychosemantics*. Cambridge, Mass.: MIT Press.

Fodor, J. A., M. Garrett, E. Walker and C. Parkes (1980). "Against Definitions." *Cognition* 8, 263–367.

Fodor, J. D., J. A. Fodor, and M. Garrett (1975). "The Psychological Unreality of Semantic Representations." *Linguistic Inquiry* 6, 515–532.

Frazier, L., and J. D. Fodor (1978). "The Sausage Machine: A New Two-Stage Parsing Model." *Cognition* 6, 291–325.

Frege, G. (1892). "On Sense and Reference." Reprinted in D. Davidson and G. Harman, eds., *The Logic of Grammar*, 116–128. Encino, Calif.: Dickenson (1975).

Freud, S. (1900). *The Interpretation of Dreams*. In *The Standard Editions of the Complete Psychological Works of Sigmund Freud*, vols. 4 and 5. Edited and translated by J. Strachey. London: Hogarth Press (1953).

Fromkin, V. (1971). "The Non-Anomalous Nature of Anomalous Utterances." *Language* 47, 27–52.

Gardner, H. (1983). *Frames of Mind*. New York: Basic Books.

Garrett, M. (1975). "The Analysis of Sentence Production." In G. H. Bower, ed., *Psychology of Learning and Motivation*, vol. 9, 133–177. New York: Academic Press.

Gee, J. P., and F. Grosjean (1983). "Performance Structure: A Psycholinguistic and Linguistic Appraisal." *Cognitive Psychology* 15, 411–458.

Gjerdingen, R. O. (1990). "Categorization of Musical Patterns by Self-Organizing Neuron-like Networks." *Music Perception* 7, 339–369.

Gould, S. J. (1980). *The Panda's Thumb*. New York: W. W. Norton.

Gould, S. J. (1981). *The Mismeasure of Man*. New York: W. W. Norton.

Gould, S. J. (1983). *Hen's Teeth and Horse's Toes*. New York: W. W. Norton.

Gruber, J. S. (1965/1976). "Studies in Lexical Relations." Ph.D. dissertation, MIT. Reprinted as part of *Lexical Structures in Syntax and Semantics*. Amsterdam: North-Holland (1976).

Gruber, J. W. (1960). *A Conscience in Conflict: The Life of St. George Jackson Mivart*. New York: Columbia University Press.

Halle, M. (1978). "Knowledge Unlearned and Untaught." In M. Halle, J. Bresnan, and G. Miller, eds., *Linguistic Theory and Psychological Reality*, 294–303. Cambridge, Mass.: MIT Press.

Halle, M., and J.-R. Vergnaud (1987). *An Essay on Stress*. Cambridge, Mass.: MIT Press.

Hawkins, B. W. (1984). "The Semantics of English Spatial Prepositions." Ph.D. dissertation, University of California at San Diego.

Heider, F., and M. Simmel (1944). "An Experimental Study of Apparent Behavior." *American Journal of Psychology* 57, 243–249.

Herskovits, A. (1986). *Language and Spatial Cognition: An Interdisciplinary Study of the Prepositions in English.* Cambridge: Cambridge University Press.

Hickok, G. (1991). "Gaps and Garden-Paths: Studies on the Architecture and Computational Machinery of the Human Sentence Processor." Ph.D. dissertation, Program in Linguistics and Cognitive Science, Brandeis University.

Hinrichs, E. (1985). "A Compositional Semantics for Aktionsarten and NP Reference in English." Ph.D. dissertation, Ohio State University.

Hochberg, J. (1978). *Perception.* 2nd ed. Englewood Cliffs, N.J.: Prentice-Hall.

Hoffman, D., and W. Richards (1984). "Parts of Recognition." *Cognition* 18, 65–96.

Horowitz, M., ed. (1988a). *Psychodynamics and Cognition.* Chicago: University of Chicago Press.

Horowitz, M. (1988b). "Unconsciously Determined Defensive Strategies." In Horowitz (1988a), 49–80.

Horowitz, M. (1990). *Introduction to Psychodynamics: A New Synthesis.* New York: Basic Books.

Hudson, S., and M. Tanenhaus (1984). "Ambiguity Resolution in the Absence of Contextual Bias." In *Proceedings of the Sixth Annual Conference of the Cognitive Science Society,* 159–165. Hillsdale, N.J.: L. Erlbaum Associates.

Humphrey, N., and D. C. Dennett (1989). "Speaking for Ourselves: An Assessment of Multiple Personality Disorder." *Raritan* 9, 68–98.

Jackendoff, R. (1972). *Semantic Interpretation in Generative Grammar.* Cambridge, Mass.: MIT Press.

Jackendoff, R. (1975). "On Belief-Contexts." *Linguistic Inquiry* 6, 53–93.

Jackendoff, R. (1976). "Toward an Explanatory Semantic Representation." *Linguistic Inquiry* 7, 89–150.

Jackendoff, R. (1980). "Belief-Contexts Revisited." *Linguistic Inquiry* 11, 395–414.

Jackendoff, R. (1983). *Semantics and Cognition.* Cambridge, Mass.: MIT Press.

Jackendoff, R. (1985a). "Multiple Subcategorization and the θ-Criterion: The Case of *Climb.*" *Natural Language and Linguistic Theory* 3, 271–295.

Jackendoff, R. (1985b). "Believing and Intending: Two Sides of the Same Coin." *Linguistic Inquiry* 16, 445–459.

Jackendoff, R. (1987a). *Consciousness and the Computational Mind.* Cambridge, Mass.: MIT Press.

Jackendoff, R. (1987b). "On Beyond Zebra: The Relation of Linguistic and Visual Information." *Cognition* 26, 89–114.

Jackendoff, R. (1990). *Semantic Structures.* Cambridge, Mass.: MIT Press.

Jackendoff, R. (1991). "Parts and Boundaries." *Cognition* 41, 9–45.

Jackendoff, R., and D. Aaron (1991). Review of Lakoff and Turner (1989). *Language* 67, 320–338.

Jakobson, R. (1941). *Child Language, Aphasia, and Phonological Universals.* Translated by Allan Keiler. The Hague: Mouton (1968).

Jakobson, R., G. Fant, and M. Halle (1952). *Preliminaries to Speech Analysis.* Cambridge, Mass.: MIT Press.

Jerison, H. (1973). *Evolution of the Brain and Intelligence.* New York: Academic Press.

Katz, J. J. (1966). *The Philosophy of Language.* New York: Harper & Row.

Katz, J. J. (1981). *Language and Other Abstract Objects.* Totowa, N.J.: Rowman and Littlefield.

Katz, J. J., and J. A. Fodor (1963). "The Structure of a Semantic Theory." *Language* 39, 170–210.

Katz, N., E. Baker, and J. Macnamara (1974). "What's in a Name? A Study of How Children Learn Common and Proper Names." *Child Development* 45, 469–473.

Kluft, R. P. (1984). "An Introduction to Multiple Personality Disorders." *Psychiatric Annals* 14, 19–24.

Koffka, K. (1935). *Principles of Gestalt Psychology*. New York: Harcourt, Brace, & World.

Kosslyn, S. (1980). *Image and Mind*. Cambridge, Mass.: Harvard University Press.

Kosslyn, S. (1987). "Seeing and Imagining in the Cerebral Hemispheres. A Computational Approach." *Psychological Review* 94, 148–175.

Kosslyn, S., R. Flynn, J. Amsterdam, and G. Wang (1990). "Components of High-Level Vision: A Cognitive Neuroscience Analysis and Accounts of Neurological Syndromes." *Cognition* 34, 203–277.

Krumhansl, C. (1990). "Tonal Hierarchies and Rare Intervals in Music Cognition." *Music Perception* 7, 309–324.

Kundera, M. (1981). *The Book of Laughter and Forgetting*. Translated by M. H. Heim. New York: Penguin Books.

Lackner, J. (1981). "Some Contributions of Touch, Pressure, and Kinesthesis to Human Spatial Orientation and Oculomotor Control." *Acta Astronautica* 8, 825–830.

Lackner, J. (1985). "Human Sensory-Motor Adaptation to the Terrestrial Force Environment." In D. Ingle, M. Jeannerod, and D. Lee, eds., *Brain Mechanisms and Spatial Vision*. Dordrecht: Martinus-Nijhoff.

Lackner, J. (1988). "Some Proprioceptive Influences on the Perceptual Representation of Body Shape and Orientation." *Brain* 111, 281–297.

Lackner, J., and P. DiZio (1984). "Some Efferent and Somatosensory Influences on Body Orientation and Oculomotor Control." In L. Spillman and B. Wooten, eds., *Sensory Experience*, 281–301. Hillsdale, N.J.: L. Erlbaum Assocs.

Lackner, J., and P. DiZio (1988). "Visual Stimulation Affects the Perception of Voluntary Leg Movements during Walking." *Perception* 17, 71–80.

Lackner, J., and A. Graybiel (1983). "Perceived Orientation in Free-Fall Depends on Visual, Postural, and Architectural Factors." *Aviation, Space, and Environmental Medicine* 54, 47–51.

Lakoff, G. (1971). "On Generative Semantics." In D. Steinberg and L. Jakobovits, eds., *Semantics: An Interdisciplinary Reader*, 232–296. New York: Cambridge University Press.

Lakoff, G. (1987). *Women, Fire, and Dangerous Things*. Chicago: University of Chicago Press.

Lakoff, G. (1990). "The Invariance Hypothesis: Is Abstract Reasoning Based on Image-Schemas?" *Cognitive Linguistics* 1, 39–74.

Lakoff, G., and M. Johnson (1980). *Metaphors We Live By*. Chicago: University of Chicago Press.

Lakoff, G., and M. Turner (1989). *More Than Cool Reason: A Field Guide to Poetic Metaphor*. Chicago: University of Chicago Press.

Landau, B., and L. Gleitman (1985). *Language and Experience: Evidence from the Blind Child*. Cambridge, Mass.: Harvard University Press.

Landau, B., L. Smith, and S. Jones (1988). The Importance of Shape in Early Lexical Learning." *Cognitive Development* 3, 299–321.

Landau, B., E. Spelke, and H. Gleitman (1984). "Spatial Knowledge in a Young Blind Child." *Cognition* 16, 225–260.

Landau, B., and D. Stecker (1990). "Objects and Places: Syntactic Geometric Representations in Early Lexical Learning." *Cognitive Development* 5, 287–312.

Langacker, R. (1986). *Foundations of Cognitive Grammar*, vol. 1. Stanford, Calif.: Stanford University Press.

Lashley, K. (1956). "Cerebral Organization and Behavior." In H. Solomon, S. Cobb, and W. Penfield, eds., *The Brain and Human Behavior*, 1–18. Baltimore, Md.: Williams and Wilkins.

Lerdahl, F., and R. Jackendoff (1983a). *A Generative Theory of Tonal Music.* Cambridge, Mass.: MIT Press.

Lerdahl, F., and R. Jackendoff (1983b). "An Overview of Hierarchical Structure in Music." *Music Perception* 1, 229–252.

Levelt, W. I. M. (1989). *Speaking.* Cambridge, Mass.: MIT Press.

Levine, D., J. Warach, and M. Farah (1985). "Two Visual Systems in Mental Imagery: Dissociation of 'What' and 'Where' in Imagery Disorders Due to Bilateral Posterior Cerebral Lesions." *Neurology* 35, 1010–1018.

Lewis, D. (1972). "General Semantics." In D. Davidson and G. Harman, eds., *Semantics of Natural Language,* 169–218. Reidel: Dordrecht.

Liberman, M., and A. Prince (1977). "On Stress and Linguistic Rhythm." *Linguistic Inquiry* 8, 249–336.

Link, G. (1983). "The Logical Analysis of Plurals and Mass Terms: A Lattice-Theoretic Approach." In R. Bauerle, C. Schwarze, and A. von Stechow, eds., *Meaning, Use, and Interpretation of Language,* 302–323. Berlin: de Gruyter.

Longuet-Higgins, C. (1987). *Mental Processes: Studies in Cognitive Science.* Cambridge, Mass.: MIT Press.

McCawley, J. D. (1968). "Lexical Insertion in a Transformational Grammar without Deep Structure." In B. Darden, C.-J. N. Bailey, and A. Davison, eds., *Papers from the Fourth Regional Meeting, Chicago Linguistic Society.* Chicago Linguistic Society, University of Chicago.

McClelland, J., and D. Rumelhart (1986). *Parallel Distributed Processing: Explorations in the Microstructure of Cognition.* Vol. 2: *Psychological and Biological Models.* Cambridge, Mass.: MIT Press.

Macnamara, J. (1986). *A Border Dispute.* Cambridge, Mass.: MIT Press.

Marcus, M. (1980). *A Theory of Syntactic Recognition for Natural Language.* Cambridge, Mass.: MIT Press.

Marr, D. (1982). *Vision.* San Francisco: Freeman.

Marr, D., and L. Vaina (1982). "Representation and Recognition of the Movements of Shapes." *Proceedings of the Research Society of London B* 214, 501–524.

Meyer, L. (1956). *Emotion and Meaning in Music.* Chicago: University of Chicago Press.

Meyer, L. (1967a). "On Rehearing Music." In *Music, the Arts, and Ideas.* Chicago: University of Chicago Press.

Meyer, L. (1967b). "Meaning and Music in Information Theory." In *Music, the Arts, and Ideas.* Chicago: University of Chicago Press.

Meyer, L. (1973). *Explaining Music.* Berkeley and Los Angeles: University of California Press.

Michotte, A. (1954). *The Perception of Causality.* English translation: New York: Basic Books.

Michotte, A. et collaborateurs (1962). *Causalité, permanence et realité phénoménales.* Louvain: Publications Universitaires de Louvain.

Michotte, A., G. Thinès, and G. Crabbé (1964). *Les compléments amodaux des structures perceptives.* Louvain: Publications Universitaires de Louvain.

Miller, G. (1956). "The Magical Number Seven, Plus or Minus Two: Some Limits on Our Capacity for Processing Information." *Psychological Review* 63, 81–97.

Miller, G., and P. Johnson-Laird (1976). *Language and Perception.* Cambridge, Mass.: Harvard University Press.

Mourelatos, A. P. D. (1981). "Events, Processes, and States." In P. J. Tedeschi and A. Zaenen, eds., *Syntax and Semantics,* vol. 14, 191–212. New York: Academic Press.

Narmour, E. (1977). *Beyond Schenkerism.* Chicago: University of Chicago Press.

Newport, E. (1990). "Maturational Constraints on Language Learning." *Cognitive Science* 14, 11–28.

Onifer, W., and D. Swinney (1981). "Accessing Lexical Ambiguities during Sentence Comprehension: Effects of Frequency of Meaning and Contextual Bias." *Memory and Cognition* 9, 225 –236.

Oura, Y. (1991). "Constructing a Representation of a Melody: Transforming Melodic Segments into Reduced Pitch Patterns Operated on by Modifiers." *Music Perception* 9, 251–266.

Parsons, L. H. (1987). "Imagined Spatial Transformations of One's Hands and Feet." *Cognitive Psychology* 7, 532–547.

Piaget, J. (1966). *Psychology of Intelligence*. Totowa, N.J.: Littlefield, Adams & Co.

Piaget, J. (1970). *Genetic Epistemology*. New York: Columbia University Press.

Piattelli-Palmerini, M., ed. (1980). *Language and Learning: The Debate between Jean Piaget and Noam Chomsky*. Cambridge, Mass.: Harvard University Press.

Pinker, S. (1989). *Learnability and Cognition: The Acquisition of Argument Structure*. Cambridge, Mass.: MIT Press.

Pinxten, R., I. van Dooren, and K. Harvey (1983). *The Anthropology of Space: Explorations into Natural Philosophy and Semantics of the Navajo*. Philadelphia: University of Pennsylvania Press.

Platzack, C. (1979). *The Semantic Interpretation of Aspect and Aktionsarten*. Dordrecht: Foris.

Postal, P. (1970). "On the Surface Verb 'Remind'." *Linguistic Inquiry* 1, 37–120.

Premack, D. (1990). "On the Coevolution of Language and Social Competence." *Behavioral and Brain Sciences* 13, 754–756.

Prince, A. (1983). "Relating to the Grid." *Linguistic Inquiry* 14, 19–100.

Putnam, H. (1975). "The Meaning of 'Meaning'." In K. Gunderson, ed., *Language, Mind, and Knowledge*, 131–193. Minneapolis, Minn.: University of Minnesota Press.

Pylyshyn, Z. (1984). *Computation and Cognition*. Cambridge, Mass.: MIT Press.

Quine, W. V. (1956). "Quantifiers and Propositional Attitudes." *Journal of Philosophy* 53.

Quine, W. V. (1960). *Word and Object*. Cambridge, Mass.: MIT Press.

Rapaport, W. J. (1988). "Syntactic Semantics: Foundations of Computational Natural-Language Understanding." In J. H. Fetzer, ed., *Aspects of Artificial Intelligence*, 81–131. Dordrecht: Kluwer.

Rappaport, M., and B. Levin (1985). "The Locative Alternation: A Case Study in Lexical Analysis." Ms., Center for Cognitive Science, MIT.

Rosch E. (1975). "Cognitive Reference Points." *Cognitive Psychology* 7, 532–547.

Rosch, E. (1978). "Principles of Categorization." In E. Rosch and B. Lloyd, eds., *Cognition and Categorization*, 27–48. Hillsdale, N.J.: L. Erlbaum Assocs.

Rosner, B., and L. Meyer (1986). "The Perceptual Roles of Melodic Process, Contour, and Form." *Music Perception* 4, 1–40.

Rueckl, J., K. Cave, and S. Kosslyn (1988). "Why Are 'What' and 'Where' Processed by Separate Cortical Visual Systems? A Computational Investigation." *Journal of Cognitive Neuroscience* 1, 171–186.

Rumelhart, D., and J. McClelland (1986). *Parallel Distributed Processing: Explorations in the Microstructure of Cognition*. Vol. 1: *Foundations*. Cambridge, Mass. MIT Press.

Russell, B. (1905). "On Denoting." *Mind* 14, 479–493.

Sacks, O. (1985). *The Man Who Mistook His Wife for a Hat*. New York: Summit Books.

Sadalla, E., W. J. Burroughs, and L. J. Staplin (1980). "Reference Points in Spatial Cognition." *Journal of Experimental Psychology: Human Learning and Memory* 6, 516–528.

Schank, R., and R. Abelson (1975). *Scripts, Plans, Goals, and Knowledge*. Hillsdale, N.J.: L. Erlbaum Assocs.

Schenker, H. (1935). *Der freie Satz*. Vienna: Universal Edition. Translation by E. Oster. New York: Longman (1979).

Schmuckler, M. (1989). "Expectation in Music: Investigation of Melodic and Harmonic Processes." *Music Perception* 7, 109–150.

Scutenaire, L. (1947). *René Magritte*. Brussels: Librairie Sélection.

Searle, J. (1980). "Minds, Brains, and Programs." *Behavioral and Brain Sciences* 3, 417–424.

Selkirk, E. (1982). *The Syntax of Words*. Cambridge, Mass.: MIT Press.

Selkirk, E. (1984). *Phonology and Syntax: The Relation between Sound and Structure*. Cambridge, Mass.: MIT Press.

Shepard, R., and L. Cooper, eds. (1982). *Mental Images and Their Transformations*. Cambridge, Mass.: MIT Press.

Shevrin, H. (1988). "Unconscious Conflict: A Convergent Psychodynamic and Electrophysiological Approach." In Horowitz (1988a), 117–167.

Snare, F. (1972). "The Concept of Property." *American Philosophical Quarterly* 9, 200–206.

Spelke, E. (1983). Perception of Unity, Persistence, and Identity: Thoughts on Infants' Conceptions of Objects." In J. Mehler, ed., *Infant and Neonate Cognition*. Hillsdale, N.J.: L. Erlbaum Assocs.

Sprague, E. (1960). "The Mind-Brain Problem." In S. Hook, ed., *Dimensions of Mind*, 71–73. New York: Collier Books.

Stich, S. C. (1983). *From Folk Psychology to Cognitive Science: The Case against Belief*. Cambridge, Mass.: MIT Press.

Swinney, D. (1979). "Lexical Access during Sentence Comprehension: (Re)consideration of Context Effects." *Journal of Verbal Learning and Verbal Behavior* 18, 645–659.

Swinney, D. (1982). "The Structure and Time-Course of Information Interaction during Speech Comprehension: Lexical Segmentation, Access, and Interpretation." In J. Mehler, E. Walker, and M. Garrett, eds., *Perspectives on Mental Representation*. Hillsdale, N.J.: L. Erlbaum Assocs.

Symons, D. (1987). "If We're All Darwinians, What's the Fuss About?" In C. Crawford, M. Smith, and D. Krebs, eds., *Sociobiology and Psychology: Ideas, Issues, and Applications*, 121–146. Hillsdale, N.J.: L. Erlbaum Associates.

Symons, D. (1991). "On the Use and Misuse of Darwinism in the Study of Human Behavior." In J. H. Barkow, L. Cosmides, and J. Tooby, eds., *The Adapted Mind*. New York: Oxford University Press.

Talmy, L. (1978). "The Relation of Grammar to Cognition." In D. Waltz, ed., *Proceedings of TINLAP-2: Theoretical Issues in Natural Language Processing*. New York: Association for Computing Machinery.

Talmy, L. (1980). "Lexicalization Patterns: Semantic Structure in Lexical Forms." In T. Shopen et al., eds., *Language Typology and Syntactic Description*, vol. 3. New York: Cambridge University Press.

Talmy, L. (1983). "How Language Structures Space." In H. Pick and L. Acredolo, eds., *Spatial Orientation: Theory, Research, and Application*. New York: Plenum.

Talmy, L. (1985). "Force Dynamics in Language and Thought." In *Papers from the Twenty-First Regional Meeting, Chicago Linguistic Society*. Chicago Linguistic Society, University of Chicago. Also in *Cognitive Science* 12, 49–100 (1988).

Tanenhaus, M., J. Leiman, and M. Seidenberg (1979). "Evidence for Multiple Stages in the Processing of Ambiguous Words in Syntactic Contexts." *Journal of Verbal Learning and Verbal Behavior* 18, 417–440.

Tenny, C. (1987). "Grammaticalizing Aspect and Affectedness." Ph.D. dissertation, MIT.

Tooby, J., and L. Cosmides (1989). "Evolutionary Psychology and the Generation of Culture, Part I." *Ethology and Sociobiology* 10, 29–49.

Trubetzkoy, N. S. (1939). *Grundzüge der Phonologie*. Translated as *Principles of Phonology*. Berkeley and Los Angeles: University of California Press (1969).

Ungerleider, L. G., and M. Mishkin (1982). "Two Cortical Visual Systems." In D. J. Ingle, M. A. Goodale, and R. J. W. Mansfield eds., *Analysis of Visual Behavior*, 549–586. Cambridge, Mass.: MIT Press.

Vandeloise, C. (1986). *L'espace en français*. Paris: Editions du Seuil. English translation by A. Bosch: *Spatial Prepositions*. Chicago: University of Chicago Press (1991).

Vendler, Z. (1957). "Verbs and Times." *Philosophical Review* 56, 143–160. Reprinted in *Linguistics in Philosophy*, 97–121. Ithaca, N.Y.: Cornell University Press (1967).

Verkuyl, H. (1972). *On the Compositional Nature of the Aspects*. Dordrecht: Reidel.

Verkuyl, H. (1989). "Aspectual Classes and Aspectual Composition." *Linguistics and Philosophy* 12, 39–94.

Verkuyl, H., and J. Zwarts (1990). "Time and Space in Conceptual and Logical Semantics: The Notion of Path." Paper given at Max Planck Conference on Space, Time, and the Lexicon, Nijmegen. Manuscript, University of Utrecht-OTS.

Von Neumann, J. (1958). *The Computer and the Brain*. New Haven, Conn.: Yale University Press.

Wanner, E., and M. Maratsos (1978). "An ATN Approach to Comprehension." In M. Halle, J. Bresnan, and G. Miller, eds., *Linguistic Theory and Psychological Reality*, 119–161. Cambridge, Mass.: MIT Press.

Weinreich, U. (1966). "Explorations in Semantic Theory." In T. Sebeok, ed., *Current Trends in Linguistics*, vol. 3. The Hague: Mouton. Reprinted in *On Semantics*, 99–201. Philadelphia: University of Pennsylvania Press (1980).

Wertheimer, M. (1923). "Laws of Organization in Perceptual Forms." In W. D. Ellis, ed., *A Source Book of Gestalt Psychology*, 71–88. London: Routledge & Kegan Paul (1938).

Wiener, N. (1954). *The Human Use of Human Beings: Cybernetics and Society*. Boston: Houghton Mifflin.

Wimmer, H., and J. Perner (1983). "Beliefs about Beliefs: Representation and Constraining Function of Wrong Beliefs in Young Children's Understanding of Deception. *Cognition* 13, 103–128.

Wittgenstein, L. (1953). *Philosophical Investigations*. Oxford: Blackwell.

Zaitchik, D. (1989). "When Representations Conflict with Reality: The Preschooler's Problem with False Beliefs and 'False' Photographs." *Cognition* 35, 41–68.

Index